Language and power

LANGUAGE IN SOCIAL LIFE SERIES

Series Editor: Professor Christopher N. Candlin

Language and Power Norman Fairclough

Language and power

Norman Fairclough

LONGMAN

LONDON AND NEW YORK

Longman Group UK Limited,
Longman House, Burnt Mill, Harlow,
Essex CM20 2JE, England
and Associated Companies throughout the world.

*Published in the United States of America
by Longman Inc., New York*

First published 1989

British Library Cataloguing in Publication Data
Fairclough, Norman, *1941–*
   Language and power.
   1. Language related to power
   I. Title
   401′.9

ISBN 0-582-03133-8 CSD
ISBN 0-582-00976-6 PPR

Library of Congress Cataloguing-in-Publication Data
Fairclough, Norman, 1941–
   Language and power.
   (Language in social life series)
   Bibliography: p.
   Includes index.
   1. Sociolinguistics. 2. Discourse analysis.
I. Title. II. Series.
P40.F35 1988   401′.9   87-36669
ISBN 0-582-00976-6

Set in 10/12pt Linotron 202 Palatino

Produced by Longman Singapore Publishers (Pte) Ltd
Printed in Singapore

Contents

General Editor's Preface

It is appropriate with the publication of its first book to indicate the intentions and scope of the new Language in Social Life Series, both to show how Norman Fairclough's Language and Power admirably provides its corner-stone and to encourage readers and other potential authors to join us in this imaginative enterprise.

Our objective is to focus on language in social life but with a particular agenda in mind. To highlight how language, in its everyday as well as professional usages enables us to understand issues of social concern. More specifically, to examine how the ways in which we communicate are constrained by the structures and forces of those social institutions within which we live and function. To display, too, how these institutions and our roles within them are in frequent measure defined by such particular language use. Such an agenda suggests three points of reference for books within the Series: on the one hand that of language, on the other that of social theory, and thirdly, that of the particular professional context providing as it were a location for critical linguistic exploration.

Each of these reference points, however, is necessarily defined in relation to each of the others. Language, in this Series, is no autonomous construct, simply a system of sentences, but language as discourse, as action; similarly, society is no mosaic of individual existences looked in some stratified structure but a dynamic formation of relationships and practices constituted in large measure by struggles for power; professions not as guilds but as institutions whose conventions are ideologically shaped by such social relationships and realised through such particular discourses.

Characteristic of books in the Series will be their attitude to the relationship between theory and practice. It is expected that they will make a theoretical contribution to our understanding of language and society, exploring especially how they interconnect, but this contribution will arise from the description and interpretation of practice, accounting for what takes place. The intimacy of theory and practice is not by chance; it is crucial if we are to relate actions that are specific and local to the social institutions that give rise to them and if we are to explain what transpires in terms of theories of modern society.

To achieve this lays a responsibility upon the writer; he or she seeks after all a triple respectability, in relation to language and linguistics, to society and sociology and, most importantly, to those professional groups whose actions provide the data and the motivation for the descriptions, interpretations and explanations of the books which the Series will publish. We have, then, by necessity a multiple audience, which, while we hope it is a supportive and not adversarial one, is unlikely to be equally conversant in these three worlds. The books will have to make the connections, show the interdependence and display the relevance of the design.

To achieve this we are constructing books which reflect a general pattern, aimed at the engagement of the reader. One which emphasises problem-sensing (what are the linguistic, social and professional dimensions of the topic in question), problem-identifying (how the topic can be illuminated through the procedures of critical discourse analysis), problem-solving (what action may be undertaken in respect of the issues explored through the analysis in question). We are in no doubt that of these the third is the most problematic. Necessarily so, since it lies outside any book and is not in our hands. To ignore it, however, would rob the Series of its engagement with social action and its raison d'etre. We hope that the various measures undertaken in the composition of the books in the Series, and their style, will make this commitment to action plain.

I referred earlier to how this book provided the cornerstone to the Language in Social Life Series. Let me expand on the reasons for saying so. Norman Fairclough begins by defining the characteristics of Critical Language Study, distinguishing it from those other orientations within Linguistics which have sought to connect language with society. Central here are two assertions; that language is social practice and not a phenomenon external to society to be adventitiously correlated with it, and that language seen as discourse rather than as accomplished text compels us to take account not only of the artefacts of language, the products that we hear and see, but also the conditions of production and interpretation of texts, in sum the process of communicating of which the text is only a part. This emphasis is of central importance for Linguistics. It marks a movement away from the merely descriptive towards the interpretative, to an inclusion of the participants in the linguistic process, to a reconciliation of the psychological and the social with the textual, which radically alters the map of conventional linguistic study.

As importantly for Sociology as for Linguistics, he constructs a theory in which the connections between the orders of discourse (in Foucault's terms) the motivated and conventionalised selections from available linguistic options, and the orders of society are shown to be co-determined. To explore the one is to begin the explanation of the other. Such an explanatory process is most conveniently and most tellingly undertaken through the analysis of communication in particular social institutions, thus tying the macro analysis of society with the micro analysis of particular social exchanges. The arguments adduced here are important for students of social theory. They tie the abstractions of Bourdieu, Foucault and Habermas to the actualities of encounters, linking the work of British and Australian "critical linguists" (Fowler, Kress, Martin and others) to the mainstream of European social theory.

In other ways, too, this book exemplifies the Series of which it is the initiator. Throughout, Norman Fairclough offers his readers a carefully illustrated guide to the practice of the theory, selecting key texts for analysis and exploration, offering his own interpretations and explanations to be challenged by the reader with a different social history to his own. In sum, providing a discrete working out of the principles of Critical Language Study announced in his introductory Chapter.

From this analysis and exploration two salient principles emerge. The first, that of the primacy of particular research sites, is one already identified in distinct circumstances by Gumperz. On this view, research sites are not of equivalent salience and value to critical linguists. Rather than expending analysis on linguistic objets trouves (in Jakob Mey's telling phrase) the texts that so to speak fall off the back of trucks and bear no special social significance, we should address our talents as explorers and explainers to those texts which evidence crucial moments in discourse where participants may be placed at social risk during the communication, suffering disadvantage in consequence of the inequalities of communication. Occasions spring to mind easily: in medical, legal, educational, caring encounters, instances of interethnic miscommunication where life chances are at stake, migrant learners in an alien society, children at school, the speech and the hearing disadvantaged.

The second principle refers to the selection from the structures and modes of language itself. Critical language study identifies particular areas of language as having the greatest meaning potential for the understanding of the social process, privileging certain options from the whole array of features which are present for analysis. Chapters 5 and 6 within the book carefully outline these features and demonstrate how such an explanatory analysis can be carried out on the chosen texts. Here Norman Fairclough's distinctions between the experiential, relational and expressive values of linguistic features are of considerable significance for discourse analysts and linguists more generally, especially those in the Hallidayan tradition. Notable here is the discussion of intertextuality, in particular how the concept of social and inter-personal struggle can be seen working out, as it were, in the structures of discourse. The extended case-study of the discourse of Thatcherism provides an exemplary model.

We identified earlier one role of the Language in Social Life Series as the advancing of particular causes in the context of the need for social change. We did so not because we naively attri-bute to language either the ultimate cause of current disorders and inequities or, more romantically perhaps, because we believe that greater awareness of language in critical linguistic terms will easily restore or create the equilibrium many seek, but because it is our belief that an understanding of the social order is most conveniently and naturally achieved through a critical awareness of the power of language. More directly even, that access to and participation in the power forums of society is dependent on knowing the language of those forums and how using that language power enables personal and social goals to be achieved. It is entirely appropriate, therefore, that Chapter 9 of this book addresses this central question and especially so in relation to language education in the school. In many countries and many educational systems there is current concern surrounding the need for an enhanced communicative competence among school children from all social backgrounds. It is in itself interesting, and not perhaps surprising, that most concern centres around the concept of language deficit and attributes causes of such deficit to the inadequate learning by certain pupils of language seen as text. Now there are notable exceptions both to this focus and to its implied remedy, some of the most imaginative in fact from within Australia; what Norman Fairclough's book demonstrates very clearly is the implausibility of such a narrow definition of communicative incompetence in terms of text, the need to connect discoursal study and teaching to an understanding of contemporary society, and to see the critical consciousness of discourse as a basis for social emancipation.

Language and power, language is power; these are the themes of this first book in this new Series. The groundwork is laid, both linguistically and social theoretically, for the volumes that will follow. Several are in production or in active preparation, illuminating different professional worlds and exploring particular crucial communicative sites. All will derive benefit and a grounding from Norman Fairclough's book. It is a source of much personal pleasure to me as an erstwhile colleague and collaborator at the University of Lancaster where many of the ideas contained here were debated in detail, that his book has set this new Series off to such a productive start.

Christopher N Candlin
General Editor
Macquarie University, Sydney

Acknowledgements

The production of a book begins long before it starts to be written, and indirectly involves many more people than those who are directly involved. Some of these indirect contributors are acknowledged in the bibliography, but there are others whose impact has not been via the printed page. I wish first and foremost to thank Vonny for helping me to acquire the confidence to embark upon this book, and for her support throughout the time it has taken to write it. I also wish to thank past and current student and staff members of the Lancaster 'Language, Ideology and Power' research group for creating a good, rich soil in which this book could take root and grow, and other colleagues who have helped: Mike Breen, Chris Candlin, Luciano Cheles, Romy Clark, Daniela Gennrich, Roz Ivanic, Anna Jordanidou, Sarah Mann, Marilyn Martin-Jones, Donatella Pallotti, Mary Talbot, Virginia Samuda, Stef Slembrouk, Jenny Thomas, Ken Turner.

As to those who have been directly involved, my thanks to Romy Clark, Anna Jordanidou, Dick Leith, Marilyn Martin-Jones and Mary Talbot for valuable comments on parts of or all of the book, and especially to Chris Candlin, who has been extremely supportive throughout, and whose constructive criticism of earlier drafts has helped to make the book better than it would otherwise have been. I am not sure, given what some have proclaimed as 'the death of the author', how much sense it makes to ritually confess my responsibility for what is in the book, but I can say with my hand on my heart that I am more responsible for its faults than any of these friends and colleagues!

We are grateful to the following for permission to reproduce copyright material: the author Michael Bretherton for an extract from 'Options' 7.12.86 original broadcast by BBC Radio 4; the Prime Minister's Office and the BBC for an extract from Michael

ONE

Introduction: critical language study

'How do we recognize the shackles that tradition has placed upon us?
For if we can recognize them, we are also able to break them.'

Franz Boas

This book is about language and power, or more precisely about connections between language use and unequal relations of power, particularly in modern Britain. I have written it for two main purposes. The first is more theoretical: to help correct a widespread underestimation of the significance of language in the production, maintenance, and change of social relations of power. The second is more practical: to help increase consciousness of how language contributes to the domination of some people by others, because consciousness is the first step towards emancipation.

The more theoretical objective stems from my own academic background, which is in linguistics. Linguists, and especially those working in sociolinguistics (which is often said to deal with 'language in its social context') have had quite a lot to say about language and power, but they have not in my opinion done justice to the rich and complex interrelationships of language and power. There are for example many studies of 'standard' and 'nonstandard' social dialects, and of how the amount of prestige which attaches to such dialects depends on the power of their users. There have also been studies of the ways in which power is exercised in conversation and other forms of talk between people, though perhaps surprisingly few. These studies have generally set out to *describe* prevailing sociolinguistic conventions in terms of how they distribute power unequally; they have not set out to *explain* these conventions as the product of relations of power and struggles for power. The point is that sociolinguistic conventions have a dual relation to power: on the one hand they incorporate differences of power, on the other hand they arise out of – and give rise to – particular relations of power.

My main focus in this book will be on the second of these – on trying to explain existing conventions as the outcome of power relations and power struggle. My approach will put particular emphasis upon 'common-sense' assumptions which are implicit in the conventions according to which people interact linguistically, and of which people are generally not consciously aware. An example would be how the conventions for a traditional type of consultation between doctors and patients embody 'common-sense' assumptions which treat authority and hierarchy as natural – the doctor knows about medicine and the patient doesn't; the doctor is in a position to determine how a health problem should be dealt with and the patient isn't; it is right (and 'natural') that the doctor should make the decisions and control the course of the consultation and of the treatment, and that the patient should comply and cooperate; and so on. A crucial point is that it is possible, as we shall see, to find assumptions of this sort embedded in the forms of language that are used.

Such assumptions are *ideologies*. Ideologies are closely linked to power, because the nature of the ideological assumptions embedded in particular conventions, and so the nature of those conventions themselves, depends on the power relations which underlie the conventions; and because they are a means of legitimizing existing social relations and differences of power, simply through the recurrence of ordinary, familiar ways of behaving which take these relations and power differences for granted. Ideologies are closely linked to language, because using language is the commonest form of social behaviour, and the form of social behaviour where we rely most on 'common-sense' assumptions. But despite its importance for language, the concept of 'ideology' has very rarely figured in discussions of language and power within linguistics, which is itself symptomatic of their limitations.

It is not just because it has been neglected that I have chosen to focus upon the relatively neglected ideological dimension. My main reason for this choice is that the exercise of power, in modern society, is increasingly achieved through ideology, and more particularly through the ideological workings of language. We live in a linguistic epoch, as major contemporary social theorists such as Pierre Bourdieu, Michel Foucault, and Jürgen Habermas have recognized in the increasing importance they have given to language in their theories. Some people refer to 'the linguistic turn' in social theory – though more recently, writers on 'postmodernism' have claimed that visual images are ousting language, and have referred to postmodernist culture as 'post-linguistic'. It is not just that language has become perhaps the primary medium of social control and power, though that is noteworthy enough; language has grown dramatically in terms of the uses it is required to serve, in terms of the range of language varieties, and in terms of the complexity of the language capacities that are expected of the modern citizen. If, as I shall argue, ideology is pervasively present in language, that fact ought to mean that the ideological nature of language should be one of the major themes of modern social science.

Language is therefore important enough to merit the attention of all citizens. In particular, so far as this book is concerned, nobody who has an interest in modern society, and certainly nobody who has an interest in relationships of power in modern society, can afford to ignore language. That, to some degree or other, means everyone. Nevertheless, many people with precisely such interests have believed they could safely ignore language. This is perhaps not surprising, for the general level of attention and sensitivity to language has been woefully inadequate, and in particular the teaching of language in schools has to a remarkable extent contrived to ignore its most decisive social functions. This cannot be blamed on the teachers, because the same is true of most of the academic work on language which the teachers have been offered as models. This gap between the level of consciousness which the contemporary position of language demands, and the level it actually attracts, is another reason for my choice of focus.

It is important to emphasize that I am not suggesting that power is *just* a matter of language. There is always a danger, in focusing upon one aspect of a social relation or process, of being tempted to reduce it to that aspect alone, especially if as in this case it is a neglected aspect. Power exists in various modalities, including the concrete and unmistakable modality of physical force. It is a fact, if a sad fact, that power is often enough exercised through depriving people of their jobs, their homes, and their lives, as recent events in for example South Africa have reminded us. It is perhaps helpful to make a broad distinction between the exercise of power through *coercion* of various sorts including physical violence, and the exercise of power through the manufacture of *consent* to or at least acquiescence towards it. Power relations depend on both, though in varying proportions. Ideology is the prime means of manufacturing consent.

The more practical objective mentioned in the opening paragraph is to help increase consciousness of language and power, and particularly of how language contributes to the domination of some people by others. Given my focus on ideology, this means helping people to see the extent to which their language does rest upon common-sense assumptions, and the ways in which these common-sense assumptions can be ideologically shaped by relations of power. Although I shall be painting a somewhat depressing picture of language being increasingly caught up in domination and oppression, this will I hope be offset by my faith in the capacity of human beings to change what human beings have created. Resistance and change are not only possible but continuously happening. But the effectiveness of resistance and the realization of change depend on people developing a critical consciousness of domination and its modalities, rather than just experiencing them. The more practical objective of this book is therefore to make a contribution to the general raising of consciousness of exploitative social relations, through focusing upon language.

My aim has been to write a book which is accessible not only to students and teachers in higher education, but also to a variety of people in other spheres, and I have correspondingly not assumed that readers have specialist backgrounds in language study or indeed in social theory, though I imagine that most readers will have some acquaintance with one or the other. I have had in mind in particular those who are or may eventually be in a position to act as educators in a broad sense – who may be able to draw upon books such as this in order to produce appropriate informative or teaching materials suited to the particular needs and circumstances of particular groupings of people. This would include, most obviously, students, teachers and teacher trainers, and those who are involved in various forms of specialist vocational or professional training (of health workers or social workers, for instance). But there may be others, such as political and trade union activists, or activists in the peace, feminist, black, or other social movements, part of whose work is educational in this broader sense.

I have tried to make this book as accessible and as practically usable as possible, but no matter how practically organized a book of this sort may be, it is clearly not enough on its own for reaching the majority of the people who could make good use of some form of critical language analysis – and that, as I have said, really includes everyone. It needs to be complemented by pamphlets, leaflets, and other types of material (film, video, cartoons) which many people find more digestible than books. My hope is that among the readers of this book there will be educators who will be able to take this work forward.

I am sure that readers will have already formed some impression of the political position from which I am writing this book. It is widely understood that people researching and writing about social matters are inevitably influenced in the way they perceive them, as well as in their choice of topics and the way they approach them, by their own social experiences and values and political commitments. I think it is important not only to acknowledge these influences rather than affecting a spurious neutrality about social issues, but also to be open with one's readers about where one stands. I shall spell out in some detail my view of the society I belong to in Chapter 2; for the moment, let me say that I write as a socialist with a generally low opinion of the social relationships in my society and a commitment to the emancipation of the people who are oppressed by them. This does not, I hope, mean that I am writing political propaganda. The scientific investigation of social matters is perfectly compatible with committed and 'opinionated' investigators (there are no others!), and being committed does not excuse you from arguing rationally or producing evidence for your statements.

The approach to language which will be adopted here will be called *critical language study*, or CLS for short. *Critical* is used in the special sense of aiming to show up connections which may be hidden from people – such as the connections between language, power and ideology referred to above. CLS analyses social interactions in a way which focuses upon their linguistic elements, and which sets out to show up their generally hidden determinants in the system of social relationships, as well as hidden effects they may have upon that system.

APPROACHES TO LANGUAGE STUDY

There are many existing approaches to the study of language, so why do we need CLS? Because, while each of the approaches which I review below has something to contribute to CLS, they all have major limitations from a critical point of view. Just as important, the relationship which is standardly assumed to hold between these various branches of language study is itself unsatisfactory in a critical perspective, a point which I develop at the end of this section. The approaches to language study which I shall review are those of: linguistics, sociolinguistics, pragmatics, cognitive psychology and artificial intelligence, conversation and discourse analysis. I shall also say something about views of language in recent social theory. My aim is only to give a brief characterization of these complex areas of study from a critical perspective, and I shall refer mostly to 'mainstream' work, although most of them include other work which is in contention with the mainstream, and sometimes closer to a critical perspective than the mainstream.

Linguistics

The term *linguistics* is used ambiguously within the mainstream: it sometimes refers to all the branches of language study which are inside the academic discipline of linguistics (some are not), but it sometimes refers just to the branch which has the most privileged status, 'linguistics proper' as people occasionally say. I am referring here to 'linguistics proper', which is the study of 'grammar' in a broad sense: the sound systems of language ('phonology'), the grammatical structure of words ('morphology') and of sentences ('syntax'), and more formal aspects of meaning ('semantics'). Linguistics has won widespread acceptance within the human sciences and beyond for the centrality of language among human phenomena, and of language study among the human sciences. It has done so by developing an impressive array of systematic techniques for the description of language which have been widely drawn upon as models in other human sciences, and which any modern approach to language study (including CLS) can benefit from.

However, the achievements of linguistics have been bought at the price of a narrow conception of language study. It is a paradoxical fact that linguistics has given relatively little attention to actual speech or writing; it has characterized language as a potential, a system, an abstract competence, rather than attempting to describe actual language practice. In the terms of Ferdinand de Saussure, a founder of modern linguistics, linguistics is concerned with the study of *langue*, 'language', rather than *parole*, 'speaking'. Mainstream linguistics has taken two crucial assumptions about *langue* from Saussure: that the language of a particular community can for all practical purposes be regarded as invariant across that community, and that the study of *langue* ought to be 'synchronic' rather than historical – it ought to be studied as a static system at a given point in time, not dynamically as it changes through time. These assumptions and the neglect of language practice result in an idealized view of language, which isolates it from the social and historical matrix outside of which it cannot actually exist. Mainstream linguistics is an asocial way of studying language, which has nothing to say about relationships between language and power and ideology.

Sociolinguistics

Sociolinguistics has developed, partly under the influence of disciplines outside linguistics (notably anthropology and sociology), in reaction to the neglect by 'linguistics proper' of socially conditioned variation in language. Some practitioners see sociolinguistics as complementary to 'linguistics proper': the latter studies the invariant language system, whereas the former studies socially variable language practice ('use'). Others see sociolinguistics as challenging socially unrealistic aspects of mainstream linguistics. Sociolinguistics has shown systematic correlations between variations in linguistic form (phonological, morphological, syntactic) and social variables – the social strata to which speakers belong, social relationships between participants in linguistic interactions, differences in social setting or occasion, differences of topic, and so on. It is thanks to sociolinguistics that the socially constituted nature of language practice can be taken as a general premiss of CLS.

But sociolinguistics is heavily influenced by 'positivist' conceptions of social science: sociolinguistic variation in a particular society tends to be seen in terms of sets of facts to be observed and described using methods analogous to those of natural science. Sociolinguistics is strong on 'what?' questions (what are the facts of variation?) but weak on 'why?' and 'how?' questions (why are the facts as they are?; how – in terms of the development of social relationships of power – was the existing sociolinguistic order brought into being?; how is it sustained?; and how might it be changed to the advantage of those who are dominated by it?).

The tendency to take facts at face value is connected with the treatment of social class. The term *social class* is used, but it is often used to refer to what might better be referred to as 'social strata' – groupings of people who are similar to one another in occupation, education or other standard sociological variables. Social classes in the classical Marxist sense are social forces which occupy different positions in economic production, which have different and antagonistic interests, and whose struggle is what determines the course of social history. In terms of this conception of social class, the sociolinguistic facts can be seen as the outcome of class struggle and represent a particular balance of forces between classes. This conception of social class points to the 'why?' and 'how?' questions.

Also connected with the positivist orientation to facts is the general insensitivity of sociolinguistics towards its own relationship to the sociolinguistic orders it seeks to describe. When one focuses on the simple existence of facts without attending to the social conditions which made them so and the social conditions for their potential change, the notion that the sociolinguist herself might somehow affect the facts hardly seems to arise. But it does arise in the alternative scenario I have sketched out: if the facts of the existing sociolinguistic order are seen as lines of tension, as a temporary configuration representing the current balance of class forces, then the effect of sociolinguistic research might either be to legitimize these facts and so indirectly the power relations which underlie them, or to show the contingency of these facts despite their apparent solidity, and so indirectly point to ways of changing them. For instance, sociolinguistics has often described sociolinguistic conventions in terms of what are the 'appropriate' linguistic forms for a given social situation; whatever the intention, this terminology is likely to lend legitimacy to 'the facts' and their underlying power relations.

Pragmatics

We need to distinguish a broad continental European conception of pragmatics as 'the science of language use' (according to the first issue of the *Journal of Pragmatics*) and a much narrower Anglo-American conception of pragmatics as just one of a number of sub-disciplines which deal with language use, including sociolinguistics and psycholinguistics. There are tendencies within pragmatics in the former sense which amount to what I am calling CLS. However, I shall comment on the Anglo-American tradition only, because that is the one most familiar in the English-language literature.

Anglo-American pragmatics is closely associated with analytical philosophy, particularly with the work of Austin and Searle on 'speech acts'. The key insight is that language can be seen as a form of action: that spoken or written utterances constitute the performance of speech acts such as promising or asking or asserting or warning; or, on a different plane, referring to people or things, presupposing the existence of people or things or the truth of propositions, and implicating meanings which are not overtly expressed. The idea of uttering as acting is an important one, and it is also central to CLS in the form of the claim, presented in Chapter 2, that discourse is social practice.

The main weakness of pragmatics from a critical point of view is its individualism: 'action' is thought of atomistically as emanating wholly from the individual, and is often conceptualized in terms of the 'strategies' adopted by the individual speaker to achieve her 'goals' or 'intentions'. This understates the extent to which people are caught up in, constrained by, and indeed derive their individual identities from social conventions, and gives the implausible impression that conventionalized ways of speaking or writing are 'reinvented' on each occasion of their use by the speaker generating a suitable strategy for her particular goals. And it correspondingly overstates the extent to which people manipulate language for strategic purposes. Of course, people do act strategically in certain circumstances and use conventions rather than simply following them; but in other circumstances they do simply follow them, and what one needs is a theory of social action – social practice – which accounts for both the determining effect of conventions and the strategic creativity of individual speakers, without reducing practice to one or the other.

The individuals postulated in pragmatics, moreover, are generally assumed to be involved in cooperative interactions whose ground rules they have equal control over, and to which they are able to contribute equally. Cooperative interaction between equals is elevated into a prototype for social interaction in general, rather than being seen as a form of interaction whose occurrence is limited and socially constrained. The result is an idealized and Utopian image of verbal interaction which is in stark contrast with the image offered by CLS of a sociolinguistic order moulded in social struggles and riven with inequalities of power. Pragmatics often appears to describe discourse as it might be in a better world, rather than discourse as it is.

Pragmatics is also limited in having been mainly developed with reference to single invented utterances rather than real extended discourse, and central notions like 'speech act' have turned out to be problematic when people try to use them to analyse real discourse. Finally, Anglo-American pragmatics bears the scars of the way in which it has developed in relation to 'linguistics proper'. While it has provided a space for investigating the interdependence of language and social context which was not available before its inception, it is a strictly constrained space, for pragmatics tends to be seen as an additional 'level' of language study which fills in gaps left by the more 'core' levels of grammar and semantics. Social context is acknowledged but kept in its place, which does it less than justice.

Cognitive psychology and artificial intelligence

One of the concerns of pragmatics has been with the discrepancies which standardly exist between what is said and what is meant, and with how people work out what is meant from what is said; but the detailed investigation of the processes of comprehension involved, as well as of processes of production, has been undertaken by cognitive psychologists, and workers in artificial intelligence concerned with the computer simulation of production and comprehension. From the perspective of CLS, the most important result of work on comprehension is the stress which has been placed upon its active nature: you do not simply 'decode' an utterance, you arrive at an interpretation through an

active process of matching features of the utterance at various
levels with representations you have stored in your long-term
memory. These representations are prototypes for a very diverse
collection of things – the shapes of words, the grammatical forms
of sentences, the typical structure of a narrative, the properties
of types of object and person, the expected sequence of events
in a particular situation type, and so forth. Some of these are
linguistic, and some of them are not. Anticipating later
discussion, let us refer to these prototypes collectively as
'members' resources', or MR for short. The main point is that
comprehension is the outcome of interactions between the utterance being interpreted, and MR.

Not surprisingly, cognitive pyschology and artificial intelligence have given little attention to the social origins or significance of MR. I shall argue later that attention to the processes of
production and comprehension is essential to an understanding
of the interrelations of language, power and ideology, and that
this is so because MR are socially determined and ideologically
shaped, though their 'common sense' and automatic character
typically disguises that fact. Routine and unselfconscious resort
to MR in the ordinary business of discourse is, I shall suggest,
a powerful mechanism for sustaining the relations of power
which ultimately underlie them.

Conversation analysis and discourse analysis

Discourse analysis has recently been described as a new 'cross-
discipline', to which many established disciplines (linguistics,
sociology, anthropology, cognitive psychology among others)
have contributed. There are strands within discourse analysis in
this extended sense which are close to what I am calling CLS. I
shall concentrate on conversation analysis, which is one prominent approach within discourse analysis that has been developed
by a group of sociologists known as 'ethnomethodologists'.

Ethnomethodologists investigate the production and interpretation of everyday action as skilled accomplishments of social
actors, and they are interested in conversation as one particularly
pervasive instance of skilled social action. One of the strengths
of conversation analysis is that it works with extended samples
of real conversation. It has demonstrated that conversation is
systematically structured, and that there is evidence of the orien-

tation of participants to these structures in the ways in which they design their own conversational turns and react to those of others. These structures are social structures: one of the main concerns is to show that social structures are present and produced in everyday action, and are not just a property of abstract societal macrostructures.

But conversation analysis has been resistant to making connections between such 'micro' structures of conversation and the 'macro' structures of social institutions and societies. As a result, it gives a rather implausible image (similar to the image I attributed to pragmatics) of conversation as a skilled social practice existing in a social vacuum, as if talk were generally engaged in just for its own sake. This image is reinforced by the privileged status assigned to casual conversation between equals, especially telephone conversation, where the determinative effect of institutional and societal structures is perhaps least evident, though nonetheless real. It is also reinforced by the focus upon conversation as an accomplishment of the social actors who produce it, and the corresponding emphasis in the analysis upon the actor's perspective, which typically experiences the conventions of everyday action as just commonsensically 'there', rather than determined by and determinative of wider social structures. Conversation analysis is open to the criticism directed above at sociolinguistics, that it answers 'what?' questions but not 'how?' and 'why?' questions.

Some recent social theory

Finally, let me briefly mention recent contributions to social theory which have explored the role of language in the exercise, maintenance and change of power. I shall refer to just three such contributions. The first is work on the theory of ideology, which on the one hand has pointed to the increasing relative importance of ideology as a mechanism of power in modern society, as against the exercise of power through coercive means, and on the other hand has come to see language as a (or indeed the) major locus of ideology, and so of major significance with respect to power. The second is the influential work of Michel Foucault, which has ascribed a central role to discourse in the development of specifically modern forms of power. And the third is the equally influential work of Jürgen Habermas, whose 'theory of communicative action' highlights the way in which our currently distorted communication nevertheless foreshadows communication without such constraints. The main limitation of these contributions from the perspective of CLS is that they remain theoretical – they are not operationalized in the analysis of particular instances of discourse.

Relationship of CLS to these approaches

Ultimately, CLS is probably best understood not as just another approach to language study which complements those I have referred to by highlighting issues which they tend to ignore, but as an alternative orientation to language study which implies a different demarcation of language study into approaches or branches, different relationships between them, and different orientations within each of them. To fully elaborate this claim would need another book, and I shall limit myself to just quickly illustrating what I have in mind.

One aspect of power is the capacity to impose and maintain a particular structuring of some domain or other – a particular way of dividing it into parts, of keeping the parts demarcated from each other, and a particular ordering of those parts in terms of hierarchical relations of domination and subordination. Mainstream linguistics has imposed such a structuring on language study: the approaches I have been referring to are some of the 'parts' it differentiates, and 'linguistics proper' is privileged within this structuring of language study. All of the other approaches tend to be regarded as sub-disciplines which extend the results of 'linguistics proper' in various specialized directions – though they sometimes resist such subordination. From a critical perspective, this is unsatisfactory, both because branches of language study which belong closely together tend to be kept apart – this is the case for sociolinguistics and pragmatics, and for sociolinguistics and psychological work on production and comprehension, for example – and because it relegates the social nature of language to a sub-discipline. CLS would place a broad conception of the social study of language at the core of language study. It would also favour certain emphases within the various branches of study: for instance, in the study of grammar it would find 'functionalist' approaches (such as that of the systemic linguistics associated particularly with Michael Halliday) more helpful than 'formalist' approaches (such as that of Noam Chomsky and his associates).

It is not, however, within the scope of the present book to put forward a fully-fledged alternative to mainstream linguistics. Readers interested in such alternatives might wish to look at various existing proposals which move to some extent in that direction, and which harmonize to a degree with CLS: systemic linguistics, continental pragmatics, or cross-disciplinary trends in discourse analysis. As far as the present book is concerned, the focus is upon doing critical analyses of discourse samples; it will make some use of all the approaches I have referred to, but attempts to go beyond them in providing a synthesis of necessary theoretical concepts and analytical frameworks for doing critical analyses.

USING THIS BOOK

This book can be used as a coursebook, for informal group discussion, or by individual readers. I am assuming that in all cases readers will wish to be actively involved in doing CLS, rather than just reading about it. This orientation to doing analysis is built into the book in two main ways. Firstly, readers are invited to comment upon texts or carry out various other short exercises in most of the chapters below. In some cases, I give my own answers to reader-directed questions, in others I do not. These answers are *not* to be regarded as 'right'; they are merely there to give readers something against which to compare their own answers, particularly when the book is being used outside a class or group context. Readers' answers are likely to differ from mine, and this should be regarded not as grounds for consternation, but as worth exploring in itself. It may be due, for instance, to differences in the MR brought to the task of interpreting the text, which are just as important in determining how a text is interpreted as what is in the text itself. The second aspect of the orientation to analysis is the procedure for analysis which is presented in Chapters 5 and 6 (see below).

Here is a summary of chapter contents:

- **Chapters 2, 3 and 4** anchor the rest of the book theoretically. They set out a view of the interrelationship of language and society, with the emphasis upon power and ideology. The gist of my position is that language connects with the social through being the primary domain of ideology, and through being both a site of, and a stake in, struggles for power. Chapter 2 gives a general picture of the place of language in society, Chapters 3 and 4 focus respectively upon power and ideology.

- **Chapters 5 and 6** give a systematic presentation of a procedure for critical analysis. Chapter 5 deals with the description of texts, and Chapter 6 focuses on processes of producing and interpreting texts, and the analysis of their social determinants and effects. See Chapter 2 for these distinctions.

- **Chapters 7 and 8** explore change in discourse in relation to change in society. In Chapter 7, the emphasis is on individual creativity and its social conditions, with a case study on the political discourse of Thatcherism, which is used for an extended application of the procedure of Chapters 5 and 6. In Chapter 8, the focus shifts to large-scale tendencies in contemporary discourse in relation to main directions of change in contemporary capitalist society, drawing loosely upon some recent social theory (especially Habermas and Foucault).

- **Chapter 9** brings into focus an issue which is present throughout the book: how CLS could contribute to struggles for social emancipation. The chapter also suggests how readers might develop their interest in CLS.

Finally, a note on style. I have written in the first person, rather than disguise my personal views and interpretations in the 'impersonal' style which is more traditional in academic work. And I have operated with an image of the reader as not just someone to whom I am telling things (though sometimes I am!), but also as a partner in a collaborative venture. This is why I have sometimes used the pronoun 'we' inclusively, to refer to the reader and myself. But as I suggest in Chapter 5, this use of 'we' can be manipulative; it can claim a spurious solidarity, for instance when a politician uses it to convince people that she is 'one of them'. I hope that readers will not feel similarly dragooned into partnership: obviously, some readers will not see themselves as partners in critical discourse analysis, but in view of the practical objectives of the book, I have found it easier to write as if they did. This connects with a general risk run by writers on CLS: their critical apparatus is liable to be applied to their own writing, almost certainly with some success, because the impress of power and ideology on language is not self-evident, and it is not something that you can necessarily escape from in particular instances by virtue of being aware of it in general.

REFERENCES

Kramarae C et al. 1984 is a recent collection of papers on language and power written generally from a perspective which is different from mine. On ideology, see McLellan D 1986, and on the relation between ideology, power and language, see Thompson J B 1984. The following are representative of the various approaches to language study referred to: Fromkin V, Rodman R 1983 (linguistics); Downes W 1984 (sociolinguistics); Levinson S 1983 (pragmatics); van Dijk T, Kintsch W 1983 (cognitive psychology); Stubbs M 1983 (discourse analysis); Atkinson J M, Heritage J 1984 (conversation analysis). The description of discourse analysis as a new 'cross-discipline' is from the editor's introduction to the first volume of van Dijk T 1985; Mey J 1985 is representative of continental pragmatics; Halliday M A K 1978 sets out the perspective of systemic linguistics. On views of language in recent social theory, see: Dreyfus H L, Rabinow P 1982; McCarthy T 1978; and Thompson J B 1984. On postmodernism, see Jameson F 1984.

TWO

Discourse as social practice

This chapter gives a general picture of the place of language in society, which is developed in more specific terms in later chapters. It is most closely linked to Chapters 3 and 4, which elaborate this general picture in terms of, respectively, the relationship between language and power, and the relationship between language and ideology. Together, these three chapters present the main elements of the position which I am adopting in this book on the place of language in society: that language is centrally involved in power, and struggles for power, and that it is so involved through its ideological properties.

Let me summarize the major themes of Chapter 2 under its main section headings:

- **Language and discourse:** the conception of language we need for CLS is *discourse*, language as social practice determined by social structures.

- **Discourse and orders of discourse:** actual discourse is determined by socially constituted *orders of discourse*, sets of conventions associated with social institutions.

- **Class and power in capitalist society:** orders of discourse are ideologically shaped by power relations in social institutions and in society as a whole.

- **Dialectic of structures and practices:** discourse has effects upon social structures, as well as being determined by them, and so contributes to social continuity and social change.

AN EXAMPLE

As I said above, this chapter will be discussing language and society in relatively general terms which will be made more specific in later chapters. It does not lend itself as easily to textual illustrations of points as chapters 3 and 4 do, and it will therefore perhaps be helpful to have a concrete example which can be used to give a preliminary illustration of some of the main themes, and which we can also refer back to later in the chapter.

This text is part of an interview in a police station, involving the witness to an armed robbery (w) and a policeman (P), in which basic information elicitation is going on. w, who is rather shaken by the experience, is being asked what happened, P is recording the information elicited in writing.

(1) P: Did you get a look at the one in the car?
(2) w: I saw his face, yeah.
(3) P: What sort of age was he?
(4) w: About 45. He was wearing a . . .
(5) P: And how tall?
(6) w: Six foot one.
(7) P: Six foot one. Hair?
(8) w: Dark and curly. Is this going to take long? I've got to collect the kids from school.
(9) P: Not much longer, no. What about his clothes?
(10) w: He was a bit scruffy-looking, blue trousers, black . . .
(11) P: Jeans?
(12) w: Yeah.

How would you characterize the relationship between the police interviewer and **w** in this case, and how is it expressed in what is said?

The relationship is an unequal one, with the police interviewer firmly in control of the way the interview develops and of w's contribution to it, and taking no trouble to mitigate the demands he makes of her. Thus questions which might be quite painful for someone who has just witnessed a violent crime are never mitigated; P's question in turn 1, for example, might have been in a mitigated form such as *did you by any chance manage to get a good look at the one in the* instead of the bald form in which it actually occurs. In some cases, questions are reduced to words or minimal phrases – *how tall* in turn 5, and *hair* in turn 7. Such reduced questions are typical when one person is filling in a form 'for' another, as P is here; what is interesting is that the sensitive nature of the situation does not override the norms of form-filling. It is also noticeable that there is no acknowledgement of, still less thanks for, the information w supplies. Another feature is the way in which the interviewer checks what w has said in 7. Notice finally how control is exercised over w's contributions: P interrupts w's turn in 5 and 11, and in 9 P gives a minimal answer to w's question about how much longer the interview will take, not acknowledging her problem, and immediately asks another question thus closing off w's interpellation.

Would we be justified in saying that these properties are *arbitrary*? In one sense, they are, because they could be different. In another sense, however, they are anything but arbitrary: they are determined by social conditions, more specifically by the nature of the relationship between the police and members of the 'public' in our society, and indeed they are *part* of that relationship. If that relationship were to undergo dramatic changes – if members of local communities were elected by those communities to act as police officers on a triennial renewable basis, for instance – we can be pretty confident that police/'public' discourse would change too. This illustrates one major contention of this chapter – that social conditions determine properties of discourse.

Another is that we ought to be concerned with the processes of producing and interpreting texts, and with how these cognitive processes are socially shaped and relative to social conventions, not just with texts themselves. Consider for instance how w interprets the absence of any acknowledgement by the policeman of the information she supplies. If something similar happened in a friendly conversation, it would be experienced by participants as a real absence and a problem, maybe an indication of disbelief or embarrassment, and one would expect to find its problematical character reflected in formal features of the text (such as an 'embarrassed silence' or signs of hesitation). In the police interview, acknowledgement would I think not generally be expected, so its absence would not be experienced as a problem for someone in tune with the conventions for such interviews. This does indeed appear to be the case for w. The example illustrates that the way people interpret features of texts depends upon which social – more specifically, discoursal – conventions they are assuming to hold.

Finally, in this chapter I shall be highlighting not only the social determination of language use, but also the linguistic determination of society. Thus, for instance, one wishes to know to what extent the positions which are set up for members of the 'public' in the order of discourse of policing are passively occupied by them. In our example, w does indeed seem to be a fully compliant witness. In so far as such positions are compliantly occupied, the social relationships which determine them are sustained by the use of language. Conversely, in so far as dominant conventions are resisted or contested, language use can contribute to changing social relationships.

Think of cases where a feature of discourse may be interpreted in different ways depending on what social conventions people are operating with – like the example of w's interpretation of the lack of acknowledgements. Can people resist a particular set of conventions by insisting on interpreting features according to another set? Try rewriting the text with w in the position of resisting the conventions which the interviewer is operating with, specifically in respect of the lack of acknowledgement of information.

LANGUAGE AND DISCOURSE

This section develops the argument that, for CLS, the conception of language we need is that of *discourse*, language as a form of social practice. Then term *language* has been used in a number of different senses, including the two which linguists have standardly distinguished as *langue* and *parole* (as mentioned in Ch. 1). Neither of these is equivalent to discourse, but a discusssion of them may help to clarify some of the various conceptions of language, and how discourse differs from others.

Langue and parole

The distinction between *langue* and *parole* was made famous in the work of the Swiss linguist Ferdinand de Saussure. What I shall refer to is the way Saussure has generally been interpreted; his ideas are less clear and less simple than this might suggest, partly because published versions of his work were compiled posthumously by others.

Saussure regarded *langue* as a system or code which is prior to actual language use, which is the same for all members of a language community, and which is the *social* side of language as opposed to *parole*, which is individual. For Saussure, *parole*, what is actually said or written, is determined purely by individual choices, not socially at all. Linguistics, according to Saussure, is concerned primarily with *langue*, not *parole*.

Language use (*parole*) is, as Saussure was aware, characterized by extensive linguistic variation, and it is the account of this variation given by modern sociolinguistics which has done most to undermine the Saussurean concept of *parole*. Sociolinguistics has shown that this variation is not, as Saussure thought, a product of individual choice, but a product of social differentiation – language varies according to the social identities of people in interactions, their socially defined purposes, social setting, and so on. So Saussure's individualistic notion of *parole* is unsatisfactory, and in preferring the term *discourse* I am first of all committing myself to the view that language use is socially determined.

But what about *langue*? Saussure understood *langue* as something unitary and homogeneous throughout a society. But *is* there such a thing as 'a language' in this unitary and homogeneous sense? It is certainly the case that a good many people talk and act as if there were – we are all familiar with 'the English language', or 'English', and there is an army of specialists who teach 'English', give lectures about 'English', and write grammars and dictionaries of 'English'. Similarly for 'German', 'Russian', 'French', etc.

A *language* has been jokingly defined as 'a dialect with an army and a navy', but this is a joke with a serious undercurrent. Modern armies and navies are a feature of the 'nation state', and so too is the linguistic unification or 'standardization' of large politically defined territories which makes talk of 'English' or 'German' meaningful. When people talk about 'English' in Britain for instance, they generally have in mind British *standard* English, i.e. the standardized variety of British English. The spread of this variety into all the important public domains and its high status among most of the population are achievements of *standardization* (see Ch. 3) as a part of the economic, political and cultural unification of modern Britain. From this perspective, 'English' and other 'languages' appear to be the products of social conditions specific to a particular historical epoch.

But there is no historical specificity about the notion of *langue*; Saussure writes as if all language communities whatever their social conditions had their *langues*, and for him the possession of *langue* is a condition for the possession of language. Moreover, Saussure assumes that everyone in a language community has equal access to and command of its *langue*, whereas in reality access to and command of standard languages are unequal.

What is striking about the Saussurean notion of *langue*, as well as analogous uses of *language* by English-speaking linguists, is its similarity to some of the *rhetoric* of standardization. The real spread of a standard variety through a population and across domains of use is one aspect of standardization; rhetorical claims made on behalf of the standard variety – that it is the language of the whole people, that everyone uses it, that everyone holds it in high esteem, and so forth – are another. What these claims amount to is the transmutation of standard languages into mythical *national languages*. A political requirement for creating and sustaining a nation state is that its unifying institutions should have legitimacy among the mass of the people, and winning legitimacy often calls for such rhetoric. I am not suggesting that Saussure and other linguists set out to deliberately reproduce a politically motivated myth in their linguistic theory. But is it accidental that the emergence of the notion of *langue* occurred during a period when the myth of the 'national language' was at its height – the turn of the twentieth century?

Let me now relate this to my decision to focus upon *discourse*. I shall not accept the Saussurean concentration on language as opposed to language use; nor, on the other hand, shall I accept the individualistic notion of language use involved in *parole*. The emphasis should be on language use, but language use conceived of as socially determined, as what I call discourse. But part of Saussure's *langue/parole* distinction is a general one between underlying social conventions and actual use, and this is a distinction which I maintain, though in different terms (see the next section). However, I don't assume (as *langue* does) that conventions are unitary and homogeneous; on the contrary, they are characterized by diversity, and by power struggle. In so far as homogeneity is achieved – as it is to some extent in the case of standardization – it is imposed by those who have power. See Chapter 3 for a more detailed statement of this view.

Discourse as social practice

I have glossed the discourse view of language as 'language as a form of social practice'. What precisely does this imply? Firstly, that language is a part of society, and not somehow external to it. Secondly, that language is a social process. And thirdly, that language is a socially conditioned process, conditioned that is by other (non-linguistic) parts of society. I shall discuss these in turn.

It is not uncommon for textbooks on language to have sections on the relationship 'between' language and society, as if these were two independent entities which just happen to come into contact occasionally. My view is that there is not an external relationship 'between' language and society, but an internal and dialectical relationship. Language is a part of society; linguistic phenomena *are* social phenomena of a special sort, and social phenomena *are* (in part) linguistic phenomena.

Linguistic phenomena are social in the sense that whenever people speak or listen or write or read, they do so in ways which are determined socially and have social effects. Even when people are most conscious of their own individuality and think themselves to be most cut off from social influences – 'in the bosom of the family', for example – they still use language in ways which are subject to social convention. And the ways in which people use language in their most intimate and private encounters are not only socially determined by the social relationships of the family, they also have social effects in the sense of helping to maintain (or, indeed, change) those relationships.

Social phenomena are linguistic, on the other hand, in the sense that the language activity which goes on in social contexts (as all language activity does) is not merely a reflection or expression of social processes and practices, it is a *part* of those processes and practices. For example, disputes about the meaning of political expressions are a constant and familiar aspect of politics. People sometimes explicitly argue about the meanings of words like *democracy, nationalization, imperialism, socialism, liberation* or *terrorism*. More often, they use the words in more or less pointedly different and incompatible ways – examples are easy to find in exchanges between leaders of political parties, or between, say, the Soviet Union and the United States of America. Such disputes are sometimes seen as merely preliminaries to or outgrowths from the real processes and practices of politics. What I am suggesting is that they are not: they *are* politics. Politics partly consists in the disputes and struggles which occur in language and over language.

But it is not a matter of a symmetrical relationship 'between' language and society as equal facets of a single whole. The whole is society, and language is one strand of the social. And whereas all linguistic phenomena are social, not all social phenomena are linguistic – though even those that are not just linguistic (economic production, for instance) typically have a substantial, and often underestimated, language element.

Let us turn now to the second implication of regarding language as social practice – that language is a social process – and approach it through looking at what differentiates discourse from *text*. I shall be making extensive use of the term *text*, and shall use the term as the linguist Michael Halliday does, for both written texts and 'spoken texts'; a spoken text is simply what is said in a piece of spoken discourse, but I shall generally use the term for a written transcription of what is said.

A text is a product rather than a process – a product of the process of text production. But I shall use the term *discourse* to refer to the whole process of social interaction of which a text is just a part. This process includes in addition to the text the *process of production*, of which the text is a product, and the *process of interpretation*, for which the text is a resource. Text analysis is correspondingly only a part of discourse analysis, which also includes analysis of productive and interpretative processes. The formal properties of a text can be regarded from the perspective of discourse analysis on the one hand as *traces* of the productive process, and on the other hand as *cues* in the process of interpretation. It is an important property of productive and interpretative processes that they involve an interplay between properties of texts and a considerable range of what I referred to in Chapter 1 as 'members' resources ' (MR) which people have in their heads and draw upon when they produce or interpret texts – including their knowledge of language, representations of the natural and social worlds they inhabit, values, beliefs, assumptions, and so on.

However, no account of the processes of production and interpretation can be complete which ignores the way in which they are socially determined, which brings us to the third implication of seeing language as social practice: that it is conditioned by other, non-linguistic, parts of society. The MR which people draw upon to produce and interpret texts are cognitive in the sense that they are in people's heads, but they are social in the sense that they have social origins – they are socially generated, and their nature is dependent on the social relations and struggles out of which they were generated – as well as being socially transmitted and, in our society, unequally distributed. People internalize what is socially produced and made available to them, and use this internalized MR to engage in their social practice, including discourse. This gives the forces which shape societies a vitally important foothold in the individual psyche, though as we shall see, the effectiveness of this foothold depends on it being not generally apparent. Moreover, it is not just the nature of these cognitive resources that is socially determined, but also the conditions of their use – for instance, different cognitive strategies are conventionally expected when someone is reading a poem on the one hand, and a magazine advertisement on the other. It is important to take account of such differences when analysing discourse from a critical perspective.

Discourse, then, involves social conditions, which can be speci-fied as *social conditions of production,* and *social conditions of interpretation.* These social conditions, moreover, relate to three different 'levels' of social organization: the level of the social situation, or the immediate social environment in which the discourse occurs; the level of the social institution which constitutes a wider matrix for the discourse; and the level of the society as a whole. What I am suggesting, in summary, is that these social conditions shape the MR people bring to production and interpretation, which in turn shape the way in which texts are produced and interpreted. (See Fig. 2.1.)

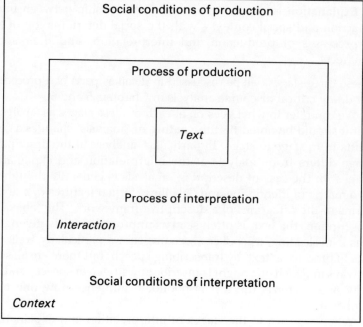

Fig. 2.1 Discourse as text, interaction and context

So, in seeing language as discourse and as social practice, one is committing oneself not just to analysing texts, nor just to analysing processes of production and interpretation, but to analysing the relationship between texts, processes, and their social conditions, both the immediate conditions of the situational context and the more remote conditions of institutional and social structures. Or, using the italicized terms in Fig. 2.1, the relationship between *texts*, *interactions*, and *contexts*.

Corresponding to these three dimensions of discourse, I shall distinguish three dimensions, or stages, of critical discourse analysis:

- **Description** is the stage which is concerned with formal properties of the text.
- **Interpretation** is concerned with the relationship between text and interaction – with seeing the text as the product of a process of production, and as a resource in the process of interpretation; notice that I use the term *interpretation* for both the interactional process and a stage of analysis, for reasons which will emerge in Chapter 6.
- **Explanation** is concerned with the relationship between interaction and social context – with the social determination of the processes of production and interpretation, and their social effects.

These three stages will be discussed in detail as parts of a procedure for doing critical discourse analysis in Chapters 5 and 6.

We can refer to what goes on at each of these stages as 'analysis', but it should be noted that the nature of 'analysis' changes as one shifts from stage to stage. In particular, analysis at the description stage differs from analysis at the interpretation and explanation stages. In the case of description, analysis is generally thought of as a matter of identifying and 'labelling' formal features of a text in terms of the categories of a descriptive framework. The 'object' of description, the text, is often seen as unproblematically given. But this is misleading, as spoken discourse shows particularly well: one has to produce a 'text' by transcribing speech, but there are all sorts of ways in which one might transcribe any stretch of speech, and the way one *interprets* the text is bound to influence how one transcribes it.

When we turn to the stages of interpretation and explanation, analysis cannot be seen in terms of applying a procedure to an 'object', even with provisos about the 'object'. What one is analysing is much less determinate. In the case of interpretation, it is the cognitive processes of participants, and in the case of explanation, it is relationships between transitory social events (interactions), and more durable social structures which shape and are shaped by these events. In both cases, the analyst is in the position of offering (in a broad sense) interpretations of complex and invisible relationships.

Although I shall for convenience use a notion of description along the lines indicated above, it should be said that description is ultimately just as dependent on the analyst's 'interpretation', in the broad sense in which I have just used the term, as the transcription of speech. What one 'sees' in a text, what one regards as worth describing, and what one chooses to emphasize in a description, are all dependent on how one interprets a text. There is a positivist (see Ch. 1 for this term) tendency to regard language texts as 'objects' whose formal properties can be mechanically described without interpretation. But try as they may, analysts cannot prevent themselves engaging with human products in a human, and therefore interpretative, way.

Verbal and visual language

Although the focus in this book will be mainly upon discourse which includes *verbal* texts, it would be quite artificial to conceive of discourse in exclusively verbal terms. Even when texts are essentially verbal – and I'm thinking here especially of spoken texts – talk is interwoven with gesture, facial expression, movement, posture to such an extent that it cannot be properly understood without reference to these 'extras'. Let's call them collectively *visuals*, on the grounds that they are all visually perceived by interpreters. Visuals can be an accompaniment to talk which helps determine its meaning – think for instance of the smirk which turns an innocent-sounding question into a nasty jibe. Or visuals can substitute for talk as a perfectly acceptable alternative; head-nodding, head-shaking and shrugging one's shoulders for *yes, no* and *I don't know* are obvious examples.

When we think of written, printed, filmed, or televised material, the significance of visuals is far more obvious. Indeed, the traditional opposition between spoken and 'written' language has been overtaken by events, and a much more helpful terminology in modern society would be *spoken* as opposed to *visual* language. It is well known, for example, that a photograph is often as important in getting across the 'message' of a report in a newspaper as the verbal report, and very often visuals and 'verbals' operate in a mutually reinforcing way which makes them very difficult to disentangle. Moreover, the relative social significance of visual imagery is increasing dramatically – think of the degree to which one of the most populous and pervasive modern discourse types, advertising, works through visuals. For all these reasons, I shall assume broad and nonrestrictive notions of discourse and text. Even though, as I have said, my focus is very much on the verbal element, visuals will feature at various points in the following chapters.

DISCOURSE AND ORDERS OF DISCOURSE

This section looks at one aspect of the social conditions of discourse and the determination of discourse by social structures: the way in which actual discourse is determined by underlying conventions of discourse. I regard these conventions as clustering in sets or networks which I call *orders of discourse*, a term used by Michel Foucault. These conventions and orders of discourse, moreover, embody particular ideologies.

The terms *discourse* and *practice* have what we might call a 'felicitous ambiguity': both can refer to either what people are doing on a particular occasion, or what people habitually do given a certain sort of occasion. That is, both can refer either to action, or to convention. The ambiguity is felicitous here because it helps underline the social nature of discourse and practice, by suggesting that the individual instance always implies social conventions – any discourse or practice implies conventional types of discourse or practice. The ambiguity also suggests social preconditions for action on the part of individual persons: the individual is able to act only in so far as there are social conventions to act within. Part of what is implied in the notion of social practice is that people are enabled through being constrained: they are able to act on condition that they act within the constraints of types of practice – or of discourse. However, this makes social practice sound more rigid than it is; as I shall argue in the final section of this chapter, being socially constrained does not preclude being creative.

I shall use the term *discourse* to refer to discoursal action, to actual talk or writing, and the term *practice* will be used in a parallel way. It can be used to refer generally to discoursal action, or to refer to specific instances (*a discourse*, and similarly *a practice*). I shall also use *discourse* when there is no risk of ambiguity to refer to a convention, a type of discourse (e.g. the discourse of police interviews). Where the meaning may be unclear, I shall use instead *discourse type*, or *discourse conventions*.

I suggested earlier that even the intimate and private interactions which occur within the family are socially determined. Think of the most personal and individual discourse of yourself and people you are close to. Do you agree even in this case with the claim that discourse always implies discoursal conventions?

Discourse and practice are constrained not by various independent types of discourse and practice, but by interdependent networks which we can call 'orders' – *orders of discourse* and *social orders*. The social order is the more general of the two. We always experience the society and the various social institutions within which we operate as divided up and demarcated, *structured* into different spheres of action, different types of situation, each of which has its associated type of practice. I will use the term *social order* to refer to such a structuring of a particular social 'space' into various domains associated with various types of practice. What I shall call an order of discourse is really a social order looked at from a specifically discoursal perspective – in terms of those types of practice into which a social space is structured which happen to be discourse types. This is summarized in Fig. 2.2.

I referred above to social orders as *structured*: social orders will differ not only in which types of practice they include, but also

Social order	Order of discourse
Types of practice	Types of discourse
Actual practices	Actual discourses

Fig. 2.2 Social orders and orders of discourse

in how these are related to each other, or structured. Similarly, orders of discourse will differ in both discourse types, and the way they are structured. For example, we find 'conversation' as a discourse type in various orders of discourse, associated with various social institutions. That is interesting in itself. But it is even more interesting to see how orders of discourse differ in terms of the relationship (complementarity, opposition, mutual exclusion, or whatever) between conversation and other discourse types. For instance, conversation has no 'on-stage' role in legal proceedings, but it may have a significant 'off-stage' role in, for example, informal bargaining between prosecution and defence lawyers. In education, on the other hand, conversation may have approved roles not only before and after classes are formally initiated by teachers, but also as a form of activity embedded within the discourse of the lesson.

In addition to the order of discourse of a social institution, which structures constituent discourses in a particular way, we can refer to the order of discourse of the society as a whole, which structures the orders of discourse of the various social institutions in a particular way. How discourses are structured in a given order of discourse, and how structurings change over time, are determined by changing relationships of power at the level of the social institution or of the society. Power at these levels includes the capacity to control orders of discourse; one aspect of such control is ideological – ensuring that orders of discourse are ideologically harmonized internally or (at the societal level) with each other. See Chapter 3 for more details.

Let us relate this to the interview example introduced earlier. This is a discourse (or more precisely a part of a discourse) which draws upon a single discourse type of witness interviews, or more specifically, an information-gathering phase or episode of such a discourse type. The relationship between convention and practice, discourse type and discourse, seems quite straightforward – quite conventional – in this case; the features which I noted earlier strike me as predictable for this type. The discourse type is an element in the order of discourse associated with policing as a social institution. It contrasts with others, such as the discourses of making an arrest, or charging a suspect, and this episode is also in contrast with others in the discourse of interviewing a witness, such as interrogation, or questioning aimed at testing out a story. Although it is the prerogative of the more powerful participants, in this case the police interviewers, to determine which discourse type(s) is/are the 'appropriate' ones to draw upon in a given situation, the choice positions all participants in a determinate place in the order of discourse and the social order of police work. It also positions them in terms of one of a number of procedures for dealing with cases, which are constituted by a series of discourse types in determinate orders: information gathering is likely to be followed by interrogation which may result in a charge being laid, for example. Thus even a small extract like this one implies not just a particular discourse type, but an order of discourse.

In saying that discourse *draws upon* discourse types (and practice upon types of practice), I have been trying to avoid any suggestion of a mechanical relationship between the two. Although we must have conventions in order to be able to engage in discourse, the latter is not simply a realization or implementation of the former. In fact, a particular discourse may well draw upon two or more discourse types, and the possible ways in which types may in principle be combined are innumerable. Rather than mechanical implementation, discourse should be thought of as the creative extension-through-combination of existing resources, with conventional cases of a discourse drawing upon a single discourse type as in the interview extract being thought of as limiting cases rather than the norm. See the section *Dialectic of structures and practices* below, and Chapter 7.

> Think of your own current or former place of work or study in terms of its social practices, as a social order and an order of discourse. List some of the major types of practice, and try to work out how they are demarcated from each other – maybe in terms of the sorts of situation, and participant, they are associated with. To what extent are they discoursal and to what extent are they non-discoursal?

CLASS AND POWER IN CAPITALIST SOCIETY

This section extends the discussion of the social conditions of discourse at the societal and institutional levels, suggesting how social structures at these levels determine discourse. The way in which orders of discourse are structured, and the ideologies which they embody, are determined by relationships of power in particular social institutions, and in the society as a whole. We therefore need to be sensitive in critical language analysis to properties of the society and institutions we are concerned with. In what follows, I shall first identify, though only schematically, some basic structural characteristics and tendencies of British society; similar features are evident in comparable capitalist societies. I shall then point to ways in which characteristics of discourse in modern Britain appear to be determined by these features. Readers will find a more detailed analysis in these terms in Chapter 8. I should stress that the interpretation of British society which I give is not a neutral one – there are none – but one which reflects my own experience, values, and political commitments.

The way in which a society organizes its economic production, and the nature of the relationships established in production between social classes, are fundamental structural features which determine others. In capitalist society, production is primarily the production for private profit of commodities, goods which are sold on the market – as opposed to the production of goods for immediate consumption by their producers, for instance. And the class relationship on which this form of production depends is between a (capitalist) class which owns the means of production, and a (working) class who are obliged to sell their power to work to the capitalists, in exchange for a wage, in order to live.

But aren't a great many people in a somewhat tangential relationship to this production process rather than directly involved? This seems to be true of the increasing number who work in 'service' and 'leisure' industries, various categories of 'professional' workers and so on. Some of these people perhaps constitute minor classes; some of them (e.g. professional workers) are standardly assigned to a 'middle class' or *petit bourgeois* class. I shall refer rather loosely to a 'middle class', but I shall also assume that the working class is internally complex in modern Britain, and includes 'service', 'leisure', 'technical' and other groups of workers, as well as a 'core' of workers who produce commodities.

Economic, state, and ideological power

The relationship between social classes starts in economic production, but extends to all parts of a society. The power of the capitalist class depends also on its ability to control the *state*: contrary to the view of the state as standing neutrally 'above' classes, I shall assume that the state is the key element in maintaining the dominance of the capitalist class, and controlling the working class. This political power is typically exercised not just by capitalists, but by an alliance of capitalists and others who see their interests as tied to capital – many professional workers, for instance. We can refer to this alliance as the *dominant bloc*.

State power – including Government, control of the police and the armed forces, the civil service, and so forth – is decisive in periods of crisis. But in more normal conditions of life in capitalist society, a whole range of social institutions such as education, the law, religions, the media, and indeed the family, collectively and cumulatively ensure the continuing dominance of the capitalist class. The people who have power in these social institutions often have very little in the way of direct links to the capitalist class. Think of the local education authorities, school governors and senior teachers who are responsible for most of what goes on in schools, for example. Nevertheless, analyses of the way in which education and other institutions train children to fit into and accept the existing system of class relations are very persuasive.

We can explain this partly in terms of the people with power in institutions mainly seeing their interests as tied in with capitalism. But a more significant factor is *ideology*. Institutional practices which people draw upon without thinking often embody assumptions which directly or indirectly legitimize existing power relations. Practices which appear to be universal and common-sensical can often be shown to originate in the dominant class or the dominant bloc, and to have become *naturalized*. Where types of practice, and in many cases types of discourse, function in this way to sustain unequal power relations, I shall say they are functioning *ideologically*.

Ideological power, the power to project one's practices as universal and 'common sense', is a significant complement to economic and political power, and of particular significance here because it is exercised in discourse. There are (as mentioned briefly in Ch. 1) in gross terms two ways in which those who have power can exercise it and keep it: through coercing others to go along with them, with the ultimate sanctions of physical violence or death; or through winning others' consent to, or at least acquiescence in, their possession and exercise of power. In short, through *coercion* or *consent*. In practice, coercion and consent occur in all sorts of combinations. The state includes repressive forces which can be used to coerce if necessary, but any ruling class finds it less costly and less risky to rule if possible by consent. Ideology is the key mechanism of rule by consent, and because it is the favoured vehicle of ideology, discourse is of considerable social significance in this connection. See Chapter 4 for a full discussion, but also further below.

> Think again of your own workplace, place of study, or some other institution you know, in terms of the balance which exists between coercion and consent, force and ideology, in the maintenance of social control. Can you identify particular types of discourse which are important ideologically in 'rule by consent'?

Power relations, class relations, and social struggle

Power relations are not reducible to class relations. There are power relations between social groupings in institutions, as we have seen, and there are power relations between women and men, between ethnic groupings, between young and old, which are not specific to particular institutions. One of the problems in analysing contemporary capitalism is how to see the connection between class relations and these other types of relation. On the one hand, there is no simple transparent connection between them which would justify *reducing* these other relations to class relations, by seeing them as merely indirect expressions of class. On the other hand, class relations define the nature of the society, and have a funda-mental and pervasive influence on all aspects of the society, including these other relations, so that it is not acceptable to regard gender, race and so forth as simply parallel to class. I shall regard class relations as having a more fundamental status than others, and as setting the broad parameters within which others are constrained to develop, parameters which are broad enough to allow many options which are narrowed down by determinants autonomous to the particular relation at issue.

Power relations are always relations of *struggle*, using the term in a technical sense to refer to the process whereby social group-ings with different interests engage with one another. Social struggle occurs between groupings of various sorts – women and men, black and white, young and old, dominating and dominated groupings in social institutions, and so on. But just as class relations are the most fundamental relations in class society, so too is class struggle the most fundamental form of struggle. Class struggle is a necessary and inherent property of a social system in which the maximization of the profits and power of one class depends upon the maximization of its exploitation and domination of another. Social struggle may be more or less intense and may appear in more or less overt forms, but all social developments, and any exercise of power, take place under conditions of social struggle. This applies also, as we shall see in Chapter 3, to language: language is both a site of and a stake in class struggle, and those who exercise power through language must constantly be involved in struggle with others to defend (or lose) their position.

Changes in capitalism

Capitalism has undergone many changes since the nineteenth century. Marx identified in his economic analyses a tendency towards *monopoly*, towards the concentration of production in an ever-decreasing number of ever-larger units. This tendency has become more pronounced with the passage of time, and the scale of concentration is now international: a relatively small number of massive multinational corporations now dominate production in the capitalist world.

At the same time, the capitalist economic domain has been progressively enlarged to take in aspects of life which were previously seen as quite separate from production. The *commodity* has expanded from being a tangible 'good' to include all sorts of intangibles: educational courses, holidays, health insurance, and funerals are now bought and sold on the open market in 'packages', rather like soap powders. And an ever greater focus has been placed upon the consumption of commodities, a tendency summed up in the term *consumerism*. As a result, the economy and the commodity market massively impinge upon people's lives, including, especially through the medium of television, their 'private' lives in the home and the family.

Another tendency which has been taking place in parallel with this is increasing state and institutional control over people through various forms of bureaucracy. On the one hand, the state has become increasingly interventionary to create the conditions for the smooth operation of the multinational corporations, in terms of currency controls, control of inflation, constraints on wages and on the capacity of trade unions to take industrial action, and so forth. On the other hand, the reverse side of the benefits which people have gained from the welfare state is a sharp increase in the extent to which individual members of 'the public' are subjected to bureaucratic scrutiny.

> Can you find examples of the expansion of the commodity? Look out particularly for cases where the language of commodities is extended to other domains (e.g. 'that's a great idea, but can you sell ideas like that to people? will they buy it, no matter how you package it?').

Analysis of society and analysis of discourse

I shall now suggest in broad terms some relationships of determination which might usefully be explored between these characteristics of modern capitalist society and characteristics of orders of discourse. In what follows, I have modern Britain particularly in mind.

I stressed the importance of ideology in the way in which various social institutions contribute to sustaining the position of the dominant class. Modern society is characterized by rather a high degree of integration of social institutions into the business of maintaining class domination. Correspondingly, one might expect a high degree of ideological integration between institutional orders of discourse within the societal order of discourse. And I think one finds this. There are for instance certain key discourse types which embody ideologies which legitimize, more or less directly, existing societal relations, and which are so salient in modern society that they have 'colonized' many institutional orders of discourse. They include advertising discourse, and the discourses of interviewing and counselling/therapy. Advertising, for instance, firmly embeds the mass of the population within the capitalist commodity system by assigning them the legitimate and even desirable role of 'consumers'.

I also suggested above a special relationship between ideology and the exercise of power by consent as opposed to coercion. I think that in modern society, social control is increasingly practised, where this is feasible, through consent. This is often a matter of integrating people into apparatuses of control which they come to feel themselves to be a part of (e.g. as consumers or as owners of shares in the 'share-owning democracy'). Since discourse is the favoured vehicle of ideology, and therefore of control by consent, it may be that we should expect a quantitative change in the role of discourse in achieving social control. For instance, the constant doses of 'news' which most people receive each day are a significant factor in social control, and they account for a not insignificant proportion of a person's average daily involvement in discourse. But the increasing reliance on control through consent is also perhaps at the root of another, qualitative feature of contemporary discourse: the tendency of the discourse of social control towards simulated egalitarianism, and the removal of surface markers of authority and power. One finds this in orders of discourse as varied as advertising, education, and government bureaucracy. Detailed discussion and examples of the points raised in this section can be found in Chapter 8.

DIALECTIC OF STRUCTURES AND PRACTICES

The relationship between discourse and social structures is not the one-way relationship which I have suggested so far. As well as being determined by social structures, discourse has effects upon social structures and contributes to the achievement of social continuity or social change. It is because the relationship between discourse and social structures is dialectical in this way that discourse assumes such importance in terms of power relationships and power struggle: control over orders of discourse by institutional and societal power-holders is one factor in the maintenance of their power.

Let us begin from a more general consideration of the relationship of social practice and reality. Social practice does not merely 'reflect' a reality which is independent of it; social practice is in an active relationship to reality, and it changes reality. The world that human beings live in is massively a humanly created world, a world created in the course of social practice. This applies not only to the social world but also to what we normally call the 'natural world', for the essence of human labour is that it creates the means of life for people by transforming the natural world. As far as the social world is concerned, social structures not only determine social practice, they are also a product of social practice. And more

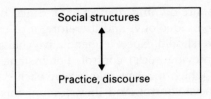

Fig. 2.3 Social structures and social practice

particularly, social structures not only determine discourse, they are also a product of discourse. This is represented in Fig. 2.3.

Example: Subject positions in schools

Let us make this claim more concrete by referring to an example of the social structure of a social institution: the school. The school has a social order and an order of discourse which involve a distinctive structuring of its 'social space' into a set of situations where discourse occurs (class, assembly, playtime, staff meeting, etc.), a set of recognized 'social roles' in which people participate in discourse (headteacher, teacher, pupil, prefect, etc.), and a set of approved purposes for discourse – learning and teaching, examining, maintaining social control, as well as a set of discourse types. Focusing upon 'social roles' or what I shall prefer to call *subject positions* (a term I shall explain shortly), there is a sense in which we can say that the teacher and the pupil *are what they do*. The discourse types of the classroom set up subject positions for teachers and pupils, and it is only by 'occupying' these positions that one becomes a teacher or a pupil. Occupying a subject position is essentially a matter of doing (or not doing) certain things, in line with the discoursal rights and obligations of teachers and pupils – what each is allowed and required to say, and not allowed or required to say, within that particular discourse type. So this is a case where social structure, in the particular form of discourse conventions, determines discourse. But it is also the case that in occupying particular subject positions, teachers and pupils *reproduce* them; it is only through being occupied that these positions continue to be a part of social structure. So discourse in turn determines and reproduces social structure.

The 'subject'

However, what I have just described is a closed circle: discourse types determine discourse practice, which reproduces discourse types. The concept of reproduction is more complex and more socially interesting and significant than that. To see why, let us look at my choice of the term *subject (position)* instead of 'social role'. *Subject* has yet another of those 'felicitous ambiguities' we have already met with in *practice* and *discourse*, though of rather a different order. In one sense of *subject*, one is referring to someone who is under the jurisdiction of a political authority, and hence passive and shaped: but the *subject* of a sentence, for instance, is usually the active one, the 'doer', the one causally implicated in action.

Social subjects are constrained to operate within the subject positions set up in discourse types, as I have indicated, and are in that sense passive; but it is only through being so constrained that they are made able to act as social agents. As I said earlier, being constrained is a precondition for being enabled. Social agents are active and *creative*. Recall my insistence that discourse (and practice generally) *draws upon* discourse types rather than mechanically implementing them, and the suggestion there that discourses typically draw upon a combination of types. Discourse types are a resource for subjects, but the activity of combining them in ways that meet the ever-changing demands and contradictions of real social situations is a creative one. See Chapter 7 for a detailed argument to this effect.

The term *reproduction* requires some comment. Whenever people produce or interpret discourse, they necessarily draw upon orders of discourse and other aspects of social structure, internalized in their MR, in order to do so. Through being drawn upon, these structures are constantly being created anew in discourse and practice generally. Discourse, and practice in general, in this sense are both the products of structures and the producers of structures. It is this process of being produced anew (re-produced) through being drawn upon that I refer to as reproduction. But structures may be produced anew with virtually no change, or (through the creative combinations referred to above) they may be produced anew in modified forms. Reproduction may be basically conservative, sustaining continuity, or basically transformatory, effecting changes.

The relations of power which obtain between social forces, and the way in which these relations develop in the course of social struggle, are a key determinant of the conservative or transformatory nature of reproduction in discourse. Thus I have been suggesting that orders of discourse embody ideological assumptions, and these sustain and legitimize existing relations of power. If there is a shift in power relations through social struggle, one can expect transformation of orders of discourse. Conversely, if power relations remain relatively stable, this may give a conservative quality to reproduction. However, this is not necessarily the case, for even if power relations remain relatively stable, they need to renew themselves in a constantly changing world, and transformations of orders of discourse may thus be necessary even for a dominant social grouping to keep its position.

> Look for examples of the creative combination of discourse types. Advertising is a good source, in that many different types are exploited as vehicles for selling things.

Reproducing class: hidden agendas

But what about the case of more abstract and diffuse aspects of social structures, such as the relationship between social classes in a society? Class relations also determine discourse (and social practice generally) on the one hand, but are reproduced in discourse on the other. But class relations and positions are not directly expressed and reproduced in most practice. The connection between class relations and discourses is a mediated one, mediated precisely by the various discourse types of the social institutions in a society. In terms of reproduction, we can say that, for example, the teacher–pupil relations, and the teacher and pupil positions, embedded in educational discourse types are directly reproduced in educational discourse, while the same discourse indirectly reproduces class relations. The general point is that education, along with all the other social institutions, has as its 'hidden agenda' the reproduction of class relations and other higher-level social structures, in addition to its overt educational agenda.

Because they are indirect and 'hidden', neither the social determination of the discourse types of the various institutions (and thereby of discourse) by more abstract levels of social structure, nor their effect on these levels of social structure, are apparent to subjects in the normal course of events. In the words of Pierre

Bourdieu, 'it is because subjects do not, strictly speaking, know what they are doing that what they do has more meaning than they know'. This *opacity* of discourse (and practice in general) indicates why it is of so much more social importance than it may on the face of it seem to be: because in discourse people can be legitimizing (or delegitimizing) particular power relations without being conscious of doing so. It also indicates both the basis for critical analysis in the nature of discourse and practice – there are things that people are doing that they are unaware of – and the potential social impact of critical analysis as a means of raising people's self-consciousness.

A word on the police interview extract in the light of these themes. Being a police officer or being a police witness is a matter of occupying the subject positions set up in discourses such as the discourse of (information-gathering in) interviews which is drawn upon in the extract. And it is only in so far as people do routinely occupy these positions that the conventional personae of police officer and witness are reproduced as a part of the social structure of policing as an institution. But mundane and conventional practice such as we have in the extract also indirectly contributes to the reproduction of the unequal social relations of our society, through naturalizing hierarchy, the routine insensitive manipulation of people in the interests of bureaucratic goals of efficiency, and the image of the police as helpers and protectors of us all (rather than an arm of the state apparatus). People who take part in such interviews, including police officers, are unlikely to be generally conscious of these reproductive effects.

> Think about a social institution you operate within yourself in the light of what I have said in this section. What are the major *subject positions* occupied by people in discourse? Focus on one such subject position – maybe one you commonly occupy yourself: what is it that you are obliged or allowed to do or not do in discourse that distinguishes the subject position? And, finally, think about how the practice of this institution might be reproducing higher-level social structures such as class relations as part of a 'hidden agenda'.

SUMMARY AND CONCLUSIONS

In this chapter, I have suggested that CLS ought to conceptualize language as a form of social practice, what I have called *discourse*; and that correspondingly it ought to stress both the determination of discourse by social structures, and the effects of discourse upon society through its reproduction of social structures. Both the determination of discourse and its effects involve not just elements in the social situations of discourse, but orders of discourse which are the discoursal aspects of social orders at the societal and social institutional levels. People are not generally aware of determinations and effects at these levels, and CLS is therefore a matter of helping people to become conscious of opaque causes and consequences of their own discourse.

This chapter has laid foundations which will be built upon in subsequent chapters. A consequence of seeing discourse as just a particular form of social practice is perhaps that language research ought to be more closely in tune with the rhythms of social research than it has tended to be. In Chapters 7 and 8 I explore linguistic dimensions of social changes with a view to determining what part discourse has in the inception, development and consolidation of social change. But more immediately, I need to put more flesh upon the relationship between discourse, power and ideology which, I have suggested, is at the centre of the social practice of discourse. This is my objective in Chapters 3 and 4, which focus respectively on power and on ideology in their relationships to discourse.

REFERENCES

For some views of 'discourse', and how it differs from 'text', see: Stubbs M 1983; Widdowson H 1979: 89–149; and Brown G, Yule G 1983. On the concepts of 'practice', 'reproduction', and 'subject', see Althusser L 1971. Henriques J *et al.* 1984 is a useful more recent compilation on the subject. The *langue–parole* distinction is drawn in de Saussure F 1966, and Culler J 1976 is a lucid commentary on Saussure. On the distinction between 'description', 'interpretation' and 'explanation' see Fairclough N 1985 and Candlin C N 1986. Barthes R 1972 and 1977 contain interesting insights about visual images. My interpretation of class and power in contemporary Britain draws upon a variety of sources including: Communist Party of Great Britain 1978; the monthly periodical *Marxism Today*; Habermas J 1984; and the writings of Marx, Engels, Lenin, Gramsci and others – see for instance: Marx K, Engels F 1968; Gramsci A 1971. Foucault uses the term 'order of discourse' in Foucault M 1971, and the Bourdieu quotation is from Bourdieu P 1977.

THREE

Discourse and power

The purpose of this chapter is to explore various dimensions of the relations of power and language. I focus upon two major aspects of the power/language relationship, power *in* discourse, and power *behind* discourse. This picks up a distinction which was made in the opening pages of Chapter 1.

The section on power in discourse is concerned with discourse as a place where relations of power are actually exercised and enacted; I discuss power in 'face-to-face' spoken discourse, power in 'cross-cultural' discourse where participants belong to different ethnic groupings, and the 'hidden power' of the discourse of the mass media.

The section on power behind discourse shifts the focus to how orders of discourse, as dimensions of the social orders of social institutions or societies, are themselves shaped and constituted by relations of power, a process already referred to in Chapter 2. The section discusses, as effects of power: the differentiation of dialects into 'standard' and 'nonstandard'; the conventions associated with a particular discourse type, the discourse of gynaecological examinations; and constraints on access to discourses within an order of discourse.

The final section of the chapter adds a vitally important proviso to what precedes it: power, whether it be 'in' or 'behind' discourse, is never definitively held by any one person, or social grouping, because power can be won and exercised only in and through social struggles in which it may also be lost.

POWER IN DISCOURSE

Let us begin the discussion of power in discourse with an example of the exercise of power in a type of 'face-to-face' discourse where participants are unequal – what we might call an *unequal encounter*. The following is an extract from a visit to a premature baby unit by a doctor (D) and a group of medical students (S), as part of the students' training programme. A spaced dot indicates a short pause, a dash a longer pause, extended square brackets overlap, and parentheses talk which was not distinguishable enough to transcribe.

(1) D: and let's gather round . the first of the infants – now what I want you to do is to make a basic . neo-natal examination just as Dr Mathews has to do as soon as a baby arrives in the ward . all right so you are actually going to get your hands on the infant . and look at the key points and demonstrate them to the group as you're doing it will you do that for me please . off you go

(2) S: well first of all I'm going to [( )

(3) D: [first . before you do that is do you wash your hands isn't it I . cos you've just been examining another baby (long silence) are you still in a are you in a position to start examining yet ( )

(4) S: just going to remove this .

(5) D: very good . it's putting it back that's the problem isn't it eh –

(6) S: come back Mum —

(7) D: that's right. OK now just get a little more room by shifting baby . er up the . thing a bit more that's very good . well now . off you go and describe what's going on

(8) S: well here's a young baby boy . who we've decided is . thirty . thirty seven weeks old now . was born . two weeks ago . um is fairly active . his er eyes are open . he's got hair on . his head[. his eyes are[open

(9) D: [yes [yes you've told me that

(10) S: um he's crying or[making

(11) D: [yeah we we we we've heard that now what other examination are you going to make I mean —

(12) S: erm we'll see if he'll respond to

(13) D: now look . did we not look at a baby with a head problem yesterday .

(14) S: right

(15) D: and might you not make one examination of the head
         almost at square one . before you begin .
(16) S: feel for the (   )
(17) D: now what ⌈. the next most important thing .
(18) S: ⌊er   gross mo-
         gross motor ⌈function
(19) D: ⌊well now you come down to the mouth
         don't we.
(20) S: yes
(21) D: now what about the mouth

Text 3.1 Source: 'The Boys from Horseferry Road', Granada Tele-
         vision 1980

One immediately striking feature, marked by the square
brackets, is the number of times the doctor interrupts the student
– in (3), (9), (11), (13), and (19). (There are no square brackets in
(13), because there is no actual overlap.) My impression is that
the doctor does not interrupt simply because he wants to do all
the talking, as people sometimes do. I think he interrupts in order
to *control* the contributions of the student – to stop him beginning
the examination before washing his hands, to stop him repeating
information or giving obvious and irrelevant information, to
ensure the student gives the key information expected.

**In what other ways does the doctor exercise control over the student's
contributions?**

Firstly, in the opening turn, where the nature of what is going to go on
in the interaction is announced to the students – including the nature
of their own contributions. Secondly, in the way in which the student
is explicitly told when to start talking and examining, at the end of
turn (1) (*off you go*) and again in (7). Thirdly, in the equally explicit
instructions to the student as to how he should sequence his actions,
in (3). Fourthly, in the way in which the student's contributions are
evaluated in (5) (*very good*) and (7) (*that's right*); positive and
encouraging as they are, these are still techniques of control which
would be regarded as presumptious or arrogant if they were addressed
to an equal or someone more powerful.

The fifth and final point is that the student is 'put on the spot' in
the series of questions of turns (13), (15), (17) and (19). The questions
constitute a strategically ordered sequence which leads the student
through the routine he has failed to master. Also, the student's

obligation to answer is underscored in each case by a pause (marked by a spaced dot) – brief silences in which all eyes are on him, and which it is definitely his responsibility to end!

Notice too the grammatical forms in which these questions are put: (13) and (15) are *negative questions – did we not, might we not*. Using negative questions is sometimes (depending on intonation and other factors) like saying 'I assume that X is the case, but you seem to be suggesting it isn't; surely it is?'. In this case, the student ought to know that X is the case, so asking him questions of this elaborate sort is a way of making him look silly. The power relationship is more baldly expressed in (17), where the reduced question forms (reduced, that is, from *now what do we do? what is the next most important thing?*) sound to me abrupt and curt. Finally, in (19) the doctor uses a *declarative* sentence rather than an *interrogative* sentence, with a *question tag: don't we*. The effect is rather like that of the negative questions.

On the basis of examples of this sort, we can say that power in discourse is to do with powerful participants *controlling and constraining the contributions of non-powerful participants*. It is useful to distinguish broadly between three types of such constraints – constraints on:

• *contents*, on what is said or done;
• *relations*, the social relations people enter into in discourse;
• *subjects*, or the 'subject positions' people can occupy.

'Relations' and 'subjects' are very closely connected, and all three overlap and co-occur in practice, but it is helpful to be able to distinguish them. Our example illustrates all three types of constraint. In terms of contents, the student is required to conduct an examination according to a learned routine, operating (relations) in a professional relationship to his audience and a subordinate relationship to the doctor, and occupying (subjects) the subject positions of (aspirant) doctor as well as student. These constraints imply particular linguistic forms.

But some of these constraints on the student do not appear to involve any direct control being exercised by the doctor. Notice for instance that all the *directive speech acts* (orders and questions) in the example come from the doctor: it appears that the doctor has the right to give orders and ask questions, whereas the students have only the obligation to comply and answer, in accordance with the subordinate relation of student to doctor. Yet the doctor is not directly controlling the student in this respect.

Rather, the constraints derive from the conventions of the discourse type which is being drawn upon. However, in an indirect sense, the doctor *is* in control, for it is the prerogative of powerful participants to determine which discourse type(s) may be legitimately drawn upon. Thus in addition to directly constraining contributions, powerful participants can indirectly constrain them by selecting the discourse type. Notice that the latter type of constraint is also a form of self-constraint: once a discourse type has been settled upon, its conventions apply to all participants, including the powerful ones. However, that is something of a simplification, because more powerful participants may be able to treat conventions in a more cavalier way, as well as to allow or disallow varying degrees of latitude to less powerful participants.

> There are obvious similarities between the text in the example above and the police interview text discussed in Chapter 2 (p. 18) in terms of the unequal power relationships between participants. Compare the two texts, and see what conclusions you can come up with on similarities and differences in the ways in which police interviewers 'handle' witnesses and doctors 'handle' medical students.

Power in cross-cultural encounters

In the example we have been looking at, I think it is safe to assume that the students are able to operate within the constraints on legitimate discourse type imposed by the doctor. But what about unequal encounters where the non-powerful people have cultural and linguistic backgrounds different from those of the powerful people? This is common for instance in 'gatekeeping encounters' – encounters such as a job interview in which a 'gatekeeper' who generally belongs to the societally dominant cultural grouping controls an encounter which determines whether someone gets a job, or gets access to some other valued objective. In contemporary Britain, for example, it is mainly white middle-class people who act as gatekeepers in gatekeeping encounters with members of the various ethnic (and cultural) minorities of Asian, West Indian, African, etc., origin.

Discourse types and orders of discourse vary across cultures. But in such gatekeeping encounters, white middle-class gatekeepers are likely to constrain the discourse types which can be drawn upon to those of the dominant cultural grouping. Sensitivity to cultural differences is growing in some cases, but slowly. Interviewers tend to assume, for instance, that interviewees are familiar with dominant ways of conducting interviews. And interviewees' contributions are correspondingly interpreted on the assumption that they are capable of working out what is required, and capable of providing it, in terms of these dominant conventions. So if an interviewee gives what is felt to be a poor or weak or irrelevant answer to a question, this is likely to be put down to her lack of the requisite knowledge or experience, her uncooperativeness, and so forth; the possibility of miscommunication because of differences in discoursal conventions rarely suggests itself. People may thus be denied jobs and other valuable social 'goods' through misconceptions based upon cultural insensitivity and dominance.

The possibilities for miscommunication are ample. For instance, the following snippet is from a simulated job interview for a post in a library with a member of an American cultural minority (C2):

Interviewer: What about the library interests you most?
C2:   What about the library in terms of the books? or the whole building?
Interviewer: Any point that you'd like to . . .
C2:   Oh, the children's books, because I have a child, and the children . . . you know there's so many you know books for them to read you know, and little things that would interest them would interest me too.

Text 3.2 Source: Akinasso F N, Ajirotutu C S 1982:124

Notice that C2's English in terms of grammar and vocabulary is native-like, which in itself is likely to lead the interviewer to dismiss any thoughts of culturally based miscommunication even if those thoughts occurred. But that *is* a possibility. C2 has failed to interpret the interviewer's question in 'the obvious way' – as an invitation to C2 to show what she could do in her professional work in the library if appointed to the post. But 'the obvious way' is the way within a specific culture of 'the interview', and there is no inherent reason why people should not show how their work interests relate to their family and other interests in response to a question of this sort.

It may be justifiable to interpret as 'miscommunication' the outcome of individual interviews where people are denied jobs or other 'goods' partly on the basis of cultural differences. But such outcomes are more regular and more systematic than that would imply, and they would appear to be based upon not only cultural differences in discourse but also upon more overt differences in skin colour and lifestyle. Power in discourse between members of different cultural groupings is in this perspective an element in the domination of, particularly, black and Asian minorities by the white majority, and of institutionalized racism.

Hidden power

The examples so far have been of face-to-face discourse, but a not inconsiderable proportion of discourse in contemporary society actually involves participants who are separated in place and time. This is true of written language generally, but the growth area for this sort of discourse has been the mass media – television, radio, film as well as newspapers. Mass-media discourse is interesting because the nature of the power relations enacted in it is often not clear, and there are reasons for seeing it as involving *hidden* relations of power.

The most obvious difference between face-to-face discourse and media discourse is the 'one-sidedness' of the latter. In face-to-face interaction, participants alternate between being the producers and the interpreters of text, but in media discourse, as well as generally in writing, there is a sharp divide between producers and interpreters – or, since the media 'product' takes on some of the nature of a commodity, between producers and 'consumers'.

There is another important difference. In face-to-face discourse, producers design their contributions for the particular people they are interacting with – they adapt the language they use, and keep adapting throughout an encounter in the light of various sorts of 'feedback' they get from co-participants. But media discourse is designed for mass audiences, and there is no way that producers can even know who is in the audience, let alone adapt to its diverse sections. And since all discourse producers must produce with *some* interpreters in mind, what media producers do is address an *ideal subject*, be it viewer, or listener, or reader. Media discourse has built into it a subject position for an ideal subject, and actual viewers or listeners or readers have to negotiate a relationship with the ideal subject.

But what is the nature of the power relations in media discourse? We can say that producers exercise power over consumers in that they have sole producing rights and can therefore determine what is included and excluded, how events are represented, and (as we have seen) even the subject positions of their audiences. But who precisely are these 'producers'? Let us take a specific example to try to answer this. Text 3.3 is an article from my local newspaper.

Quarry load-shedding problem

UNSHEETED lorries from Middlebarrow Quarry were still causing problems by shedding stones on their journey through Warton village, members of the parish council heard at their September meeting.

The council's observations have been sent to the quarry management and members are hoping to see an improvement.

Text 3.3 Source: *Lancaster Guardian*, 12 September 1986

Who is actually exercising power in this little article? Perhaps it is the journalist who wrote the piece. But it is well-known that journalists work under editorial control. So perhaps it is the editor, or rather more nebulously the newspaper itself, as a sort of institutional collective. But is the representation of the parish council meeting *only* the newspaper's, or is not the newspaper perhaps transmitting someone else's representation? And if so, does that not give a certain amount of power to that 'someone else'?

Let us generalize from this example, but keep the reporting of news particularly in mind. It is rather obvious that the people and organizations that the media use as *sources* in news reporting do not represent equally all social groupings in the population: Government ministers figure far more than unemployed people, and industrial managers or trade union officials figure far more than shopfloor workers. While the unequal influence of social group-

ings may be relatively clear in terms of who gets to be inter-
viewed, for example, it is less clear but nevertheless highly
significant in terms of whose *perspective* is adopted in reports. If, for
instance, industrial disputes are systematically referred to as *trouble*
or *disruption*, that is systematically building the employer's
perspective into industrial news coverage.

In the British media, the balance of sources and perspectives and
ideology is overwhelmingly in favour of existing power-holders.
Where this is the case – and it sometimes is not the case – we can
see media power relations as relations of a *mediated* (NB media-ted!)
sort between power-holders and the mass of the population. These
mediated relations of power include the most fundamental relation,
the *class* relation; on balance again, though with all sorts of provisos and limitations, the media operate as a means for the
expression and reproduction of the power of the dominant class and
bloc. And the mediated power of existing power-holders is also a
hidden power, because it is implicit in the practices of the media
rather than being explicit.

Let us make the case more concretely, though, in respect of the
example above. What I want to focus upon is *causality*: who is
represented as causing what to happen, who is represented as
doing what to whom. The grammatical form in which the headline is cast is that of *nominalization* (see p. 124): a process is
expressed as a *noun*, as if it were an entity. One effect of this
grammatical form is that crucial aspects of the process are left
unspecified: in particular, we don't know who or what is shedding loads or causing loads to be shed – causality is unspecified.

The first paragraph of the report makes things clearer, but not
much. Causality is attributed to *unsheeted lorries from Middlebarrow
Quarry*. This itself contains unspecified causality again, for *unsheeted*
implies the failure of a process to happen – someone did not put
sheets over the loads, when (one assumes) they ought to have
done. It is difficult to take literally the notion that the *lorries* are the
cause of the problem, and it is evident that in a different representation it could be this 'someone' – presumably the *quarry
management* or people under their control. Yet the quarry management figure only in the second paragraph in this representation as
in receipt of the council's *observations*, a term which again avoids
attributing any responsibility (it might have been *complaints*).

The report (and maybe the meeting it reports, though one cannot
be sure) seems geared to representing what *might* have come across,

from a quite different perspective, as the antisocial consequences of unscrupulous corner-cutting on the part of the quarry owners, in a way that presents the consequences without the causes, or the responsibilities. The power being exercised here is the power to disguise power, i.e. to disguise the power of quarry owners and their ilk to behave antisocially with impunity. It is a form of the power to constrain *content*: to favour certain interpretations and 'wordings' of events, while excluding others (such as the alternative wording I have just given). It is a form of hidden power, for the favoured interpretations and wordings are those of the power-holders in our society, though they appear to be just those of the newspaper.

Let us take another and rather different example. The extract in Text 3.4 is taken from the beginning of a front-page newspaper article during the Falklands war.

How is Jenny Keeble represented here? What picture of army officers' wives do you get from this extract? What impression of Major Keeble do you get from the photograph? Do you find yourself having to negotiate with an ideal *subject position* built into the text by its producer? What is that position?

What is at issue in the representation of Jenny Keeble is another form of constraint on contents: such representations cumulatively stereotype 'army wives' and more generally the wives of favoured public figures, and so constrain the meanings people attach to them. The process is profoundly sexist: it works by attaching to Jenny Keeble attributes which are already conventionally definers of 'a good wife'. Notice that at no point here (or in the rest of the article) is Jenny Keeble explicitly *said* to be 'a good wife', or an admirable person; the process depends entirely on an 'ideal reader's' capacity to *infer* that from the list of attributes – she expresses confidence in her husband's professional abilities, she is concerned for his safety, she 'prays' he has 'done enough', she tries to 'maintain an air of normality for the children's sake'. But this indicates that what is being constrained is not only contents but also subjects: the process presupposes an ideal reader who will indeed make the 'right' inference from the list, i.e. have the 'right' ideas about what a 'good wife' is. Texts such as this thus reproduce sexists, provided that readers generally fall into the subject position of the ideal reader, rather than opposing it.

Not all photographs are equal: any photograph gives one image of a scene or a person from among the many possible images. The choice is very important, because different images convey different meanings.

The Paras' new leader

He'll do his job well says major's wife

THE wife of the new CO of the 2nd Parachute Battalion spoke last night of her fears for her husband's safety.

As she played in the sunshine with her four children, Jenny Keeble said she hoped her husband would not have to go into battle again.

She said: "I pray he and his men have done enough. But if they do go on I know that he is a man who will do his job to the best of his ability and I am certain he and the 2nd Parachute Battalion will succeed.

Major Christopher Keeble, a 40-year-old devout Roman Catholic, is to succeed Colonel Herbert Jones who died leading his men against an Argentine machine-gun post in the battle for Goose Green.

Yesterday Jenny Keeble's family and friends gathered around in the garden of her old vicarage home—a rambling Tudor building at Maddington on Salisbury Plain—for a picnic afternoon as she tried to maintain an air of normility for the children's sake.

Major Keeble . . . will lead the paras into battle

Text 3.4 Source: *Daily Mail*, 1 June 1982

In this example, for instance, I find my attention drawn particularly by the Major's eyes; he is looking straight ahead, looking the reader in the face, so to speak, rather appraisingly, with a serious expression mitigated by a hint of a smile at the corners of his mouth (possibly a cynical one). Notice the ambiguous function of the caption: does it register for us what the picture 'says', or does it lead us to 'read' the picture in that way? Be that as it may, the photograph in its verbal matrix shows me that Major Keeble is all I would expect a leader of an elite military unit to be.

Look at some further examples of the way in which images and words interact in the press, on television, on hoardings, and so forth. Can you spot particular techniques for giving particular impressions of people?

The hidden power of media discourse and the capacity of the capitalist class and other power-holders to exercise this power depend on systematic tendencies in news reporting and other media activities. A single text on its own is quite insignificant: the effects of media power are cumulative, working through the repetition of particular ways of handling causality and agency, particular ways of positioning the reader, and so forth. Thus through the way it positions readers, for instance, media discourse is able to exercise a pervasive and powerful influence in social reproduction because of the very scale of the modern mass media and the extremely high level of exposure of whole populations to a relatively homogeneous output. But caution is necessary: people do *negotiate* their relationship to ideal subjects, and this can mean keeping them at arm's length or even engaging in outright struggle against them. The power of the media does not mechanically follow from their mere existence.

Is the hidden power of the media *manipulative*? It is difficult to give a categorical answer to this question: sometimes and in some ways it is, sometimes and in some ways it isn't. We can perhaps approach the problem by asking *from whom* exactly the power of media discourse is hidden: is it just audiences, or is it not also at least to some degree media workers? There are of course cases where media output is consciously manipulated in the interests of the capitalist class – a case which is often referred to is that of BBC Radio during the British General Strike in 1926, when the BBC openly supported the Government in a context where the class issues were clear to its Director-General, Lord Reith. But for many media workers, the practices of production which can be interpreted as facilitating the exercise of media power by power-holders, are perceived as *professional* practices with their own internal standards of excellence and their own rationalizations in terms of the constraint of the technical media themselves, what the public want, and other factors. Indeed, the professional beliefs and assumptions of media workers are important in keeping the power of media discourse hidden from the mass of the population.

Power is also sometimes hidden in face-to-face discourse. For instance, there is obviously a close connection between *requests* and power, in that the right to request someone to do something often derives from having power. But there are many grammatically different forms available for making requests. Some are *direct* and mark the power relationship explicitly, while others are *indirect* and leave it more or less implicit. Direct requests are typically expressed grammatically in imperative sentences: *type this letter for me by 5 o'clock*, for instance. Indirect requests can be more or less indirect, and they are typically expressed grammatically in questions of various degrees of elaborateness and corresponding indirectness: *can you type this letter for me by 5 o'clock, do you think you could type this letter for me by 5 o'clock, could I possibly ask you to type this letter for me by 5 o'clock*. There are also other ways of indirectly requesting – through *hints*, for instance: *I would like to have the letter in the 5 o'clock post*.

Why would a business executive (let us say) choose an indirect form to request her secretary to type a letter? It could be, particularly if a hint or one of the more elaborate questions is used, for manipulative reasons: if the boss has been pressurizing the secretary hard all day, such a form of request might head off resentment or even refusal. But less elaborate forms of indirect request (*can you/will you/could you type* . . .) are conventionally used in the sort of situation I have described, so the question becomes why business executives and other power-holders systematically avoid too much overt marking of their power. This leads us to the relationship of hidden power and social struggle, which is discussed in the final section of this chapter.

The examples I have given in this section are of hidden power being exercised within discourse. But what I have called the 'power behind discourse' is also a hidden power, in that the shaping of orders of discourse by relations of power is not generally apparent to people. This is an appropriate point, then, to move behind discourse.

POWER BEHIND DISCOURSE

The idea of 'power behind discourse' is that the whole social order of discourse is put together and held together as a hidden effect of power. In this section I begin with just one dimension of this – *standardization*, the process which I have already referred to in Chapter 2, whereby a particular social dialect comes to be elevated into what is often called a standard or even 'national' language. I will focus upon standard British English.

Standard language

I suggested in Chapter 2 that we ought to see standardization as a part of a much wider process of economic, political and cultural unification, which was tied in with the emergence of capitalism out of feudal society in Britain. There is an economic basis for this connection between capitalism and unification: the need for a unified home market if commodity production is to be fully established. This in turn requires political and cultural unification. Standardization is of direct economic importance in improving communication: most people involved in economic activity come to understand the standard, even if they don't always use it productively. It is also of great political and cultural importance in the establishment of nationhood, and the nation-state is the favoured form of capitalism.

The social dialect which developed into standard English was the East Midland dialect associated with the merchant class in London at the end of the medieval period. This underlines the link to capitalism, for these feudal merchants became the first capitalists, and the rise of standard English is linked to the growing power of the merchants. The beginnings of standard English were very modest in comparison with its pre-eminence now: the emergent standard form was used in very few places for very few purposes by very few people. Standardization initially affected written language, and has only gradually extended to various aspects of speech – grammar, vocabulary and even pronunciation.

We can think of its growth as a long process of colonization, whereby it gradually 'took over' major social institutions, pushing out Latin and French, vastly extending the purposes it was used for and its formal resources as a result, and coming to be accepted (if not always widely used) by more and more people. By coming to be associated with the most salient and powerful institutions – literature, Government and administration, law, religion, education, etc. – standard English began to emerge as the language of political and cultural power, and as the language of the politically and culturally powerful. Its successful colonization of these institutions cannot be separated from their modernization in the period of transition from feudalism to capitalism, or from the growing power within them of the emergent 'middle class' (*bourgeoisie*).

Standard English developed not only at the expense of Latin and French, but also at the expense of other, 'non-standard' social dialects (and the expense of the other languages of Britain – Welsh and Gaelic, and especially since the Second World War many others, including a number of Asian languages). Standard English was regarded as *correct* English, and other social dialects were stigmatized not only in terms of correctness but also in terms which indirectly reflected on the lifestyles, morality and so forth of their speakers, the emergent working class of capitalist society: they were *vulgar, slovenly, low, barbarous*, and so forth. The establishment of the dominance of standard English and the subordination of other social dialects was part and parcel of the establishment of the dominance of the capitalist class and the subordination of the working class.

The *codification* of the standard was a crucial part of this process, which went hand-in-hand with *prescription*, the designation of the forms of the standard as the only 'correct' ones. Codification is aimed at attaining minimal variation in form through setting down the prescribed language code in a written form – in grammars, dictionaries, pronouncing dictionaries, spelling books. The highpoint of codification was the second half of the eighteenth century, and much of the readership for the vast numbers of grammar books and dictionaries which were produced at the beginning of the industrial revolution came from the industrialists and their families.

There is an element of schizophrenia about standard English, in the sense that it aspires to be (and is certainly portrayed as) a *national* language belonging to all classes and sections of the society, and yet remains in many respects a *class dialect*. The power of its claims as a national language even over those whose use of it is limited is apparent in the widespread self-depreciation of working-class people who say they do not speak English, or do not speak 'proper' English. On the other hand, it is a class dialect not only in the sense that its dominance is associated with capitalist class interests in the way I have outlined, but also because it is the dominant bloc that makes most use of it, and gains most from it as an asset – as a form of 'cultural capital' analogous to capital in the economic sense, as Pierre Bourdieu has put it.

Standard English is an asset because its use is a passport to good jobs and positions of influence and power in national and local communities. This applies naturally enough to standard English as a written form, but also to standard spoken English including the use of forms of *Received Pronunciation* (RP) – the type of pronunciation which most politicians, television and radio reporters, university teachers, senior industrial managers, senior civil servants use, which is precisely my point!

As I have suggested at one or two points above, people generally may acknowledge the dominance of the standard language, but that does not mean that they always use it, or indeed *accept* it in the full sense of the term. In fact it meets stiff resistance from speakers of other social dialects, as well as from speakers of other languages in modern multilingual Britain. (See the last section of this chapter.) This in itself indicates that the schizophrenia I have referred to is sensed by people – people know it is someone else's language and not theirs, despite the claims to the contrary. However, it does not mean that people are aware of the power basis of standardization: they may know the standard in a sense belongs to the dominant bloc, but the responsibility of the dominant bloc for articulating and defining the relationship and pecking order between languages and social dialects is generally hidden.

> We quite often hear nonstandard social dialects on radio and TV these days, but my impression is that certain key broadcasting roles are still restricted to standard spoken forms. Listen out for *accents* other than Received Pronunciation (RP for short). In what 'capacities' (e.g. newsreader, interviewer, announcer, interviewee, entertainer) do non-RP-speakers mainly appear? Do they tend to appear in particular sorts of programme (such as news, comedy shows, quizzes, documentaries)? Are there certain capacities and types of programme which don't feature non-RP-speakers? What about TV advertisements? Are there particular roles within them which are open to non-RP-speakers?

Power behind discourse: a discourse type

I want now to shift focus, still with reference to 'power behind discourse', and look at a particular discourse type as 'an effect of power' – as having conventions which embody particular power relations. The example I have chosen is the discourse of medical examinations, and more specifically *gynaecological examinations*. I focus especially on how medical staff and patients are positioned in relation to each other in the conventions of the discourse type, and how this positioning can be seen as an effect of the power of those who dominate medical institutions over conventions, and so over staff as well as patients.

According to one account of gynaecological examinations, participants are subject to contradictory pressures: staff feel obliged to treat patients in a nonchalant and disengaged way, as technical objects, in order to establish that their interest in their bodies is medical and not sexual; yet they also feel obliged to treat the patient sensitively as a person to cancel out the indignity of treating her as a technical object, and to try to overcome her likely embarrassment given the overwhelming taboo on exposing one's sexual organs to non-intimates. These contradictory pressures are evident in the conventions for the discourse type.

For instance, the constraints on the *settings* of gynaecological examinations are of major significance in guaranteeing that the encounter is indeed a medical one and not, for instance, a sexual one. Such examinations can legitimately be undertaken only in 'medical space' – a hospital or a consulting room – which implies the presence of a whole range of medical paraphernalia which help to legitimize the encounter. There are also constraints on the *subjects* who can take part: there is a restricted set of legitimate subject positions, those of the doctor, the nurse, and the patient, and strict limitations on who can occupy them. There are requirements for modes of dress which reinforce properties of the setting in defining the encounter as medical, and (as we shall see) for 'demeanour'. There are constraints on *topic* – questions from medical staff on bodily functions and sexual experience must relate strictly to the medical problem at issue, disallowing for instance the sort of topical development we find elsewhere which would allow a transition to a general discussion of one's sex life.

The sequence of activities which constitutes the examination is highly routinized, following a standard procedure, and this routine property extends also to the verbal and non-verbal aspects of the ways in which medical staff relate to patients. Medical staff show their disengagement in the quality of their *gaze*, the professionally appraisive (rather than aesthetically evaluative) way in which they look at the patient's body. It emerges also in the brisk, efficient handling of the patient's body by the doctor, and, too, in questions and requests to the patient which, for example, depersonalize the patient's sexual organs by referring to, say, *the vagina* rather than *your vagina*.

But efforts of medical staff to balance disengagement with sensitivity, in accordance with the pressures referred to above, are also evident in their discourse. They often avoid using terms which might embarrass patients, by euphemizing (*Did you wash **between your legs**?*) or by relying upon *deictic* expressions (*When did you first notice difficulty **down below?***). And doctors use a soft, soothing voice to encourage the patient to relax (when they say things like *now relax as much as you can, I'll be as gentle as I can*), which contributes to 'personalizing' the examination. It is important to emphasize that despite the impression some patients may have that they are really being given individual treatment, these are just as much routine devices as those mentioned in the previous paragraph.

So far I have referred mainly to ways in which medical staff are positioned, but the same is true for patients, as the following resumé of how medical staff think patients should behave in gynaecological examinations will indicate.

> The patient's voice should be controlled, mildly pleasant, self-confident and impersonal. Her facial expression should be attentive and neutral, leaning towards the mildly pleasant and friendly side, as if she were talking to the doctor in his office, fully dressed and seated in a chair. The patient is to have an attentive glance upward, at the ceiling or at other persons in the room, eyes open, not 'dreamy' or away, but ready at a second's notice to revert to the doctor's face for a specific verbal exchange. Except for such a verbal exchange, however, the patient is supposed to avoid looking into the doctor's eyes during the actual examination because direct eye contact between the two at this time is provocative. Her role calls for passivity and self-effacement. The patient should show willingness to relinquish control to the doctor. She should refrain from speaking at length and from making inquiries which would require the doctor to reply at length. So as not to point up her undignified position, she should not project her personality profusely. The self must be eclipsed in order to sustain the definition that the doctor is working on a technical object and not a person.

> Have you ever been in a position where you were expected to behave at all similarly? How were those expectations communicated to you? Have male readers ever felt themselves required to 'eclipse the self' in

anything like this way? Are these expectations motivated entirely by the nature of the occasion, or are they to do with the sex of the patient?

Let us now bring power into the picture. The medical staff and particularly the doctor exercise power over the patient (and over other medical staff, in the case of the doctor) within encounters based upon this discourse type, in accordance with its conventions, which attribute rights to control encounters to medical staff and especially doctors. And as part of their power, the medical staff are likely to impose the discourse type upon patients, in the sense of putting pressure on them in various ways to occupy the subject position it lays down for patients, and so behave in certain constrained ways. These are aspects of power *in* discourse, but what I am interested in here is power *behind* discourse: the power effect whereby this discourse type with these properties comes to be imposed upon all of those involved, medical staff as well as patients, apparently by the medical institution or system itself.

But the power behind the conventions of a discourse type belongs not to the institution itself (whatever that would mean) but to the power-holders in the institution. One indication of this is the *policing* of conventions, the way they are enforced, both in the negative sense of what sanctions are taken against those who infringe them and in the positive sense of what affirmations there are for those who abide by them. The policing of conventions is in the hands of institutional power-holders, at various levels. Thus in the case of medical examinations, it is mainly the medical staff who come into contact with patients, and are power-holders in relation to them, who enforce patients' compliance with conventions, while the compliance of medical staff themselves is enforced by those higher in the institutional hierarchy – through procedures for disciplining people and dealing with professional malpractice, through promotions, and so forth.

Consideration of the ways in which conventions are shaped by those who have the power behind discourse takes us on to the concerns of Chapter 4, because such shaping is achieved through ideology. In our example, the conventions which position medical staff and patients in relation to each other can be regarded as embodying the dominant ideologies of medicine as a social institution, i.e. the ideologies of those who control medicine. Evidently, what a doctor is, what a nurse is, what a patient is, what constitutes 'professional' behaviour towards patients, and so forth, are all matters which are open to argument. The conventions for positioning staff and patients in gynaecological examinations are premised upon the way in which the dominant ideology answers these questions. I come to how this is done in Chapter 4.

But the sense in which these conventions are an effect of power behind discourse does not end there. The same conventions can be regarded, from the perspective of the societal (rather than the institutional) order of discourse, as a particular case of a general tendency in the way in which 'professionals' and 'clients' are positioned in relation to each other, in a variety of institutional settings and discourse types where people who have some official status in institutions ('professionals') come into contact with 'the public' ('clients'). The contradictory pressures upon medical staff to treat patients on the one hand nonchalantly as 'technical objects', and on the other hand sensitively as persons, are not I think (as the account of gynaecological examinations I referred to suggested) a peculiarity of the circumstances of gynaecological or even more generally medical examinations – though those peculiar circumstances would seem to give these pressures a special colouring. One finds techniques for efficiently and nonchalantly 'handling' people wherever one looks in the public institutions of the modern world. Equally, one finds what I shall refer to as a *synthetic personalization*, a compensatory tendency to give the impression of treating each of the people 'handled' *en masse* as an individual. Examples would be air travel (*have a nice day!*), restaurants (*welcome to Wimpy!*), and the simulated conversation (e.g. chat shows) and *bonhomie* which litter the media. These general tendencies in the order of discourse of modern society accord with the nature of its power relations and modern techniques for exercising power, as I shall show in some detail in Chapter 8.

Power and access to discourse

The third and final aspect of 'power behind discourse' that I want to look at is not to do with the constitution of orders of discourse and their component discourse types, but with access to them. The question is, who has access to which discourses, and who has the power to impose and enforce constraints on access?

The myth of *free speech*, that anyone is 'free' to say what they like, is an amazingly powerful one, given the actuality of a plethora of constraints on access to various sorts of speech, and writing. These are part and parcel of more general constraints on social practice – on access to the more exclusive social institutions, their practices, and especially the most powerful subject positions constituted in their practices. And in terms of discourse in particular, on access to the discourse types, and discoursal positions of power. In a sense, these 'cultural goods' are analogous to other socially valued 'goods' of a more tangible nature – accumulated wealth, good jobs, good housing, and so forth. Both sorts of goods are unequally distributed, so that members of what I referred to in Chapter 2 as the *dominant bloc* (the capitalist class, the 'middle class', the professions) have substantially more of them than members of the working class – they are richer in *cultural capital* (see p. 57).

Religious rituals such as church services will serve to illustrate constraints on access. You can only officiate at a church service if you are a priest, which is itself a constraint on access. Furthermore, you can only get to be a priest through a rather rigorous process of selection, during the course of which you must show yourself to meet a range of 'entry conditions' – being a believer, having a vocation, having some academic ability, conforming to certain standards of honesty, sincerity, sexual morality, and so on. These are further constraints on access.

Religion is not really that much different in this respect from medicine, or education, or law. Medical examinations, or lessons, or litigation, may not be as ritualized as a religious service, but nevertheless there are strict constraints on who can do them, and strict constraints on who can acquire the qualifications required to do them. In principle (as well as in law and in the rules of the professions), anyone is free to obtain such qualifications. But in practice, the people who do obtain them come mainly from the dominant bloc. For most people, the only involvement with medicine, education or the law is in the capacity of 'client' – patient, pupil or student, legal client – and 'clients' are not really 'insiders' in an institution.

Another less institutionally specific example of unequally distributed cultural capital is access to the various reading and writing abilities that can be summed up with the word *literacy*. Literacy is highly valued in our society, and a great deal of socially important and prestigious practice takes place in 'the written word'. Access to a high level of literacy is a precondition for a variety of socially valued 'goods', including most rewarding and well-paid jobs. Yet it is evident that access to literacy is unequally distributed – indeed, an estimated one million adults in Britain lack 'basic literacy skills', as defined by UNESCO, and the overwhelming majority of these are working-class people.

Among the more obvious and visible effects of constraints on access is the way in .which having access to prestigious sorts of discourse and powerful subject positions enhances publicly acknowledged status and authority. One reason for this is that becoming a doctor or a teacher or a lawyer is generally regarded as a purely individual achievement which merits the 'rewards' of status and authority, with social constraints on who *can* achieve these positions being correspondingly glossed over. As support for this view, people often refer to the fact that training in these professions involves spending years acquiring special knowledge and skills. Thus professional knowledge and skills act as emblems of personal achievement, mystifying social constraints on access – as well as being membership cards for those who achieve access, and a means of excluding outsiders. The discourses of these professions, including specialist vocabularies or *jargons*, serve all these functions.

Conversely, exclusion of people from particular types of discourse and subject positions lowers their publicly acknowledged status, but also as I suggested above their job and other social 'prospects'. Let us go back to the position of cultural minority groupings in interviews, which I was discussing in the section *Power in cross-cultural encounters*. I probably gave the impression that there is a great deal more homogeneity within cultural groupings than there really is. In fact, many white working-class British people from the dominant cultural grouping are as unfamiliar with the conventions of interviewing as members of black or Asian communities. But it is increasingly the case, as a result of the spread of interviewing practices across social institutions and the more intensive use of them within many institutions, that everybody is expected to be able to deal with interviews – from the interviewee end, of course! Those who cannot, either because of their cultural experience or because they belong to generations for which access to interviewing was constrained, are likely to be socially disabled.

The educational system has the major immediate responsibility for differentials in access. In the words of Michel Foucault, 'any system of education is a political way of maintaining or modifying the appropriation of discourses, along with the knowledges and powers which they carry'. And what is striking is the extent to which, despite the claims of education to differentiate only on the grounds of merit, differentiation follows social class lines: the higher one goes in the educational system, the greater the predominance of people from capitalist, 'middle-class', and professional backgrounds. The educational system reproduces without dramatic change the existing social division of labour, and the existing system of class relations. However, it will not do to blame the education system for constraints on access, or to attribute to it alone power over access. This power is diversified through the various social institutions, not just education, and its origins are, as I have been implying, in the system of class relations at the societal level.

Constraints on access: 'formality'

'Formality' is one pervasive and familiar aspect of constraints on access to discourse. Formality is a common property in many societies of practices and discourses of high social prestige and restricted access. It is a contributory factor in keeping access restricted, for it makes demands on participants above and beyond those of most discourse, and the ability to meet those demands is itself unevenly distributed. It can also serve to generate awe among those who are excluded by it and daunted by it.

Formality is best regarded as a property of social situations which has peculiar effects upon language forms. As a property of social situations, it manifests in an accentuated form the three types of constraint upon practice which I have associated with the exercise of power: constraints on contents, subjects, and relations. In terms of contents, discourse in a formal situation is subject to exceptional constraints on topic on relevance, and in terms of more or less fixed interactive routines. In terms of subjects, the social identities of those qualified to occupy subject positions in the discourses of formal situations are defined more rigorously than is usual, and in terms of public positions or statuses, as in the constraints referred to above on who may officiate at a religious service. In terms of relations, formal situations are characterized by an exceptional orientation to and marking of position, status, and 'face'; power and social distance are overt, and consequently there is a strong tendency towards *politeness*. Politeness is based upon recognition of differences of power, degrees of social distance, and so forth, and oriented to reproducing them without change.

The peculiar effects of formality on language forms follow from these accentuated constraints. We find levels of structuring of language above and beyond what is required in non-formal discourse. This extra structuring can affect any level of language. For example, the allocation of turns at talking to participants may be regulated by a formula (e.g. participants must speak in order of rank), whereas in conversation people work it out as they go along. Or encounters may have to proceed according to a strict routine which lays down stages in a fixed sequence. There may be requirements to do with the rhythm or tempo or loudness of talk – people may have to talk at a particular speed, for instance; or to do with the grammar of sentences – highly complex structures may be favoured. There is likely to be a general requirement for *consistency* of language forms, which will mean for instance that the vocabulary must be selected from a restricted set throughout. There is also a heightened self-consciousness which results in care about using 'correct' grammar and vocabulary, including a whole set of vocabulary which is reserved for more formal occasions, and is often itself referred to as 'formal'.

The following text is an extract from a transcript of part of the United States Senate investigation into the Watergate affair, and is part of the testimony of one of President Nixon's most senior aides, John Ehrlichman:

(1) Q: Mr. Ehrlichman, prior to the luncheon recess you stated that in your opinion, the entry into the Ellsberg psychiatrist's office was legal because of national security reasons. I think that was your testimony.

(2) A: Yes.

(3) Q: Have you always maintained that position?

(4) A: Well, I don't know –

(5) Q: Well, do you recall when we had our first interview in my office, and we discussed this issue you expressed shock that such a thing had occurred, and indicated that you had

informed Mr. Young or Mr. Krogh to see that this thing
should not happen again but you did not take any action
such as ordering the firing these people because of the
general sensitive issues that were involved. Do you recall
that?

(6) A: Well, that is not on the ground of illegality, Mr. Dash. I do
not think you asked me at that time whether – what my
legal opinion was, for whatever it was worth. What you
were asking me was what I did, and that is what I did.

(7) Q: Well, if it was legal you would ordinarily have approved it
would you not?

(8) A: Well, no, the thing that troubled me about it was that it
was totally unanticipated. Unauthorized by me.

(9) Q: Who was it authorized by?

(10) A: Well, I am under the impression that it was authorized by
Mr. Krogh, but it is not based on any personal knowledge.

(11) Q: Well, now, as a matter of fact, Mr. Ehrlichman, did you
not personally approve in advance a covert entry into the
Ellsberg psychiatrist office for the purpose of gaining
access to the psychoanalyst's reports?

(12) A: I approved a covert investigation. Now, if a covert entry
means a breaking and entering the answer to your
question is, no.

Text 3.5 Source: *New York Times*, 1973:512

The questioner is challenging Ehrlichman, yet in a manner which is
perhaps constrained by the formality of the situation. How is it
constrained? What aspects of the language are indicative of formality?

The taking of turns is constrained within a question-plus-answer
pattern, with Dash asking and Ehrlichman answering. Any challenges
or accusations and attempts to refute them must be fitted into this
format. Turn (7) is a challenge, for instance, but it is forced to be an
implicit and indirect challenge because Dash has to put it in question
form. Consequently it comes across as restrained. This is a case of
formality limiting the nature of relations between participants. Perhaps
the other linguistic feature which is most strikingly indicative of
formality is the vocabulary – the consistent selection of 'formal' words.
The opening turn, for example, may in a less formal scenario have
started: *John, you were making out before lunch that* . . . . Notice also the
polite title + surname modes of address that are used (*Mr Ehrlichman*).

Formal situations could be regarded as adding an extra constraint to the three I have associated with the exercise of power – a *constraint on language form* – as well as heightening the three. This means that discourse, and practice generally, in formal situations are difficult and demanding; they depend on special knowledge and skill which has to be learnt. Many people do not acquire even the necessary knowledge and skill to occupy peripheral positions in formal situations, and consequently find formal situations *per se* daunting and frightening – or ridiculous. A formidable axis is set up between social position and knowledge; since those in prestigious social positions do learn to operate formally, an easy conclusion for those who don't is 'I can't because I'm not clever enough' rather than 'I can't because I'm working class'. Thus formality both restricts access and generates awe. However, I shall discuss in the final section a contrary trend in contemporary society against overt marking of power and thus against formality.

SOCIAL STRUGGLE IN DISCOURSE

In this section I add a vitally important proviso to what has gone before. Power, 'in' discourse or 'behind' discourse, is not a permanent and undisputed attribute of any one person or social grouping. On the contrary, those who hold power at a particular moment have to constantly reassert their power, and those who do not hold power are always liable to make a bid for power. This is true whether one is talking at the level of the particular situation, or in terms of a social institution, or in terms of a whole society: power at all these levels is won, exercised, sustained, and lost in the course of social struggle (see Ch. 2, p. 34).

Let us begin with a text where struggle is overt – an interview between a youth (Y) suspected of involvement in a crime, and his headmaster (H).

(1) H: Why didn't you go straight down Queen Street?
(2) Y: I'm not walking down there with a load of coons from St Hilda's coming out of school.
(3) H: Why's that?
(4) Y: Well that's obvious, isn't it? I don't want to get belted.
(5) H: Well there isn't usually any bother in Queen Street, is there?

(6) Y: No. None of us white kids usually go down there, do we? What about that bust-up in the Odeon carpark at Christmas?

(7) H: That was nearly a year ago, and I'm not convinced you lot were as innocent as you made out. So when you got to the square, why did you wait around for quarter of an hour instead of going straight home?

(8) Y: I thought my mate might come down that way after work. Anyway, we always go down the square after school.

Compare this with the premature baby unit text in the section *Power in discourse* at the beginning of this chapter, in terms of the degree of control exercised by the headmaster over the youth's contributions, and the extent to which they both stick to the discoursal 'rights' and 'obligations' you would expect in such an interview – for instance, I don't think you would expect the youth to ask questions and the headmaster to answer them.

There are various ways in which Y exercises more control over the discourse than one might expect, exceeds his discoursal 'rights' and does not fulfil his 'obligations'. Firstly, he challenges H's questions on two occasions (turns 2 and 4) rather than answering them directly, though an answer is implied in 2 and offered after the challenge in 4. Secondly, in turn 6 Y asks a question which H answers: as I said above, you would expect neither Y to ask nor H to answer questions. Thirdly, the answers which Y does give to H's questions go beyond what is directly relevant in turns 6 and 8; recall that in the medical text, a requirement of relevance is strictly enforced by the doctor. Fourthly, Y shows no sign of adapting his style of talk to the relatively formal setting; he appears to treat the interview to an extent as if it were a conversation, and to treat the policeman as a peer. This is most evident in Y's vocabulary (*belted, kids, bust-up*) and especially in his use of the racist word *coons*. I think we would expect people who would use this sort of vocabulary with their friends to be influenced by the setting, occasion, and the power and distance separating them from the police to avoid it.

H does maintain quite a lot of control nevertheless. Most of the questions are asked by him, and some at least are answered fairly compliantly, indicating a level of adherence to conventional rights and obligations. It is always possible in cases of this sort that the person with institutional power – H in this case – is tactically yielding some ground in order to be able to pursue a longer-term strategy. Perhaps this is how we should interpret H's failure to immediately challenge or dissociate himself from the racist *coons*: by letting it pass, he appears to be accepting it.

But are we to regard such a case as just a struggle between an individual youth showing how unimpressed he is with school authority by flouting conventional constraints, and a headmaster adopting tactics to deal with that? Recall the distinction on p. 25 of chapter 2 between three levels of social organisation: situational, institutional, and societal. This seems a fair description of what is going on at the situational level. But it misses the social pattern to which this individual example seems to belong: the youth seems typical of many young people, and the tactics which the headmaster uses are perhaps fairly standard for dealing with this sort of situation. In other words, the extract can also be interpreted in terms of struggle at the institutional level. Moreover, we could surely find other pieces of discourse from quite different institutional settings – the law and the family might be examples – showing analogous struggles between young people and 'authority'; correspondingly, one can see the text both as an example of social struggle at the institutional level within the school as a social institution, and as an example of a more general struggle at the societal level between (certain groupings of) young people and power-holders of various sorts.

Of course one cannot get far in investigating social struggle between young people and the schools, or young people and public authorities more generally, on the basis of a single piece of discourse! What I am suggesting, however, is that any given piece of discourse may simultaneously be a part of a situational struggle, an institutional struggle, and a societal struggle (including class struggle). This has consequences in terms of our distinction between 'power in discourse' and 'power behind discourse'. While struggle at the situational level is over power in discourse, struggle at the other levels may also be over power behind discourse.

I referred earlier in the chapter to a tendency against the overt marking of power relationships in discourse – a tendency which is of considerable interest from the perspective of social struggle. Let me illustrate it with a well-known grammatical example, the so-called 'T' and 'V' pronoun forms which are found in many languages – French, German, Italian, Spanish, Russian among the European languages – but not (modern) standard English. These languages have two forms for the second-person pronoun where standard English has just the one, *you*, and although these forms are in origin just singular (T) and plural (V), both have come to be used for singular reference. Let us take French as an example. Its T-form (*tu*) and its V-form (*vous*) are now both used to address a single person. At one stage, the difference between them was one of power: *tu* was used to address subordinates, *vous* to address superiors, and either (depending on the class of the speakers) could be used reciprocally between social equals.

More recently, however, there has been a shift towards a system based upon *solidarity* rather than power: *tu* is used to address people one is close to in some way (friends, relations, co-workers, etc.), and *vous* is used when there is social 'distance'. There is tension between the power-based and solidarity-based systems: what happens, for instance, if you want to address a social 'superior' who you are close to (your parents, say), or a subordinate who is socially distant (e.g. a soldier, if you happen to be an officer)? The answer used to be that you would use *vous* and *tu* respectively on grounds of power, but now it is that you would probably use *tu* and *vous* respectively on grounds of solidarity.

The particular development of T/V away from the power-based system towards the solidarity-based system seems to be in line with long-term developments across whole ranges of institutions which have been documented in various languages: a movement away from the explicit marking of power relationships. For instance, this is true in Britain for higher education, for a range of types of discourse in social services, and now for industry – where Japanese management techniques which eliminate surface inequalities between managers and workers are increasingly influential. It is of course easy enough to find unreformed practice in any of these cases, but the trend over three decades or more is clear enough.

Does this trend mean that unequal power relationships are on the decline? That would seem to follow if we assumed a mechanical connection between relationships and their discoursal expression. But such a conclusion would be highly suspect in view of the evidence from elsewhere that power inequalities have not substantially changed – evidence about the distribution of wealth, the increase in poverty in the 1980s, inequalities in access to health facilities, education, housing, inequalities in employment prospects, and so forth. Nor is it credible that those with power would give it up for no obvious reason.

One dimension of power in discourse is arguably the capacity to determine to what extent that power will be overtly expressed. It is therefore quite possible for the expression of power relationships to be played down as a tactic within a strategy for the continued possession and exercise of power. That would seem to be a reasonable interpretation of the conscious and deliberate adoption of Japanese management styles referred to above. This is a case of hiding power for manipulative reasons – see the section on *Hidden power* above. But can it account for the longer-term trend across diverse institutions and indeed across national and linguistic frontiers? It is hardly credible to interpret it as an international conspiracy!

What both the optimistic explanation that inequality is on the way out and the conspiratorial explanation fail to take into account is the relationship between power and social struggle. I would suggest that the decline in the overt marking of power relationships should be interpreted as a concession on the part of power-holders which they have been forced to make by the increase in the relative power of working-class people and other groupings of formerly powerless and disregarded people – women, youth, black people, gay people, etc. (That shift in power relations has been checked and partly reversed in places during the crises of the late 1970s and 1980s.) However, this does not mean that the power-holders have surrendered power, but merely that they have been forced into less direct ways of exercising and reproducing their power. Nor is it a merely cosmetic tactic: because of the constraints under which they have been forced to operate, there are severe problems of legitimacy for power-holders.

Discourse is part and parcel of this complex situation of struggle, and we can deepen our understanding of discourse by keeping this matrix in mind, and our understanding of the struggle by attending to discourse. I shall explore for instance in Chapter 8 the way in which certain discourse types acquire cultural salience, and 'colonize' new institutions and domains, a perspective which I briefly aired in Chapter 2. Shifting patterns of salience are a barometer of the development of social struggle and a part of that process. For example, *counselling* is a salient discourse type which has colonized workplaces, schools, and so forth. This is superficially indicative of an unwonted sensitivity to individual needs and problems. But it seems in some cases at least to have been turned into a means to greater institutional control of people through exposing aspects of their 'private' lives to unprecedented institutional probing. The apparent sensitivity to individuals is a concession by power-holders to the strength of the (relatively) unpowerful; the containment of counselling is their counter-offensive. See Chapter 8 for examples and further discussion.

Access to prestigious discourse types and their powerful subject positions is another arena of social struggle. One thinks for instance of the struggles of the working class through the trade unions and the Labour Party around the turn of the century for access to political arenas including Parliament, and by implication to the discourses of politics in the 'public' domain. Or of the struggles of women and black people as well as working-class people to break into the professions, and more recently the higher echelons of the professions.

Struggles over access merge with struggles around standardization. I suggested earlier that an important part of standardization is the establishment of the standard language as the form used in a range of 'public' institutions. In the context of the increasing relative power of the working class in Britain after the Second World War, certain concessions have had to be made to nonstandard dialects in some institutions – in broadcasting and some of the professions, for example, certain forms of relatively prestigious nonstandard speech are tolerated. Again, cultural minorities have demanded rights for their own languages in various institutional spheres, including education, and these have again resulted in certain limited concessions.

SUMMARY AND CONCLUSIONS

In this chapter I have argued on the one hand that power is exercised and enacted in discourse, and on the other hand that there are relations of power behind discourse. I have also argued that in both cases power is won, held and lost in social struggles. We might say that, in terms of 'power in discourse', discourse is the site of power struggles, and, in terms of 'power behind discourse', it is the stake in power struggles – for control over orders of discourse is a powerful mechanism for sustaining power.

To conclude this chapter, I want to suggest a broad framework within which we can think about longer-term tendencies in and consequences of social struggles over discourse. This will prepare the way for later chapters. I shall start from the distinction I have been using between three types of constraint which powerful participants in discourse can exercise over the contributions of non-powerful participants: constraints on contents, relations, and subjects. We can think of these contraints either in relatively immediate and concrete terms (which was the way I introduced them) as a matter of power in discourse, or we can think of them in a relatively 'structural' and long-term way as a matter of power behind discourse – a matter, that is, of the conventions of discourse types constraining participants' contributions in these three ways. When we think of them in the second of these ways, we can see that such constraints on discourse may have long-term structural effects of a more general sort. I have been arguing that discourse is part of social practice and contributes to the repro-duction of social structures. If therefore there are systematic constraints on the contents of discourse and on the social relation-ships enacted in it and the social identities enacting them, these

Constraints	Structural effects
Contents	Knowledge and beliefs
Relations	Social relationships
Subjects	Social identities

Fig. 3.1 Constraints on discourse and structural effects

can be expected to have long-term effects on the knowledge and beliefs, social relationships, and social identities of an institution or society. This is represented in Fig. 3.1.

In any society there will be mechanisms for achieving coordination and commonality of practice in respect of knowledge and beliefs, social relationships, and social identities. Let us distinguish three main types of mechanism. First, there may be practices and discourse types which are universally followed and necessarily accepted because no alternative seems conceivable, which have built into them coordinated knowledge and beliefs, social relationships, and social identities. Secondly, coordination can be imposed in the exercise of power, in a largely hidden fashion, as the 'power behind discourse' which has been discussed in this chapter. Let us call this mechanism *inculcation*. Thirdly, coordination can be arrived at through a process of rational communication and debate. Let us call this mechanism *communication*.

All three mechanisms exist in contemporary society, but it is the struggle between communication and inculcation that is most salient. Inculcation can be thought of as motivated by a wish to re-create the universality and 'naturalness' of the first mechanism under conditions of class domination and division. It attempts to *naturalize* partial and interested practices to facilitate the exercise and maintenance of power. Broadly speaking, inculcation is the mechanism of power-holders who wish to preserve their power, while communication is the mechanism of emancipation and the struggle against domination. Correspondingly, a long-term focus of the struggle over discourse is the issue whether constraints on contents, relations and subjects are to be imposed through inculcation (and it is their imposition through inculcation that is the main concern of CLS) or coordinated through communication.

REFERENCES

This distinction between three types of constraint on social practice (contents, relations, subjects) and the distinction between 'inculcation' and 'communication' were prompted by Habermas J 1984. I have found Foucault (e.g. Foucault M 1972) as well as Habermas to be rich in ideas about language and power. The example of cross-cultural interaction is taken from Akinasso F N, Ajirotutu C S 1982. Both Gumperz J 1982a and Gumperz J 1982b are valuable sources on interaction of this type. On media discourse, see Davis H, Walton P 1983, and Gurevitch M *et al.* 1982 (especially the paper by Stuart Hall). There is an interesting discussion of standardization in Leith D 1983. The information and quotation about gynaecological examinations is taken from Emerson J 1970. In the discussion of formality, I have found Irvine J 1979 helpful. The classic study of T and V pronouns is Brown R, Gilman A 1972.

FOUR

Discourse, common sense and ideology

In this chapter, I take further the view of ideology and its relationship to discourse which I introduced in Chapter 2 – the view that conventions routinely drawn upon in discourse embody ideological assumptions which come to be taken as mere 'common sense', and which contribute to sustaining existing power relations. Given this intimate relationship between ideology and power, this chapter will inevitably overlap with Chapter 3. Both are concerned with power, but they differ in focus. Whereas Chapter 3 was a wide-ranging discussion of language and power, Chapter 4 is specifically targetted upon *common sense in the service of power* – upon how ideologies are embedded in features of discourse which are taken for granted as matters of common sense.

The sociologist Harold Garfinkel has written of 'the familiar common sense world of everyday life', a world which is built entirely upon assumptions and expectations which control both the actions of members of a society and their interpretation of the actions of others. Such assumptions and expectations are implicit, backgrounded, taken for granted, not things that people are consciously aware of, rarely explicitly formulated or examined or questioned. The common sense of discourse is a salient part of this picture. And the effectiveness of ideology depends to a considerable degree on it being merged with this common-sense background to discourse and other forms òf social action.

Let me preview the content of this chapter by giving a list of the questions which are raised, in their approximate order of appearance:

- What is 'common sense' in discourse, how does common sense relate to the *coherence* of discourse and to processes of discourse interpretation, and what is the relationship between common sense, coherence and ideology?

- To what extent are ideologies variable within a society, and how are such variations manifested in discourse?

- What is the relationship between ideological variation and social struggle, and how is the ideological common sense of discourse generated in the course of struggle?

- How does ideological common sense affect the meanings of linguistic expressions, conventional practices of speaking and writing, and the social subjects and situations of discourse?

- How can analysts bring this backgrounded common sense into the foreground?

IMPLICIT ASSUMPTIONS, COHERENCE AND INFERENCING

What must you do to make sense of a whole text (remembering, from Chapter 2, that texts may be written or spoken), to arrive at a coherent interpretation of it, assuming you already know the meanings of its constituent parts? Without trying to answer this rather big question exhaustively, let me suggest two things you must do. Firstly, you certainly need to work out how the parts of the text link to each other. Secondly, you also need to figure out how the text fits in with your previous experience of the world: what aspects of the world it relates to, or indeed what conception of the world it presupposes. In short, you need to establish a 'fit' between text and world.

I shall use the term *coherence* in a way which brings in both of these types of connection: (i) between the sequential parts of a text; and (ii) between (parts of) a text and 'the world'. These are connections which *we* make as interpreters of texts; they are not made by the text itself. But in order to make them, we have to draw upon those background 'assumptions and expectations' I have just been referring to. The sense or coherence of a whole text is generated in a sort of chemical reaction which you get when you put together what's in the text and what's already 'in' the interpreter – that is, the common-sense assumptions and expectations of the interpreter, part of what I have called 'members' resources' (MR).

Let's begin with a brief example of the second of these types of connection, between text and world. It is just one sentence from an article about 'birthstones' taken from a 'true romance' magazine: *For many centuries, the opal was reputed to be an unfortunate stone, bringing the wearer bad luck.* (*True Story* Summer Special, Argus Press 1986.) What conception of the world do you need to at least temporarily entertain, if not accept, in order to make sense of this sentence? We presumably need a world in which objects such as stones are capable of affecting human lives and human fortunes! Texts of this sort are interesting in presupposing a view of the world that is 'common sense' for some people, but strikes others as somewhat odd. Implicit assumptions can be more easily recognized in such cases than they are elsewhere.

But this is just a single sentence; what about the coherence of whole texts? Here is a rather different sort of example, the opening of a story in a 'true romance' magazine entitled 'His kind of loving':

His kind of loving . . .

Driving rain almost obscured the wooded hills as I made my way along the winding roads towards the village *where I had my craft shop.*

As I drove over the bridge and towards the shop *I was excited about Geoff's arrival* that evening. I hadn't seen him since I'd left Hampshire for Scotland three months before.

Geoff had been annoyed. 'I can see there's no use my trying to change your mind, Carrie. Go ahead, move to Scotland and open your shop.'

'We can be married next year,' *I pleaded. 'I have to take this chance of running my own business, Geoff.'*

'Just when I think you're going to settle down, *you get this hare-brained idea.'*

I sighed as I remembered our conversation . . .

Text 4.1 Source: *True Story*, Summer Special 1986

I have highlighted certain expressions in italics. What do you think they tell you about the sort of person Carrie is? Is their 'message' consistent through the extract, or are you being told contradictory things? What implicit assumptions about women do you need in order to derive this message, or these messages, from these expressions?

I think there are two 'messages' about Carrie, the one giving the text a superficial colouring of feminism, and the other firmly patriarchal: that she is an independent person (with a craft shop, her own business), and that she is a traditional subservient woman (who gets excited, pleads with 'her man', sighs, and accepts without protest her projects being called 'hare-brained'). Readers arrive at these messages by relating the italicized textual elements to implicit *frames*, which constitute accounts of what women are and do (or ought to be and do), roughly along these lines: (i) 'women are as much persons as men, and have the right to a career, to make decisions about their own lives, etc.'; (ii) 'women are subject to men's judgements on significant aspects of their lives, they are more prone to emotion and the expression of emotion, etc.'. A group of textual elements act as *cues* for a particular frame, and the frame provides a place for each textualized detail within a coherent whole, so that the apparently diverse italicized elements are given coherence, in the process of interpretation, by the frame. Or in terms of what I said above, it is the expectations and assumptions that are already 'in' the interpreter as part of MR that give coherence to the text. (On 'frames' see Ch. 6, pp. 158–159.)

As is often the case, the 'traditional-subservient-woman' message is reinforced visually. It is contained in a picture (of Carrie and Geoff) which accompanies the opening of the story: Carrie is petite, blond, and starry-eyed, Geoff is tall, dark and handsome, and is leaning towards Carrie, and towering over her, with a protective hand clasping her arm. Even the typeface in which the headline (*His kind of loving* . . .) is printed seems to have been chosen to evoke the 'true romance' paradigm.

Notice that, paradoxical as it may seem, both the production of a text and the interpretation of a text have an interpretative character. The producer of the text constructs the text as an interpretation of the world, or of the facets of the world which are then in focus; formal features of the text are *traces* of that interpretation. The traces constitute *cues* for the text interpreter, who draws upon her assumptions and expectations (incorporated in frames) to construct her interpretation of the text. Thus text interpretation is *the interpretation of an interpretation*. For neither the world nor the text does the interpretation of what is 'there' impose itself; both the production and the interpretation of texts are creative, constructive interpretative processes.

> How much of your routine interpretations of the texts you routinely see or hear come from *you* rather than from *them*? Bear in mind that images do not impose their own interpretations any more than words – the interpreter always bears some responsibility! Think about the snippets of advertising with which we are totally surrounded these days – in the underground, on buses, on hoardings, in shop windows, or coming through your letter box. What frames are you using to interpret them? What *cues* are you reacting to?

Now let's turn to the first of the aspects of coherence distinguished above, coherence between the sequential parts of a text. Implicit assumptions chain together successive parts of texts by supplying 'missing links' between explicit propositions, which the hearer/reader either supplies automatically, or works out through a process of *inferencing*, a concept we met briefly in connection with the 'Jenny Keeble' text in Chapter 3 (p. 53). Look for example at the second and third sentences of *His kind of loving* (*As I drove over the bridge* . . .). There is a coherent connection between them only if you assume a world in which the immediate prospect of seeing someone you love is likely to be exciting when you have not seen them for three months. How much working out or inferencing do you need to do to get to this assumption? None, I'd imagine; since that *is* the world for most of us, it is part of our frames for loving relationships, and it wouldn't occur to us that the sequence of sentences was anything but logical as it stands! We supply the linking assumption automatically, by a process of automatic *gap-filling*. (We can also apply the distinction between inferencing and automatic gap filling to the text/world aspect of coherence: texts can be 'fitted' to worlds either automatically, or through inferential work.)

There is no sharp dividing line between automatic gap-filling and inferencing, both because there is probably a scale from links which need no working out to links which need a lot of inferential 'work', and because a link which is supplied automatically by one person may need inferential work from another (or indeed from the same person on another occasion). Text 4.2 would probably not require any inferential work from regular readers of the sort of magazine it comes from, but it might from other people.

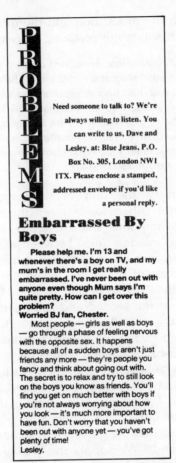

P R O B L E M S

Need someone to talk to? We're always willing to listen. You can write to us, Dave and Lesley, at: Blue Jeans, P.O. Box No. 305, London NW1 1TX. Please enclose a stamped, addressed envelope if you'd like a personal reply.

Embarrassed By Boys

Please help me. I'm 13 and whenever there's a boy on TV, and my mum's in the room I get really embarrassed. I've never been out with anyone even though Mum says I'm quite pretty. How can I get over this problem?
Worried BJ fan, Chester.

Most people — girls as well as boys — go through a phase of feeling nervous with the opposite sex. It happens because all of a sudden boys aren't just friends any more — they're people you fancy and think about going out with. The secret is to relax and try to still look on the boys you know as friends. You'll find you get on much better with boys if you're not always worrying about how you look — it's much more important to have fun. Don't worry that you haven't been out with anyone yet — you've got plenty of time!
Lesley.

Text 4.2 Source: *Blue Jeans* No. 488, 24 May 1986

My feeling is that the common-sense assumptions which give coherence to the heading (which was printed as a 'sideline' down the left-hand side of the page) are, first, that the way to deal with 'problems' is to find someone to talk to, and, second, that the role of this 'someone' is essentially to 'listen'. In other words, the folk wisdom that you should talk to a 'good listener' with a 'sympathetic ear' about your problems rather than trying to deal with them alone. These assumptions are necessary to connect the heading proper (*Problems*) with the sentences in small print beside it. Notice you also need to assume that talking and listening can go on in writing (and print) to make the third of these sentences cohere with the first two!

> But what about the letter and reply? What implicit assumptions do you need for a coherent interpretation? Do you think you supply them automatically through 'gap-filling', or by working them out through inferencing? Do you find it difficult to bring such matters to consciousness?

First, I think that in order to coherently link the letter as a request for 'help' and the reply, we need to assume that the giving of advice in writing *is* giving help. Secondly, the word *though* in the letter is the cue for an assumption necessary to give coherence to the two parts ('clauses') of sentence 3: that a 'quite pretty' girl can expect to have been out with a boy by the age of 13. Thirdly, the content of sentence 2 (and maybe also 3) is referred back to in sentence 4 as 'this problem', on the basis of the implicit assumption that her embarrassment *is* a 'problem'. Finally, to make a coherent link between the third sentence of the reply and the sentences that precede it, we need the assumption that the solution to a 'problem' lies in a 'secret', a remedy known only to some (but passed on to 'worried BJ fan' by 'Lesley').

What is perhaps thought-provoking about examples like this is that it is the *reader* who is responsible for bringing all these contentious assumptions into the process of interpretation, not the text. None of them is asserted in the text. This suggests a powerful way in which to impose assumptions upon readers and interpreters generally: by so placing the interpreter through textual cues that she has to entertain these assumptions if she is to make sense of the text. Persuasive discourse and propaganda do this all the time, often in quite obvious ways – for instance, when a journalist begins an article with *The Soviet threat to western Europe* . . ., she presupposes there *is* a Soviet threat. Fortunately, readers do not always accept being placed where writers place them!

This is a convenient point at which to pass on to the next question I want to address – that of the relationship between 'common sense' and ideology. For the common sense of the implicit assumptions I have referred to in the above example is clearly of an ideological order. I shall explain why in the next section. Moreover, the operation of ideology can be seen in terms of ways of constructing texts which constantly and cumulatively 'impose assumptions' upon text interpreters *and* text producers, typically without either being aware of it.

Common sense and ideology

'Common sense' is substantially, though not entirely, *ideological*, in the sense in which that term was introduced in Chapter 2, and it is this important relationship between common sense and ideology that I am primarily concerned with here. The relationship was explored by the Italian Marxist Antonio Gramsci, who refers to 'a form of practical activity' in which a 'philosophy is contained as an implicit theoretical "premiss"', and 'a conception of the world that is implicitly manifest in art, in law, in economic activity and in all manifestations of individual and collective life'. It is this conception of ideology as an 'implicit philosophy' in the practical activities of social life, backgrounded and taken for granted, that connects it to 'common sense' – a term extensively used by Gramsci himself in this connection. The rest of this chapter will be concerned to specify properties of ideological common sense.

Recall that I suggested in Chapter 2 that ideology be regarded as essentially tied to power relations. Let us correspondingly understand ideological common sense as *common sense in the service of sustaining unequal relations of power*. This is a matter of degree. In some cases the relationship to asymmetrical power relations may be a direct one, like the commonsensical assumption referred to in the last chapter, that everybody has 'freedom of speech', which disguises and helps to maintain the actuality of barriers to speech of various sorts for most people. In other cases, the relationship may be rather indirect – the 'problem page' texts in the last section, for instance, as I shall argue below. And rather than assuming a classification of common sense into 'ideological' and 'non-ideological', it will be more helpful to say that common-sense assumptions may *in varying degrees* contribute to sustaining unequal power relations.

They also do other things, also in varying degrees, such as establishing and consolidating solidarity relations among members of a particular social grouping. If you listen to the discourse of your family or friends or colleagues, you will notice just how many assumptions are taken for granted. You could argue that this is just a matter of efficiency – there's no point in spelling out what everyone assumes. But isn't being able to take so much for granted also an important sign that you 'belong'?

So what is it that makes the 'problem page' text (indirectly) ideological in its implicit assumptions? Isn't it dealing with purely *personal* problems, which have nothing to do with social power? On the face of it, it is: 'worried' of Chester is given advice on how she can overcome *her* 'problem', by adjusting to the reality of teenage gender relations. However, 'her' problem is clearly not just hers, it is shared by millions. And isn't it a social problem, rather than a personal problem? No doubt puberty has always caused difficulties for young people. But the difficulties seem particularly acute in contemporary society – because of the nature of teenage gender relations, of gender relations and their power asymmetries more generally, and ultimately because of our somewhat distorted social relationships. I think the ideological role of implicit assumptions in this instance is in providing a commonsensical framework and procedure for treating the *social* problems this girl is experiencing in a purely *individual* way. This is 'common sense sustaining unequal relations of power' in the sense that it helps deflect attention away from an idea which could lead to power relations being questioned and challenged – that there are social causes, and social remedies, for social problems.

Ideology is most effective when its workings are least visible. If one becomes aware that a particular aspect of common sense is sustaining power inequalities at one's own expense, it ceases to *be* common sense, and may cease to have the capacity to sustain power inequalities, i.e. to function ideologically. And invisibility is achieved when ideologies are brought to discourse not as explicit elements of the text, but as the background assumptions which on the one hand lead the text producer to 'textualize' the world in a particular way, and on the other hand lead the interpreter to interpret the text in a particular way. Texts do not typically spout ideology. They so position the interpreter through their cues that she brings ideologies to the interpretation of texts – and reproduces them in the process!

For that reason, what I referred to in the last section as automatic 'gap-filling', the supplying of 'missing links' needed for sequential coherence without inferential 'work', and automatic 'fitting' of text to world, are of particular interest from an ideological perspective. The more mechanical the functioning of an ideological assumption in the construction of coherent interpretations, the less likely it is to become a focus of conscious awareness, and hence the more secure its ideological status – which means also the more effectively it is reproduced by being drawn upon in discourse.

> How do your implicit assumptions about women differ from your implicit assumptions about men? Try to spot instances in your own discourse or other behaviour where your assumptions underpin coherence. Watch out for ways in which the texts you come across (including visual images) routinely cue ideological assumptions which are needed to interpret the texts.

VARIATION AND STRUGGLE IN IDEOLOGY

There is a constant endeavour on the part of those who have power to try to impose an ideological common sense which holds for everyone, as we shall see shortly. But there is always *some* degree of ideological diversity, and indeed conflict and struggle, so that ideological uniformity is never completely achieved. That is why we are sometimes able (thankfully!) as interpreters to keep at arm's length assumptions which text producers put across as commonsensical.

Everyone will be familiar with one domain of ideological diversity: political ideologies. This is perhaps a good starting point, because we can all find political texts whose ideological common sense is at odds with our own. This certainly holds true for me in the case of this extract:

As a whole, and at all times, the efficiency of the truly national leader consists primarily in preventing the division of attention of a people, and always concentrating it on a single enemy. The more uniformly the fighting will of a people is put into action, the greater will be the magnetic force of the movement and the more powerful the impetus of the blow. It is part of the genius of a great leader to make adversaries of different fields appear as always belonging to one category only, because to weak and unstable characters the knowledge that there are various enemies will lead only too easily to incipient doubts as to their own cause.

As soon as the wavering masses find themselves confronted with too many enemies, objectivity at once steps in, and the question is raised whether actually all the others are wrong and their own nation or their own movement alone is right.

Also with this comes the first paralysis of their own strength.

Therefore, a number of essentially different enemies must always be regarded as one in such a way that in the opinion of the mass of one's own adherents the war is being waged against one enemy alone. This strengthens the belief in one's own cause and increases one's bitterness against the attacker.

Text 4.4 Source: Adolf Hitler, *Mein Kampf*

What implicit assumptions about the nature of 'a people', and about the relationship between people and 'leader' are there here? Do you find them problematic?

It is assumed (and this is an ancient rhetorical device) that 'a people' is a sort of composite individual with the attributes of a single person (*attention, will, strength, bitterness*, having enemies), and the capacity to 'act as one', but these attributes can be sapped by disease (*paralysis*) as a result of weakness and instability. Since the people cannot sustain unity and clarity of objectives for itself (the masses are *wavering*), it falls to a 'leader' to do so – to *prevent division* and *concentrate attention*. It is assumed that the leadership of a people or nation is lodged in (*the genius of*) a single person, rather than collective.

These assumptions about the relationship between people and leader may seem extreme, but the idea of a people as a composite individual, for example, is actually quite common.

Find a passage from a political text (maybe a speech or an interview or a leaflet) whose implicit assumptions about people and leaders are alien to you, and try to spell them out as explicitly as you can. Then try the rather more difficult task of doing the same thing with a passage which accords with your political outlook!

There is certainly a great deal of variation in the extent of ideological diversity between societies, or between different periods in the history of a particular society. What determines the level of diversity? Basically the state of social relationships and social struggle, including class relationships and class struggle. In a society where power relationships are clear cut and stable, one would not expect to find a great deal of ideological diversity. What about contemporary capitalist society? Can we for instance interpret it in terms of a simple classical model of ideology, where the whole population is unified beneath a dominant ruling-class ideology? Probably not, though this model did make rather more sense in, say, the 1950s than it does now. The contemporary picture is characterized in some areas at least by a proliferation of ideologies which Therborn has compared to 'the cacophony of sounds and signs of a big city'. Furthermore, within a society, there may well be variation between different institutions in respect of degrees of ideological diversity.

Ideological diversity sets limits on what I have been calling *ideological common sense*. Although we have seen that there are cases where ideologies with very limited constituencies are nevertheless treated as common sense (the 'birthstone' text, and the Hitler text), the most effective form of ideological common sense will be 'common' in the sense of being shared by most if not virtually all of the members of a society or institution. Obviously, the greater the ideological diversity in a society, the less this will be so.

So where do these diverse ideologies come from? Are they for instance generated at random by individuals? They come rather from differences in position, experience and interests between social groupings, which enter into relationship (and, as we shall see, ideological conflict) with each other in terms of power. These groupings may be social classes, they may be women versus men, they may be groupings based on ethnicity, and so on. Often they are groupings of a more 'local' sort, associated with a particular institution. (Recall the discussion in Chapter 2 of the relationship between institutional groupings and class, gender, etc. groupings.) For instance, in education, children, parents, and teachers, and groupings *within* each of these (based upon age, class, political allegiance, etc.) may in principle develop different educational ideologies. The situation in which they are likely to do so is where there is a struggle between them over institutional power.

Among the various forms which social struggle may take, it is *ideological struggle* that is of particular concern in the present context because ideological struggle pre-eminently takes place in language. We can think of such struggle as not only *in* language in the obvious sense that it takes place in discourse and is evidenced in language texts, but also *over* language. It is over language in the sense that language itself is a *stake* in social struggle as well as a *site* of social struggle. We saw this in discussing 'power behind discourse' in Chapter 3. Having the power to determine things like which word meanings or which linguistic and communicative norms are legitimate or 'correct' or 'appropriate' is an important aspect of social and ideological power, and therefore a focus of ideological struggle. Seeing existing language practices and orders of discourse as reflecting the victories and defeats of past struggle, and as stakes which are struggled over, is, along with the complementary concept of 'power behind discourse', a major characteristic of critical language study (CLS) which differentiates it from descriptive 'mainstream' language study (in the terms of Ch. 1).

There are many different forms of ideological struggle in discourse, but here is a relatively simple example from a left-wing weekly, illustrating the use of *scare quotes*. Note that this is not a connected text – I have put together some extracts from a longer article by Zoë Tillotson.

Thatcher's fortress family

The left has been occupied of late grappling with shifts on the economic and industrial terrain. Too preoccupied, it seems, to focus any attention on another area that is also under reconstruction: the family.

Last week Thatcher, Gillick and the Mary Whitehouse posse closed ranks to launch a further onslaught on the 'permissive society'.

The demands for cheap, part-time semi-skilled labour in non-unionised industries is ensuring women's 'right to work'. Many women have no choice but to work, as men are increasingly unable to provide a 'family wage'.

However, as the state skulks off through the back door, one meddling hand remains to ensure that a 'good, moral' sex education, emphasizing a diet of 'self-restraint' and 'stable family life' will act as salvation to all potential hippies and homosexuals.

Text 4.5 Source: *7 Days*, June 1986

What is the effect of putting expressions like *permissive society* in 'scare quotes' on the way in which the reader regards these expressions? Do 'scare quotes' invariably have the sort of effect they have here? Note your own reactions when they occur in the newspaper you generally read.

The effect in this case is I think to warn the reader that these expressions are problematic in some way. It dissociates the writer from these expressions, and makes it clear they belong to someone else: the writer's and 'assumed reader's' political opponents. In some cases, conversely, putting an expression in scare quotes is a way of endorsing it.

An interesting question is how readers know in a particular case whether to interpret this cue one way rather than the other. It is, again, evidently something to do with the implicit assumptions (MR) they draw upon in interpreting text. In the case of *the permissive society*, for instance, most readers of 7 *Days* (a Communist Party publication) will be aware before they see the article that this expression belongs to an ideology alien to that of the newspaper, and so will unproblematically interpret it in a dissociating way. If they happened not to be aware of this, the immediate context would help them: since *posse* distances the writer of the article from Thatcher and company, one is likely to interpret the scare quotes which follow as also distancing.

Monitor your own practice, and try to work out what assumptions determine how you interpret scare quotes in different instances.

Dominant and dominated discourse types

The struggle over language can manifest itself as a struggle between ideologically diverse *discourse types*. Recall that in Chapter 2 I introduced this term to refer to conventions, norms, codes of practice underlying actual discourse. Discourse types are ideologically particular and ideologically variable.

Why then a struggle between discourse types? What is at stake? What is at stake is the establishment or maintenance of one type as the *dominant* one in a given social domain, and therefore the establishment or maintenance of certain ideological assumptions as commonsensical. Let's take another example from the relatively transparent case of political discourse. In politics, each opposing party or political force tries to win general acceptance for its own discourse type as the preferred and ultimately the 'natural' one for talking and writing about the state, government, forms of political action, and all aspects of politics – as well as for demarcating *politics* itself from other domains. Think for example of the contrasting accounts of Britain's economic crisis given in the discourses of Thatcherite Toryism, Social Democracy (with left and right variants), Liberalism, and Communism since the late 1970s, and how the first of these came to dominate British politics in the early 1980s. (See Ch. 7 for texts and further discussion.) The stake is more than 'mere words'; it is controlling the contours of the political world, it is legitimizing policy, and it is sustaining power relations.

The primary domains in which social struggle takes place are the social institutions, and the situation types which each institution recognizes. Institutions tend to be rather complex structures, and a single institution is likely to involve various sorts of discourse in its various situation types. We can thus have a number of different sets of ideologically competing discourse types corresponding to these situation types. Nevertheless, there are important similarities and overlaps between the discourse types associated with a particular ideological position, not only across situation types within an institution, but also across institutions. See Chapter 7 for discussion.

What forms do dominance relationships between discourse types take? A dominated type may be in a relationship of *opposition* to a dominant one. The linguist Michael Halliday calls one type of oppositional discourse the *anti-language*. Anti-languages are set up and used as conscious alternatives to the dominant or established discourse types. Examples would be the language of the criminal underworld, or a social dialect which comes to be a consciously oppositional language – as may happen with the 'nonstandard' social dialect of a minority ethnic grouping, for example, or of a working-class community in one of the large cities.

Another possibility is for a dominated discourse type to be *contained* by a dominant one. A case in point is the way in which Thatcherite discourse has attempted to incorporate popular anti-bureaucratic and anti-State discourse by deflecting it towards a critique of the *welfare* state and of, in Thatcherite terms, 'state socialism'. (See Ch. 7 for details.) Where dominated discourses are oppositional, there will be pressure for them to be suppressed or eliminated; whereas containment credits them with a certain legitimacy and protection – with strings attached!

Naturalization and the generation of common sense

One can think of the ultimate objective for a dominant discourse type as, in the words of the French anthropologist Pierre Bourdieu, 'recognition of legitimacy through misrecognition of arbitrariness'. To put the same point less tersely (and less elegantly), if a discourse type so dominates an institution that dominated types are more or less entirely suppressed or contained, then it will cease to be seen as arbitrary (in the sense of being one among several possible ways of 'seeing' things) and will come to be seen as *natural*, and legitimate because it is simply *the* way of conducting oneself. I will refer to this, as others have done, as the *naturalization* of a discourse type. Naturalization is a matter of degree, and the extent to which a discourse type is naturalized may change, in accordance with the shifting 'balance of forces' in social struggle.

What is the connection of naturalization to the ideological common sense I have been discussing? Naturalization is the royal road to common sense. Ideologies come to be ideological common sense to the extent that the discourse types which embody them become naturalized. This depends on the power of the social groupings whose ideologies and whose discourse types are at issue. In this sense, common sense in its ideological dimension is itself an *effect of power*. What comes to be common sense is thus in large measure determined by who exercises power and domination in a society or a social institution.

But in the naturalization of discourse types and the creation of common sense, discourse types actually appear to *lose* their ideological character. A naturalized type tends to be perceived not as that of a particular grouping within the institution, but as simply that of the institution itself. So it appears to be *neutral* in struggles for power, which is tantamount to it being placed outside ideology. One consequence is that the learning of a dominant discourse type comes to be seen as merely a question of acquiring the necessary skills or techniques to operate in the institution. An example would be learning how to operate discoursally in the classroom when a child first goes to school, or learning at a later educational stage how to 'come across' well in an interview. The apparent emptying of the ideological content of discourses is, paradoxically, a fundamental ideological effect: ideology works through disguising its nature, pretending to be what it isn't. When linguists take language practices at face value, as I suggested they did in Chapter 1, they help sustain this ideological effect.

Acknowledging the phenomenon of naturalization is tantamount to insisting upon a distinction between the superficial common-sense *appearances* of discourse and its underlying *essence*. But what then are we to make of the *explanations* people give, or can be persuaded by the analyst to give, of their own discourse practices? Explanations should be seen as *rationalizations* which cannot be taken at face value but are themselves in need of explanation. We can see rationalizations as part and parcel of naturalization: together with the generation of common-sense discourse practices comes the generation of common-sense rationalizations of such practices, which serve to *legitimize* them.

Think of the apparently most 'neutral' discourse types you know as effects of a process of naturalization, and of the explanations people give for them as rationalizations. Are there any types you believe to be *really* neutral?

IDEOLOGY AND MEANING

One dimension of 'common sense' is the meaning of words. Most of the time, we treat the meaning of a word (and other linguistic expressions) as a simple matter of fact, and if there is any question about 'the facts' we see the dictionary as the place where we can check up on them. For words we are all perfectly familiar with, it's a matter of mere common sense that they mean what they mean! I shall suggest below that common sense is as suspect here as elsewhere. But a brief discussion of two aspects of meaning in language will be helpful in the critique of commonsensical meaning: firstly, the variability of meaning, and secondly, the nature of *meaning systems*.

Because of the considerable status accorded by common sense to 'the dictionary', there is a tendency to generally underestimate the extent of variation in meaning systems within a society. For, although some modern dictionaries do attempt to represent variation, 'the dictionary' as the authority on word meaning is very much a product of the process of *codification* of standard languages and thus closely tied to the notion that words have fixed meanings. (Recall the discussion of standardization in Ch. 3.) It is easy enough to demonstrate that meanings vary between *social dialects* (discussed in Ch. 2), but they also vary *ideologically*: one respect in which discourse types differ is in their meaning systems. Let us take as an example a word which figures prominently in this book; the word *ideology* itself.

Ideology certainly does not give the impression of having a single fixed meaning – far from it! Indeed, it is not unusual to find words like *ideology* described as 'meaningless' because they have so many meanings. But the situation is not quite that desperate: *ideology* does have a number of meanings, but it is not endlessly variable in meaning, and the meanings it has tend to cluster together into a small number of main 'families'.

I shall just identify two such families. One belongs particularly to the USA after the Second World War, though it is familiar enough today in Britain: *ideology* is interpreted as 'any social policy which is in part or in whole derived from social theory *in a conscious way*'. The other is in the Marxist tradition: *ideologies* are 'ideas which arise from a given set of material interests' in the course of the struggle for power. The definitions I have used here are from Williams R 1976.

The point to stress is that the variable meanings of *ideology* are not just randomly generated, but themselves correspond to different ideological positions, and have been generated in the course of struggle between these positions. Thus the first of these senses of *ideology* labels Marxism as an ideology, along with fascism, and therefore uses 'the term which Marx and his followers had done so much to popularize' as 'a weapon *against* Marxism', in the words of David McLellan.

But, to come to the second of the aspects of meaning I referred to above, the meaning of a word is not an isolated and independent thing. Words and other linguistic expressions enter into many sorts of relationship – relationships of similarity, contrast, overlap and inclusion. And the meaning of a single word depends very much on the relationship of that word to others. So instead of the vocabulary of a language consisting of an unordered list of isolated words each with its own meaning, it consists of clusters of words associated with *meaning systems*.

Thus a full account of the variability of a word such as *ideology* would require comparison of *meaning systems*, not just word meanings. For instance, in the postwar American sense of *ideology* mentioned above, *ideology* is closely related to *totalitarianism*, and *totalitarian* and *ideological* are sometimes used as near synonyms. Furthermore, *totalitarianism* is a superordinate term which subsumes *fascism, communism, Marxism*, and so forth; the meaning system is structured so as to make *ideology* 'a weapon against Marxism'! In the Marxist meaning system, by contrast, *totalitarianism* does not figure at all, nor of course do we find *communism/Marxism* and *fascism* as co-*homonyms* of *totalitarianism*. For *homonym* and *synonym*, see Chapter 5, p. 116.

Let us now come back to the observation at the beginning of this section, that meaning appears as a matter of common sense. 'Common sense' in this case actually turns out to be something of an ideological sleight of hand! Imagine, for instance, *ideology* one day apparently coming to have a fixed meaning which one could check up on in 'the dictionary', and which was not contested. This could only mean that one 'side' in the struggle between meaning systems had gained undisputable dominance. The fixed meaning would in this sense be an *effect of power* – in fact the sort of ideological effect I have called *naturalization*.

But perhaps this is always the case with fixed meanings? What about an apparently quite unfavourable case like the word *nose*, in its most mundane anatomical sense of that part of the face which lies above the mouth and contains the nostrils? In contrast with *ideology*, there is (as far as I am aware) no variation in or struggle around the meaning of *nose*. Nevertheless, the meaning system which embodies the familiar classification of body parts *does* have some of the properties associated with naturalization. Firstly, there is an element of what Bourdieu called 'the misrecognition of arbitrariness', in that the meaning system seems to have a transparent and natural relationship to the body, as if it could be named in no other way. For instance, one can perfectly well imagine a meaning system which included a term for the groove between the nose and the upper lip, yet there happens to be no such term in English. Secondly, the meaning system is sustained by power: by the power of the relevant 'experts', medical scientists, and by the power of those sections of the intelligentsia (teachers, dictionary-makers, etc.) who are guarantors of this as of other elements of the codified standard language.

I shall assume that the fixed dictionary meanings that present themselves as simple matters of fact to common sense are always the outcome of a process of naturalization, in so far as the arbitrariness of meaning systems is hidden, though only in certain cases (*ideology* but not *nose*, for instance) is naturalization the outcome of ideological struggle and hence of particular interest in CLS.

What I have said about meaning so far applies to words and expressions as a resource for discourse, as the 'dictionary items' of particular discourse types, rather than the meanings of utterances in discourse. However, naturalization has parallel effects on both cases: both involve a *closure* or restriction of the plenitude of potential meanings. In the case of words and expressions thought of as dictionary items, this is a matter of the fixing of their meaning, as we have seen. In the case of an utterance in discourse, this is a matter of giving it the appearance of having only one possible interpretation, so that its meaning is given the appearance of being transparent. Think, for instance, of the meaning of *Can I help you?* uttered by a police officer standing at a reception counter in a police station to a person who has just entered the station. 'Obvious!', most people would say: the officer is inviting the person to give an account of her 'problem', her reason for being there, so that the officer can 'deal with' it. But *Can I help you?* could mean all sorts of quite different things: its meaning is closed, as transparently obvious, within the particular naturalized practice of this discourse of police/public encounters. (See the next section for discussion of the naturalization of practices, and a real example of *Can I help you?*.)

As the beginning of the last paragraph suggests, there is a sense in which texts draw upon words and expressions, and meaning

THE STILL SMALL VOICE OF TRUTH

Since the invasion of the Falklands on April 2, there has been the sound of many voices. *Yet at the heart of the matter, it was an evil thing, an injustice, an aggression.* Nobody disputes that. Even loyal Argentines — let alone Argentina's apologists — accept that force should not have been used to prosecute the Argentine case. But force *was* used; and it was not necessary. Beneath the roll of Argentine drums there are voices, however small, however still, which say that too, and they recognize that the unity achieved by the junta in Buenos Aires may only be a passing one, since it was born of an injustice. Unity in Britain, on the other hand, is based on recognition of the invasion as an incontrovertibly evil act. Obviously there have been disagreements about the method of coping with that evil, but there should be recognition that to compromise with evil — to appease it — is to run the risk of having to share responsibility for it. How we react to evil must therefore be conditioned by the need to compromise with it as little as possible, while taking care to see that our reaction to it does not compound the original evil.

Text 4.6 Source: *The Times,* 20 May 1982

systems, as a 'resource'. However, texts don't merely instantiate prior meaning systems, they can also to varying degrees generate their own. Texts are in this sense ideologically creative. Text 4.6 is the first paragraph of a newspaper editorial.

What sort of meaning relationship is there between *invasion, evil, injustice, aggression*? How does their relationship in this text differ from their relationship in discourse types you can think of? Do you think this text can reasonably be described as 'ideologically creative'?

The second sentence, which I have italicized, is an *attributive* (SVC) sentence (see Chapter 5, p. 122), which establishes a 'member of a class: class' relationship between *the invasion of the Falklands,* and *evil (thing), injustice* and *aggression*. The listing of these three expression as *attributes* suggests a relationship of meaning equivalence between them. This happens because the word for a class can generally be used to refer to a member of the class, so in this case *evil, injustice* and *aggression* can be used interchangeably to refer to the invasion. In this special sense, we can say they are textual *synonyms*. But they are not synonymous in the meaning system of any discourse type I can think of. Ideologically, this suggests a conflation of political/military acts with morality (*evil*) and legality (*injustice*); *aggression* is already a conventionalized partial expression of this conflation. In the last two sentences of the paragraph, this conflation seems to be 'put to use': the invasion is referred to as *(that) evil*, and this slides into general references to evil which are assumed to carry over to the invasion. The writer can thus say things that make no sense in terms of the invasion without appearing to be incoherent; notice for instance how peculiar it sounds if one replaces *evil* with *the invasion* in 'to compromise with evil – to appease it – is to run the risk of having to share responsibility for it', for instance.

What sort of purposes is ideological creativity in texts most commonly used for? Presumably in this text from *The Times*, it is being used politically, in something of a crisis, to blacken 'the enemy' and legitimize British military action. My impression is that ideological creativity is often associated with managing crises of one sort or another. Look for more examples, perhaps especially in the 'mass media', and try to check out this impression. You might also like to compare this text with the extract from *Mein Kampf* we had earlier.

INTERACTIONAL ROUTINES AND THEIR BOUNDARIES

Common sense gives us not only meaning systems, but also what we might call the 'interactional routines' associated with particular discourse types – the conventional ways in which participants interact with each other. For most of the time, we take part in buying-and-selling transactions in shops, interviews with social workers or clients, consultations with doctors or patients, and so forth, without giving a moment's thought to the conventional routines for relating to other participants which are built into these types of discourse. It's generally only when things go wrong that they draw themselves to our attention.

> For example, this is the opening of an exchange in a police station between a man (M) who has just come into the station, and a police woman (PW). A spaced dot indicates a short pause, a dash a longer one, round brackets indicate indistinguishable talk, and the series of dots shows that turn (8) has been curtailed. Do you agree that something appears to be going wrong? What?
>
> (1) PW: can I help you?
> (2) M: oh . yes . police?
> (3) PW: yes—
> (4) M: reckon you can help me can you? .
> (5) PW: yes
> (6) M: are you a police lady? good
> (7) PW: (unclear) what's the problem?
> (8) M: I've got to . renew my car licence . . .
>
> What appears to me to be going wrong is that M seems to find problematic things which are generally regarded as commonsensically given when we ask for information at a police station; that those behind the reception desk are indeed police, that all such people are competent to 'help' members of 'the public', that a woman at reception will indeed be a police woman ('lady'). This could almost be a script for part of a comedy routine – laughter is one established way of handling those who refuse to accept the obvious! Look out for examples of comedy routines based upon that principle.

These common-sense assumptions underlie the normal inter-actional routine of the opening of exchanges in this type of situation: one expects PW's utterance (1) to be taken as eliciting a statement of the 'problem', which actually comes only in (8), as the first utterance on the part of M. It is evident from formal features of the text that the way the exchange actually develops is treated as problematic by both PW and M. PW for instance hesitates before her turn in (5), pronounces the *yes* in (5) with a marked 'surprised' tone (though that is not evident from the transcription), and finds it necessary (which it normally isn't) to ask M to identify 'the problem'; whereas M has a long hesitation before his turn in (4), and answers his own question in (6).

But could we not regard these textual traces of discomfort and of an attempt to 'repair' the exchange as evidence that participants do expect, as a matter of common sense, that an exchange will follow a 'normal course'? Notice that these common-sense expectations are institutionally specific: although for example there are generic 'family resemblances' between *interviews* across institutions, interviews and our expectations of them differ from a police station to a workplace to a university. For that reason, it will generally make sense to investigate language practices by reference to specific social institutions. (See Ch. 2 for discussion of social institutions, and Ch. 8 on cross-institutional genres such as the interview.)

What I have said generally about *naturalization* applies also here: there is no inherent reason why enquiries at police stations should be conventionally structured the way they are, there are conceivable if not actual alternatives, and the naturalization of a particular routine as *the* common-sense way of doing things is an effect of power, an ideological effect. An interesting aspect of cases like the extract above where things are going wrong is that the arbitrariness of practices and the way in which they sustain power, normally hidden, can become apparent. In this example, M asks *reckon you can help me can you*. This highlights the normal assumption of a general police competence to 'help' the public and responsibility for helping the public (rather than, say, keeping them in check), which underlies the way in which *Can I help you?* standardly elicits a statement of 'the problem' without further preliminaries. This assumption is an important element in relations between police and public, and in the legitimacy and power of the police.

Another way in which the arbitrariness of naturalized dominant interactional routines becomes apparent is when they are

confronted or contrasted with other non-dominant practices. The
following is an extract from a consultation between a doctor (D)
and his patient (P), a woman alcoholic.

P: she said that I could she thought that it might be possible
to me for me to go to a council ⌈flat
D: ⌊right yes ⌈yeah
P: ⌊but she said it's a
very em she wasn't pushing it because . my mother's got to
sign
D: hm
a whole lot of things and e: . she said it's difficult and em
D: hm   hm   hm
. there's no rush over it . I I don't know whether . I mean one
thing they say in AA is that you shouldn't change anything .
for
D: hm
a year.
D: hm yes I think I think that's wise . I think that's wise (5-second
pause) well look I'd like to keep you know seeing you keep .
you know hearing how things are going from time to time if
that's possible
P: yeah
D: you know if you like to pop in once every em . two weeks or so
P: yes
D: and just let me know of how things are getting on

Text 4.7 Source: 'The Healing Arts', BBC2, 8 August 1986

This differs in a number of ways from what experience has taught me
to expect from a doctor/patient consultation. Do you feel the same
about it? If so, what are the differences?

These are the points that strike me: the patient is allowed to say what
she has to say in her own time – notice the 5-second pause before D
moves towards closing the consultation; D gives a great deal of
evidence of listening to and taking in what P says – notice all the
'feedback' he gives her in the form of what are sometimes
called *back-channels* (*hm, right, yes, yeah*); when D moves to a
conclusion by talking about future consultations, he talks in a way that
is minimally directive (*if you'd like to pop in*, etc.), and tries to interact
with P by appealing to her understanding (*you know*) and giving her

opportunities to respond to his 'proposals'. However, one comment I have had on this text is 'I thought the doctor sounded bored!', which underlines the fact that there might be various ways of interpreting D's behaviour.

This text is from a programme about the work of a leading member of the British Holistic Medical Association, which appears to operate as a pressure group within the National Health Service for 'holistic medicine', the treatment of the whole person rather than just the disease, and the use where appropriate of methods of treatment from homeopathy and other forms of 'alternative' medicine. Struggles within medicine between pressure groups like this and the medical establishment can be expected to be in part struggles over language – over what sort of language medical consultations ought to be conducted in, for instance.

What experience do you have of varying interactional routines, of dominant and non-dominant types, in medicine? Think of differences in age and gender between doctors, and differences between orthodox practitioners and (if you have experience of them) homeopathic, naturopathic, or other 'alternative' practitioners.

Such struggles are also over *boundaries*, which brings us to the second part of the title of this section. One way of seeing the holistic medicine text is as a mixture of interactional routines associated with different discourse types – perhaps the medical consultation, counselling, and ordinary conversation. I suspect that from the point of view of establishment medicine and the dominant type of discourse in consultation, 'counselling talk' and conversational talk would be seen as having no place in the consultation proper. Doctors do of course chat with their patients, and counsel them; but my impression is that the chat tends to come as a demarcated preface or postface to the consultation proper; and for most doctors, counselling is probably also seen as something at least partially separated from consultation. These are suggestions which would need confirming or disconfirming through detailed research. The main point for present purposes is that the way in which different discourse types are related to each other, and the extent to which they are kept apart or mixed together, is another aspect of struggle over language. This connects back to what I was saying in Chapters 2 and 3 about *orders of discourse*: the way in which an order of discourse is structured – the relationships between constituent discourse types – is determined by power relations, and therefore contested in power struggles.

SUBJECTS AND SITUATIONS

The French philosopher Louis Althusser pointed to an important connection between common-sense assumptions (what he calls 'obviousnesses') about meaning, and common-sense assumptions about social identity or the 'subject' (a concept I introduced in Ch. 2): 'Like all obviousnesses, including those that make a word "name a thing" or "have a meaning" (therefore including the obviousness of the "transparency" of language), the "obviousness" that you and I are subjects – and that that does not cause any problems – is an ideological effect, the elementary ideological effect.' And Althusser adds that 'linguists and those who appeal to linguistics for various purposes often run up against difficulties which arise because they ignore the action of the ideological effects in all discourses – including even scientific discourses'.

The 'transparency of language' is a general property which is illustrated for instance by what I said about meaning in the last section but one: the social processes constituting languages in general (and meanings in particular) are hidden beneath their appearance of being just naturally, commonsensically 'there'.

But are we to regard Althusser's analogy between the 'evident facts' of words having meaning and you and I being subjects as simply fortuitous? I don't think so. The point is that the ideological effect of one's 'subjecthood' being perceived as commonsensically given, rather than socially produced, is an effect that comes about pre-eminently in language and in meaning. That is, the socialization of people involves them coming to be placed in a range of *subject positions*, which they are exposed to partly through learning to operate within various discourse types; for, as I said in Chapter 2, each discourse type establishes its particular set of subject positions, which those who operate within it are constrained to occupy.

Subject positions are specific to discourse types, and ideologically variable. Consider again the holistic medicine text: one aspect of the contrast between medical consultations in the discourse of holistic medicine and those in the discourse of conventional medicine will be in the subject positions set up for patients. This is implicit in the comments I made about the text earlier: the contribution of the patient to the discourse is different from what one has learnt to expect in medical consultations, which suggests different subject positions for patients in the two types of discourse. Notice the power which is at stake in the struggle between discourses in this respect: it is the power to *create* the 'patient' in the image, so to speak, of the ideological ideal – for 'patients' are made what they are through the subject positions in which 'patienthood' is enacted. People sometimes feel the lack of an ideologically neutral term for referring to a person in receipt of medical care – for instance, when the term *patient* is used to refer to a woman in childbirth, inevitably portraying her as helpless, sick, and having things done to her rather than doing things (like giving birth!) herself.

Text 4.8 is another example, this time written, in which the issue is what subject position is created for the reader. What attributes do you think you would need to have to be an ideal example of the reader 'built into' this text?

The 'ideal reader' is looking for *success*, the capacity to *dominate* and *influence* others, an end to *boredom and frustration* . . . and so on. Part of the way in which this ideal reader is built into the text is to do with the nature of the *speech acts* (see Ch. 6, pp. 155–58) that are being performed here. They include what we might call *assurances* – for instance, the heading seems to contain the assurance that a command of good English will bring recognition, etc., and the two sentences following the sub-head *Command Respect* both contain assurances. One only normally gives people assurances that something will happen if they *want* it to happen. Assurances are like promises in this respect, though unlike the promiser the assurer is not committed to bringing whatever it is about personally. So, it is assumed that the reader *wants* 'new recognition and success', and so forth.

The social process of producing social subjects can be conceived of in terms of the positioning of people progressively over a period of years – indeed a lifetime – in a range of subject positions. The social subject is thus constituted as a particular configuration of subject positions. A consequence is that the subject is far less coherent and unitary than one tends to assume.

> ### How A Command Of Good English Will Bring You New Recognition And Success
>
> Language – the everyday act of speaking and writing, of reading and thinking – plays a much more important part in our daily lives than we usually realise. Indeed, it is a success "secret" of most outstanding men and women.
>
> This booklet describes a new, unique way to improve your English, to increase your business and social success, to find new power of thought and expression, and to get more out of life.
>
> ### Command Respect
>
> You will learn in detail how to dominate and influence every situation simply by using the right words at the right time. What's more, you can confidently look forward to ending boredom and frustration and gaining the attention and respect that win friends and influence people.
>
> Yes, a command of good English is the most important single aid you could have in your search for success.

Text 4.8 Source: *Good English – The Language of Success*, 1979

Instead, we have to assume that social subjects are, in Gramsci's words, 'composite personalities'. Or as Foucault has put it, the subject is 'dispersed' among the various subject positions: 'discourse is not the majestically unfolding manifestation of a thinking, knowing, speaking subject, but, on the contrary, a totality, in which the dispersion of the subject and his discontinuity with himself may be determined'. This has, as Foucault points out, profound implications for our tendency to see a speaker or writer as the *author* of her words: there is a sense, on the contrary, in which the speaker or writer is a *product* of her words. We must not take this too far, however: as I argued in Chapter 2, there is a dialectical process in discourse wherein the subject is both created and creative. See further Chapter 7.

What is the import of Althusser's designation of the 'obviousness' that one is a subject as 'an ideological effect, the elementary ideological effect'? It is I think partly that people are not conscious of being socially positioned as subjects, and standardly see their own subjective identities as somehow standing outside and prior to society. Such ideological misperceptions are the basis for various idealist theories of human society which are built around the 'individual' as pre-social, and which try to see societies as emanating from (properties of) the individual rather than the other way round. In calling this the 'elementary' ideological effect, Althusser is suggesting that constituting subjects is what ideology is all about – *all* ideology is in one way or another to do with positioning subjects.

What I have said about the subjects in discourse applies also to the *situations* of discourse. We also take the situations in which we discourse as 'obviousnesses' which cause no problems. Yet, again, far from those situations existing prior to and independently of discourse as we tend to commonsensically assume, they are in a sense the products of discourse, particular discourse types and orders of discourse having their own particular inventories of situation types, and there being consequently different ideologically contrastive inventories.

Both the subject positions and the situation types of dominant discourse types are (like the meanings of their words, and the properties of their interactional routines) liable to be *naturalized*, and we have now reached a point in the argument where it will I hope be apparent just how much is at stake in struggles in, and especially over, language, and just how much is to be gained through the achievement of naturalization. Consider the relationship between naturalization and the three ways in which I claimed power constrained the practice of others in Chapter 3. The naturalization of the meanings of words is an effective way of constraining the contents of discourse and, in the long term, knowledge and beliefs. So too is the naturalization of situation types, which helps to consolidate particular images of the social order. The naturalization of interactional routines is an effective way of constraining the social relations which are enacted in discourse, and of constraining in the longer term a society's system of social relationships. Finally, the naturalization of subject positions self-evidently constrains subjects, and in the longer term both contributes to the socialization of persons and to the delimitation of the 'stock' of social identities in a given institution or society. Naturalization, then, is the most formidable weapon in the armoury of power, and therefore a significant focus of struggle.

'MAKING TROUBLE': FOREGROUNDING COMMON SENSE

In Chapter 9, there will be a discussion of the complex issues involved in the relationship between CLS, (self-)consciousness and social emancipation, and I do not want to pre-empt that discussion too much here. However, given the emphasis I have placed in this chapter on the backgrounded and unconscious nature of ideological common sense, this is perhaps an appropriate place to say something about how common sense can be *foregrounded*, which it must be if people are to become self-conscious about things which they unreflectingly take for granted.

We saw in the section *Interactional routines and their boundaries* that one situation in which the common-sense elements of discourse are brought out into the open is when things go wrong in discourse. CLS can correspondingly focus upon instances of communication breakdown and miscommunication, and instances where people attempt to 'repair' their discourse, as a way of highlighting and foregrounding discoursal common sense.

Another situation where common-sense elements are 'spontaneously' foregrounded is where there is a sufficiently large social or cultural divide between participants in an exchange, or between participants in and observers of an exchange, for the arbitrariness and social relativity of the common sense of one to be evident to others. It follows from what has been said in this chapter about ideological variability and struggle that this happens extensively within as well as across societies, and we saw one example in the Hitler text. Again, the analyst can build upon this, focusing upon ideological struggle in discourse, or exposing people to samples of talk or writing which they are likely to find ideologically alien.

A third possibility is the deliberate disturbance of common sense through some form of intervention in discourse. The experimental tasks which the sociologist Harold Garfinkel assigned to his students are an example. Here is an excerpt from the student accounts of these experiments:

> The subject was telling the experimenter, a member of the subject's car pool, about having a flat tire while going to work the previous day.
> (s) I had a flat tire.
> (e) What do you mean, you had a flat tire?
> She appeared momentarily stunned. Then she answered in a hostile way: 'What do you mean "What do you mean?" A flat tire is a flat tire. That is what I meant. Nothing special. What a crazy question!'
>
> *(Garfinkel H 1967:42)*

The responses of subjects to experimenters' attempts to estrange the common-sense world of discourse show just how solid and real that world is for people. As we can see in this example, people quickly become incredulous, irritated, and angry when this world is disturbed, and may well conclude that whoever disturbs it is playing the fool, or mentally ill. This is therefore a technique to use cautiously!

SUMMARY

Let me now summarize what I have been saying in this chapter. I started from the *common-sense* nature of discourse, and suggested that the *coherence* of discourse is dependent on discoursal common sense. I then claimed that discoursal common sense is *ideological* to the extent that it contributes to sustaining unequal power relations, directly or indirectly. Ideology, however, is not inherently commonsensical: certain ideologies acquire that status in the course of ideological struggles, which take the linguistic form of struggles in social institutions between ideologically diverse discourse types. Such struggles determine dominance relations between them and their associated ideologies. A dominant discourse is subject to a process of *naturalization*, in which it appears to lose its connection with particular ideologies and interests and become the common-sense practice of the institution. Thus when ideology becomes common sense, it apparently ceases to be ideology; this is itself an ideological effect, for ideology is truly effective only when it is disguised.

I went on to discuss naturalization in several dimensions of discoursal common sense. In the case of the *meanings of linguistic expressions* and meaning systems, naturalization was shown to result in a closure of meaning, reflected in the apparent fixity of the 'dictionary' meanings of words, and in the apparent transparency of utterance meanings. In the case of *interactional routines*, the self-evidentness of conventional (and ultimately arbitrary) ways of interacting is an effect of naturalization, as also is the way these are related and demarcated. And, finally, in the case of the *subjects* and *situations* of discourse, their self-evidentness and apparent independence of discourse are illusory effects of naturalization, for they are both to a significant degree *products* of discourse. I concluded the chapter with a discussion of ways in which ideological common sense can be foregrounded.

REFERENCES

For discussion of the 'common-sense world of everyday life', see Garfinkel H 1967. There is a helpful discussion of inferencing, and its relation to automatic 'gap filling', in Chapter 7 of Brown G, Yule G 1983. On ideology, see: Althusser L 1971; McLellan D 1986; and Williams R 1976. Gramsci's remarks on common sense and ideology are to be found in Gramsci A 1971. See also Therborn G 1980 (quoted on p. 88). Hall S 1982 is useful on ideology and naturalization. On 'anti-languages', see the paper with that title in Halliday M 1978. There are valuable treatments of many of the themes of the chapter in: Bourdieu P 1977; Pecheux M 1982; and Thompson J B 1984. Althusser's statement about meaning and subjects comes from Althusser L 1971. Foucault's comments on the subject appear in Foucault M 1982.

FIVE

Critical discourse analysis in practice: description

The textual samples in the preceding chapters have contained quite a range of linguistic features – features of vocabulary, grammar, punctuation (recall the 'scare quotes' example in the last chapter), turn-taking, types of speech act and the directness or indirectness of their expression, and features to do with the overall structure of interactions – as well as examples of non-linguistic textual features ('visuals'). I hope that by this stage in the book, readers without a background in language analysis will appreciate how a close analysis of texts in terms of such features can contribute to our understanding of power relations and ideological processes in discourse.

But text analysis is just one part of discourse analysis. Recall Fig. 2.1 (on p. 25), which identified text, interaction, and social context as three elements of a discourse, and the corresponding distinction I drew between three stages of critical discourse analysis; *description* of text, *interpretation* of the relationship between text and interaction, and *explanation* of the relationship between interaction and social context.

In this chapter and the next, I shall present a procedure for critical discourse analysis, based upon these three stages. This chapter deals with description, and Chapter 6 with interpretation and explanation. This division of labour accords with the contrast I drew in Chapter 2 between description on the one hand, and interpretation and explanation on the other, in terms of the sorts of 'analysis' they involve. And there are corresponding differences in the organization of the two chapters: the sort of analysis associated with the description stage allows this chapter to be organized as a mini reference manual, whereas Chapter 6 is more discursive. However, as I pointed out in Chapter 2, there is a sense in which description presupposes interpretation, so this contrast, while convenient in procedural terms, should not be given too much weight. Readers will also find that some topics (including *speech acts* and *presupposition*) which might be expected in the description stage are partly or wholly delayed until Chapter 6, for reasons I shall explain there.

The present chapter is written at an introductory level for people who do not have extensive backgrounds in language study. It is organized around ten main questions (and some sub-questions) which can be asked of a text; this will I hope make it relatively easy for readers to assimilate and use the framework. Under each question, readers will find analytical categories or concepts briefly introduced, and exemplified. I have presented the procedure in a purely expository way, without examples for readers to work on. There will be an opportunity in Chapter 7 to apply the procedure to an extended example. Let me stress that the procedure should not be treated as holy writ – it is a guide and not a blueprint. In some cases, readers using it may find that some parts are overly detailed or even irrelevant for their purposes. In other cases, they (especially those with a background in language study) may find it insufficiently detailed and in need of supplementation – the references at the end of the chapter should help. The set of textual features included is highly selective, containing only those which tend to be most significant for critical analysis.

A final point before I list the ten questions. The set of formal features we find in a specific text can be regarded as particular choices from among the options (e.g. of vocabulary or grammar) available in the discourse types which the text draws upon. In order to interpret the features which are actually present in a text, it is generally necessary to take account of what other choices might have been made, i.e. of the systems of options in the discourse types which actual features come from. Consequently, in analysing texts, one's focus is constantly alternating between what is 'there' in the text, and the discourse type(s) which the text is drawing upon. This alternation of focus is reflected in the discussion below.

A. Vocabulary

1. What *experiential* values do words have? (See *Note* below for terminology.)

   What classification schemes are drawn upon?

   Are there words which are ideologically contested?

Is there *rewording* or *overwording*?
What ideologically significant meaning relations (*synonymy, hyponymy, antonymy*) are there between words?

2. What *relational* values do words have?
   Are there euphemistic expressions?
   Are there markedly formal or informal words?

3. What *expressive* values do words have?

4. What metaphors are used?

B. Grammar

5. What experiential values do grammatical features have?
   What types of *process* and *participant* predominate?
   Is agency unclear?
   Are processes what they seem?
   Are *nominalizations* used?
   Are sentences active or passive?
   Are sentences positive or negative?

6. What relational values do grammatical features have?
   What *modes (declarative, grammatical question, imperative)* are used?
   Are there important features of *relational modality*?
   Are the pronouns *we* and *you* used, and if so, how?

7. What expressive values do grammatical features have?
   Are there important features of *expressive modality*?

8. How are (simple) sentences linked together?
   What logical connectors are used?
   Are complex sentences characterized by *coordination* or *subordination*?
   What means are used for referring inside and outside the text?

C. Textual structures

9. What interactional conventions are used?
   Are there ways in which one participant controls the turns of others?

10. What larger-scale structures does the text have?

Note: experiential, relational, and expressive values

I distinguish between three types of value that formal features may have: experiential, relational, and expressive. A formal feature with *experiential* value is a trace of and a cue to the way in which the text producer's experience of the natural or social world is represented. Experiential value is to do with *contents* and knowledge and beliefs, in the terms of Chapter 3. A formal feature with *relational* value is a trace of and a cue to the social relationships which are enacted via the text in the discourse. Relational value is (transparently!) to do with *relations* and social relationships. And, finally, a formal feature with *expressive* value is a trace of and a cue to the producer's evaluation (in the widest sense) of the bit of the reality it relates to. Expressive value is to do with *subjects* and social identities, though only one dimension of the latter concepts is to do with subjective values. Let me emphasize that any given formal feature may simultaneously have two or three of these values. These are shown diagrammatically in Fig. 5.1.

Dimensions of meaning	Values of features	Structural effects
Contents	Experiential	Knowledge/beliefs
Relations	Relational	Social relations
Subjects	Expressive	Social identities

Fig. 5.1 Formal features: experiential, relational and expressive values

In addition, a formal feature may have *connective value*, i.e. in connecting together parts of a text. See Question 8 for discussion and examples.

QUESTION 1: WHAT EXPERIENTIAL VALUES DO WORDS HAVE?

The aspect of experiential value of most interest in the context of this book is how ideological differences between texts in their representations of the world are coded in their vocabulary. The following pair of texts is an example: they constitute, according to a study of the language of the 'helping professions', two different wordings of the same psychiatric practices.

deprivation of food, bed, walks in the open air, visitors, mail, or telephone calls; solitary confinement; deprivation of reading or entertainment materials; immobilizing people by tying them into wet sheets and then exhibiting them to staff and other patients; other physical restraints on body movement; drugging the mind against the client's will; incarceration in locked wards; a range of public humiliations such as the prominent posting of alleged intentions to escape or commit suicide, the requirement of public confessions of misconduct or guilt, and public announcements of individual misdeeds and abnormalities. (*Psychiatric text 1*)

discouraging sick behaviour and encouraging healthy behaviour through the selective granting of rewards; the availability of seclusion, restraints, and closed wards to grant a patient a respite from interaction with others; enabling him to think about his behaviour, to cope with his temptations to elope and succumb to depression, and to develop a sense of security; immobilizing the patient to calm him, satisfy his dependency needs, give him the extra nursing attention he values, and enable him to benefit from peer confrontation; placing limits on his acting out; and teaching him that the staff cares. (*Psychiatric text 2*)

Text 5.1 Source: Edelman M. 1974:300

The second text words these practices from the perspective of psychiatrists who favour them, whereas the first is an 'oppositional' wording. We can in fact see it as a 'rewording': an existing, dominant, and naturalized, wording is being systematically replaced by another one in conscious opposition to it.

In some cases, what is ideologically significant about a text is its vocabulary items *per se*: for instance, *subversive* and *solidarity* belong respectively to 'right' and 'left' ideological frameworks, and the occurrence of either one will tend to ideologically 'place' a text. In other cases, it is the way words co-occur or *collocate*: thus in psychiatric text 2, *behaviour* collocates with *sick* and *healthy*, giving an ideologically specific (and dominant) scheme for classifying behaviour. In yet other cases, it is the metaphorical transfer of a word or expression from one domain of use to another (see Question 4 below): for instance, *solitary confinement* in psychiatric text 1 metaphorically represents a medical situation in terms of imprisonment.

Some words are *ideologically contested*, the focus of ideological struggle, and this is sometimes evident in a text – like the word *socialism* in a letter which claimed that it is 'a semantic error' to believe that 'a term like *socialism* has one true and "literal" meaning, which is an *absolute* belief in the common ownership of the means of production, distribution and exchange'. The word's various meanings do, however, have a common core: 'the belief that social control should be exercised in the interests of the majority of working people in society'. The letter would appear to be a surreptitious piece of ideological struggle under the veil of semantics.

In answering Question 1, it is generally useful to alternate our focus between the text itself and the discourse type(s) it is drawing upon, including *classification schemes* in terms of which vocabulary is organized in discourse types. Let us look at Text 5.2 from this point of view.

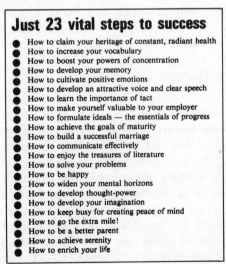

Just 23 vital steps to success
- How to claim your heritage of constant, radiant health
- How to increase your vocabulary
- How to boost your powers of concentration
- How to develop your memory
- How to cultivate positive emotions
- How to develop an attractive voice and clear speech
- How to learn the importance of tact
- How to make yourself valuable to your employer
- How to formulate ideals — the essentials of progress
- How to achieve the goals of maturity
- How to build a successful marriage
- How to communicate effectively
- How to enjoy the treasures of literature
- How to solve your problems
- How to be happy
- How to widen your mental horizons
- How to develop thought-power
- How to develop your imagination
- How to keep busy for creating peace of mind
- How to go the extra mile!
- How to be a better parent
- How to achieve serenity
- How to enrich your life

Text 5.2 Source: *Twenty-Three Steps to Success and Achievement*, Lumsden R, 1984

The list itself constitutes a classification of 'steps to success', but it also draws upon pre-existing classification schemes. One is a scheme for the psyche, or aspects of it which a person may 'develop' herself: (*powers of*) *concentration, memory*, (*positive*) *emotions, mental horizons, thought(-power), imagination*. Notice the mechanistic view of the psyche suggested by *power(s)*: as with car engines, one gets a better performance from a more powerful machine! Another scheme is for ways of evaluating a person's language; it is implicit in the collocations *increase your vocabulary, clear speech, communicate effectively*, as well as others in materials from the same advertiser such as *converse easily, speak effectively, write faster, read better*. Verbal performances are rated in terms of facility, efficiency and social impact, but not let us say in terms of empathy and communicative sharing. This is an instrumental ideology of language – language as a tool for getting things done – which we shall meet again in a different context in Chapter 9 (p. 236). In both cases, the classification scheme constitutes a particular way of dividing up some aspect of reality which is built upon a particular ideological representation of that reality. In this way, the structure of a vocabulary is ideologically based.

Classification schemes in different discourse types may differ quantitatively, in the sense of wording particular aspects of reality to different degrees, with a larger or smaller number of words. We sometimes have 'overwording' – an unusually high degree of wording, often involving many words which are near synonyms. Overwording shows preoccupation with some aspect of reality – which may indicate that it is a focus of ideological struggle. *Just 23 steps to success* is much preoccupied with growth and development, and this is evident in the vocabulary for these meanings, including the verbs *increase, boost, develop, cultivate, build, widen, enrich*.

The value of alternating focus between the text and the discourse type holds also for *meaning relations* between words. Recall the discussion of the *Times* editorial (*The still small voice of truth*; Text 4.6, p. 96). I suggested that a relation of *synonymy* was set up in the text between words which are not synonymous in any discourse type. In other cases, a text might draw directly upon meaning relations set up in a discourse type. In that example, these relations of synonymy were ideologically determined, and in fact meaning relations like synonymy can often be regarded as relative to particular ideologies; either the ideology embedded in a discourse type, or the ideology being creatively generated in a text. So one aspect of Question 1 is both to identify meaning relations in texts and underlying discourse types, and to try and specify their ideological bases.

The main meaning relations are *synonymy*, *hyponymy*, and *antonymy*. Synonymy as we have seen is the case where words have the same meaning. It is difficult to find many instances of absolute synonyms, so in reality one is looking for relations of near synonymy between words. A rough test for synonymy is whether words are mutually substitutable with little effect on meaning. *Hyponymy* is the case where the meaning of one word is, so to speak, included within the meaning of another word; in an example in Chapter 4, the meaning of *totalitarianism* was included in the meanings of *communism, Marxism, fascism* (which are thus its hyponyms) in one ideologically particular discourse type. *Antonymy* is meaning incompatibility – the meaning of one word is incompatible with the meaning of another (e.g. the meanings of *woman* and *man*, or of *dog* and *cat*).

QUESTION 2: WHAT RELATIONAL VALUES DO WORDS HAVE?

This question focuses on how a text's choice of wordings depends on, and helps create, social relationships between participants. As I have already suggested, words are likely to have such relational values simultaneously with other values. For instance, the use of racist vocabulary (such as *coons* in the text on p. 68) has experiential value in terms of a racist representation of a particular ethnic grouping; but its use – and the failure to avoid it – may also have relational value, perhaps assuming that racist ideology is common ground for the speaker and other participants.

Here is another example from a *Guardian* article by Chris Hawkes, Jo Morello and John Howard (my italics):

We suspect that industrialists are at the point of realising that they need to do something, but are not sure what that something is. We are not suggesting that industry *becomes voyeuristic about personal problems*, or that it *intrudes unnecessarily into private grief and sorrow*! It would be counterproductive to give the impression that it owns its workforce. Nor are we advocating a return to the nineteenth century *paternalism* of chocolate and soap barons. But their concept of *engaging with their employees as whole persons* is one we cannot ignore.

Text 5.3 Source: *The Guardian*, 17 December 1986

The italicized expressions could be regarded as ideologically different formulations of precisely the same actions on the part of employers, so this text could be an example of experiential values of wordings. However, the authors appear to reject the first three of these formulations in favour of the fourth as part of the process of negotiating a relationship of trust and solidarity with the assumed readership, which is where relational value comes into the picture. But expressive value is also involved: the writers presumably assume that the first three formulations would constitute negative evaluations for readers, and that the fourth would constitute a positive evaluation. Hence in favouring the fourth the writers are assuming commonality of values with readers.

Text producers often adopt strategies of avoidance with respect to the expressive values of words for relational reasons. A *euphemism* is a word which is substituted for a more conventional or familiar one as a way of avoiding negative values. Psychiatric text 2 appears to contain a number of euphemisms. It has *seclusion* where text 1 has *solitary confinement, closed wards* versus *locked wards, elope* versus *escape, succumb to depression* versus *commit suicide*.

One property of vocabulary which has to do with relational values is *formality*, which I discussed in Chapter 3. Here is the opening turn of the cross-examination text which was introduced there:

Q: Mr. Ehrlichman, prior to the luncheon recess you stated that in your opinion, the entry into the Ellsberg psychiatrist's office was legal because of national security reasons. I think that was your testimony?

The formality of the situation here demands formality of social relations, and this is evident (among other places) in the vocabulary, which consistently opts for more formal choices as against less formal available alternatives (*prior to, luncheon recess, stated* instead of *before, lunch break, said*, for example), expressing politeness, concern from participants for each other's 'face' (wish to be liked, wish not to be imposed upon), respect for status and position.

QUESTION 3: WHAT EXPRESSIVE VALUES DO WORDS HAVE?

There are a number of examples in psychiatric text 1 where the writer's negative evaluation of the practices described is implicit in the vocabulary – *exhibiting, incarceration, humiliations*, for instance. There are more examples in Text 5.4, which is publicizing one session in a political and cultural festival.

For many more traditional left-wing readers, there is likely to

LEFT . . . AFTER A FASHION

Fashion is propaganda in clothing – it tells you about who people are, what they want to be and their politics. The fashion industry is in constant flux, pumping out new images: street fashions meet haut couture – offspring – high street fashion. With personal politics and style high on the left's political agenda should fashion consciousness be part of political consciousness, or is it just an excuse for consumerism? What's radical about a radical look?

Left Unlimited is proud to present the first ever left fashion show. The very latest designers from college will present their work, followed by some of the old favourites: Ken Livingstone's flares and Safari jacket; the trotskyite flat top; the workerist donkey jacket and badges; ageing *Marxism Today* Euro chic, and much more.

And on hand will be 'street fashion' editor of *ID* magazine **Caryn Franklin**; and high fashion designer **Paul Smith**; 'High Street' fashion writer **Angela Stephens** of *Just 17*; commentator **Chris Kirk**, and *City Limits* journalist **Kathy Myers**. Lights. music, a catwalk   ... and politics.

Text 5.4 Source: 'Left Unlimited', 1986

be a clash of expressive values in this passage, for instance in the third sentence (*With personal politics* . . .). *Political consciousness* and *left* would be likely to have positive expressive values for such readers, *consumerism*, *fashion* (*consciousness*), and possibly *style* negative values. Moreover, *fashion* and *style* would probably be seen as out of place in political discourse. *Personal politics* would I suspect have no established expressive value, because the collocation is relatively new to left political discourse. The overall effect may be puzzling or indeed infuriating for such readers.

Differences between discourse types in the expressive values of words are again ideologically significant. A speaker expresses evaluations through drawing on classification schemes which are in part systems of evaluation, and there are ideologically contrastive schemes embodying different values in different discourse types. So the above example can be interpreted in terms of an ideological clash between different left discourse types and classification schemes: in a less traditional left discourse, *fashion* (*consciousness*) and *style* and *personal politics* are positively evaluated elements in classification schemes associated with politics.

The expressive value of words has always been a central concern for those interested in persuasive language. While it is still important in terms of our focus here on ideology, it is rather less so, and from a somewhat different perspective. It is not so much the mobilization of expressive values for particular persuasive ends that is of interest here, as the fact that these expressive values can be referred to ideologically contrastive classification schemes.

QUESTION 4: WHAT METAPHORS ARE USED?

Metaphor is a means of representing one aspect of experience in terms of another, and is by no means restricted to the sort of discourse it tends to be stereotypically associated with – poetry and literary discourse. But any aspect of experience can be represented in terms of any number of metaphors, and it is the relationship between alternative metaphors that is of particular interest here, for different metaphors have different ideological attachments.

This is the beginning of an article in a Scottish newspaper about the 'riots' of 1981:

As the cancer spreads

As the riots of rampaging youths spread from the south, even the most optimistic have fears for the future, afraid worse is yet to come. How far can the trouble spread? If it comes to Scotland, where will it strike?

The metaphorical representation of social problems as diseases illustrated here is extremely common. Notice it incorporates a metaphor for disease itself, as a vague, subhuman and unthinking force (*where will it strike*). The ideological significance of disease metaphors is that they tend to take dominant interests to be the interests of society as a whole, and construe expressions of non-dominant interests (strikes, demonstrations, 'riots') as undermining (the health of) society *per se*. An alternative metaphor for the 'riots' might for instance be that of the argument – 'riots' as *vociferous protests* for example. Different metaphors imply different ways of dealing with things: one does not arrive at a negotiated settlement with cancer, though one might with an opponent in an argument. Cancer has to be eliminated, cut out.

QUESTION 5: WHAT EXPERIENTIAL VALUE DO GRAMMATICAL FEATURES HAVE?

The experiential aspects of grammar have to do with the ways in which the grammatical forms of a language code happenings or relationships in the world, the people or animals or things involved in those happenings or relationships, and their spatial and temporal circumstances, manner of occurrence, and so on. The first sub-question below deals centrally and generally with these matters, and the other sub-questions deal with more specific related issues.

What types of *process* and *participant* predominate?

When one wishes to represent textually some real or imaginary action, event, state of affairs or relationship, there is often a choice between different grammatical process and participant types, and the selection that is made can be ideologically significant. That is the import of this question. To explore it further, we need to look at an aspect of the grammar of simple sentences in English.

A simple sentence of the 'declarative' sort (see Question 6) consists of a subject (S) followed by a verb (V); the V may or may not be followed by one or more other elements from this list: object (O), complement (C), adjunct (A). There are three main types of simple sentence, each with a different combination of elements. In the examples below, I have placed labels *after* each element; notice any of the elements can consist of one word or more than one word.

S V O   Reagan(S) attacks(V) Libya(O)
         South African police(S) have burnt down(V) a black township(O)
         contras(S) have killed(V) many peasants(O)

S V   Reagan(S) was fishing(V)
         a black township(S) has burnt down(V)
         many peasants(S) have died(V)

S V C   Reagan(S) is(V) dangerous(C) (or: a dangerous person(C))
         many peasants(S) are(V) dead(C)
         Libya(S) has(V) oil(C)

Notice that both O and C come after V in these examples. The difference is that O, but not C, can be turned into the S of an equivalent passive sentence. This is possible with all the SVO examples (e.g. *a black township has been burnt down by South African police*), and none of the SVC examples (e.g. you can't turn the first example into *dangerous is been by Reagan*!).

There are also differences in which sorts of words can operate as these different elements. S or O can be a noun (e.g., *Reagan*, or *boys*) or pronoun (*I, me, she*, etc.), or a phrase including a noun, known as a *noun phrase* (e.g. *a black township, many peasants*), or a *nominalization* (explained below). C can be the same, but it can also be an adjective (e.g. *dangerous, dead*). A can be an adverb (sometimes they end in – *ly*) or a *prepositional phrase*. A prepositional phrase consists of a preposition (*in, after, over*, etc.) followed by a noun or noun phrase (e.g. *in the country* or *near Preston*). There are no As in the examples illustrating the three sentence types, though in fact any of these types can freely occur with a variety of different As. Try adding these adverbs to the examples: *frequently, unmercifully, in South Africa, since 1985, unfortunately, once.* You'll find that each example can take at least one of them.

These three main types of sentence most typically (but not always – see below) express respectively the three main types of *process: actions* (SVO), *events* (SV), and *attributions* (SVC). An *action* involves two *participants,* an *agent* and a *patient,* and the agent acts upon the patient in some way. So in the SVO examples above, *Reagan, South African police* and *contras* are agents, while *Libya, a black township* and *many peasants* are patients. Not all participants are animate, incidentally, and although agents generally are, patients are sometimes animate (e.g. *many peasants*) and sometimes inanimate (e.g. *a black township*).

An *event* involves just one participant, which may be animate (*many peasants* in the SV examples above) or inanimate (*a black township*). However, SV sentences are not always events; if they have animate participants, they may be a special sort of patient-less action, or what I'll call *non-directed* action. A test is what sort of question the SV sentence naturally answers: if it most naturally answers the question *What (has) happened?*, it's an event, but if it most naturally answers the question *What did (the subject) do?*, it's a non-directed action. On this basis, *many peasants have died* is event, but *Reagan was fishing* is non-directed action.

An *attribution* also involves just one participant, but there is also some sort of *attribute* after the verb, either a *possessive* attribute if the verb is a form of *have,* or a nonpossessive attribute with other verbs (notably *be,* but also *feel, seem, look* and a number of others). Nonpossessive attributes show up sometimes as adjectives (e.g. *Reagan is dangerous*), sometimes as nouns (*Reagan is a menace*).

The ideological possibilities of the choice between process types are shown by some of the examples I have given above: representing the death of Nicaraguan peasants as an action with responsible agents, an event, or an attributed state, are choices with clear significance; similarly the representation of the burning of South African townships as an event or an action on the part of agents. Such choices to highlight or background agency may be consistent, automatic and commonsensical, and therefore ideological; or they may be conscious hedging or deception. It is difficult to know which the following example is; it was written by a newspaper columnist (Hugo Young) arguing that politicians manipulate the media more than the media manipulate politicians:

Having agreed some time ago to an interview next Sunday, he (Mr Kinnock) plainly thought it could take its place in the mushery surrounding the launch of Investing in People [= a Labour Party campaign]. But meanwhile the defence issue came to the front, and the programme, responding to the news, became a programme about Labour's defence policy – which the leader doesn't want to talk about . . .

Text 5.5 Source: *The Guardian*, 16 October 1986

Notice the absence of agency in the second sentence: the defence issue *came to the front* (event process), and the programme *became* . . . (attribution process). Where, one asks, are the agents who brought the defence issue to the front and changed the nature of the programme? A relevant piece of situational information, perhaps, is that at the Conservative Party Conference which took place the week before this column was written, Labour's defence policy was selected as the issue which the Conservatives would highlight in the imminent election campaign.

Is agency unclear?

Here is the first part of a text which we met in Chapter 3, which provides a further illustration, and also shows how the obfuscation of agency can be ideologically motivated:

Quarry load-shedding problem
Unsheeted lorries from Middlebarrow Quarry were still causing problems by shedding stones . . .

There are actually two simple sentences here, both of the SVO type: *unsheeted lorries from Middlebarrow Quarry(S) were still causing(V) problems(O)* and *(lorries – 'understood' S) shedding (V) stones(O)*. In the former, S is an untypically inanimate agent of an action process; agency in causing problems is attributed to the lorries, but as I noted in Chapter 3 it would be more properly attributed to the people who control them. I said earlier that agents are animate, and this is generally so. But agents can be realized as inanimate nouns, abstract nouns, or nominalizations (see below). In all such cases, as in this example, one should be sensitive to possible ideologically motivated obfuscation of agency, causality and responsibility.

Are processes what they seem?

In the second simple sentence, we have what would more normally be represented as an event (stones(S) were falling(V) from the lorries(A)) being represented as an action, which again gives us lorries as an inanimate agent, thus reinforcing the agentive status it has in the first sentence. It is generally worth being alert to what are usually processes of one type appearing as processes of another type, and possible ideological reasons for this.

Are *nominalizations* used?

Notice also the headline *Quarry load-shedding problem*. In addition to occurring in the grammatical shape of a sentence, a process can occur in the reduced form of a *nominalization*, as in this case. A nominalization is a process converted into noun (or a multi-word compound noun, as here). It is reduced in the sense that some of the meaning one gets in a sentence is missing – tense, so there is no indication of the timing of the process; modality (see below); and often an agent and/or a patient. In this example, we have a nominalization which compresses the two processes which are spelt out in the simple sentences in the text, though exactly how we break down the nominalization to tease out the processes is unclear. Notice the absence of agents: neither problem-causer nor load-shedder are identified, and so the headline is consistent with the text in leaving attributions of causality and responsibility unclear.

Are sentences active or passive?

Action processes can appear as *active* sentences or as *passive* sentences. All the examples of SVO sentences given above are active. Their passive equivalents would be: *Libya attacked by Reagan, a black township has been burnt down by South African police, many peasants have been killed by contras.* It is also possible in each case to delete the agent phrase (introduced with *by*) – *Libya attacked*, etc. – to get an *agentless passive* sentence. Agentless passives again leave causality and agency unclear. In some cases – and this is also true of nominalization – this may be to avoid redundancy, if that information is already given in some way. In other cases, it can be obfuscation of agency and causality.

Are sentences positive or negative?

Finally, all of the three sentence types can be either positive or negative (*contras have not killed many peasants*, and so forth). Negation obviously has experiential value in that it is the basic way we have of distinguishing what is not the case in reality from what is the case. But its main interest lies in a different direction – *intertextuality* and the *intertextual context* of a text. These are discussed in Chapter 6 (pp. 152–155).

QUESTION 6: WHAT RELATIONAL VALUES DO GRAMMATICAL FEATURES HAVE?

There is a variety of grammatical features of texts which have relational values. I shall focus upon three: *modes* of sentence, *modality*, and *pronouns*.

What modes are used?

There are three major modes: *declarative, grammatical question*, and *imperative*. All the examples we have had so far are declarative; declaratives are marked by having an S followed by a V. Imperatives do not have an S at all, and they start with a V: *open(V) the door(O)*, or *come(V) here(A)*, for instance. Grammatical questions are rather more complicated because there are different types. First, there is the type which begins with *who? what? when? where? why? how? which? – wh–*questions for short – such as *why are you advising your members to strike?* or *where were you born?*. Secondly, there is the type which begins with a verb – *can you pass the salt?* or *do you enjoy music?* or *are you Frederick Forsyth?* – and which often gets a *yes* or *no* answer. Hence they are known as *yes/no* questions.

These three modes position subjects differently. In the case of a typical declarative, the subject position of the speaker/writer is that of a giver (of information), and the addressee's position is that of a receiver. In the case of the imperative, the speaker/writer is in the position of asking something of the addressee (action on the latter's part), while the addressee is (ideally!) a compliant actor. In a grammatical question, the speaker/writer is again asking something of the addressee, in this case information, and the addressee is in the position of a provider of information. Systematic asymmetries in the distribution of modes between participants are important *per se* in terms of participant relations: asking, be it for action or information, is generally a position of power, as too is giving information – except where it has been asked for.

But the picture is a great deal more complicated than this, because: (a) there is not a one-to-one relationship between modes and the positioning of subjects, and (b) there is a much richer set of subject positions than those I have identified so far. In respect of (a), it is evident for example that a declarative may have the value of a request for information (*you must be Alan's sister*, for instance), a grammatical question may have the value of demand for action (*will you kindly go away*), and an imperative can be, say, a suggestion (*try taking the lid off*). In respect of (b), there is a host of *speech acts* which may be variously grammaticized in the three modes, with a corresponding host of more specific subject positions – promiser in promises, accuser in accusations, complainant in complaints, and so forth. But these various speech act values are not distinguished by formal features. Rather, interpreters assign utterances such values, partly on the basis of their formal features, but also partly on the basis of the interpreter's assumptions. For this reason, I am dealing with them in Chapter 6, in terms of *interpretation* (see pp. 155–157).

Are there important features of relational modality?

Let us turn now to the concept of *modality*, which is an important one for both relational and expressive values in grammar. Modality is to do with speaker or writer authority, and there are two dimensions to modality, depending on what direction authority is oriented in. Firstly, if it is a matter of the authority of one participant in relation to others, we have *relational modality*. Secondly, if it is a matter of the speaker or writer's authority with respect to the truth or probability of a representation of reality, we have *expressive modality*, i.e. the modality of the speaker/writer's evaluation of truth. There is some discussion of expressive modality under Question 7. Modality is expressed by *modal auxiliary verbs* like *may, might, must, should, can, can't, ought,* but also by various other formal features including adverbs and tense.

Here is a short text which illustrates relational modality.

> Your library books are overdue and your library card may not be used until they are returned. If the books are not returned within a fortnight, you must pay the cost of replacing them before you borrow more books.

There are two modal auxiliaries, *may not* and *must*. *May* on its own as a relational modal can signal permission (*you may go*), but with *not* the meaning is 'not permitted'. *Must* signals obligation – 'you are required to pay the cost of replacement'. Notice that the authority and power relations on the basis of which the producers of this text withhold permission from, or impose obligations upon, the people it is sent to, are not made explicit. It is precisely implicit authority claims and implicit power relations of the sort illustrated here that make relational modality a matter of ideological interest.

Are the pronouns *we* and *you* used, and if so, how?

I have already referred, in Chapter 3, to second-person T and V pronouns, and the way in which the choice between them is tied in with relationships of power and solidarity. English does not have a T/V system, and to some extent the sort of values which attach to, say, *tu* and *vous* in French are expressed outside the pronoun system in English – as in the choice between different titles and modes of address (the choice between *Bert, Bert Smith, Mr Smith, Smith,* for instance).

However, pronouns in English do have relational values of different sorts. For instance, this sentence appeared in a *Daily Mail* editorial during the 'Falklands War': 'We cannot let our troops lose their edge below decks while Argentine diplomats play blind man's buff round the corridors of the United Nations'. (*Daily Mail* 4/5/87). The editorial uses (as editorials often do) the so-called 'inclusive' *we*, inclusive that is of the reader as well as the writer, as opposed to 'exclusive' *we*, which refers to the writer (or speaker) plus one or more others, but does not include the addressee(s). The newspaper is speaking on behalf of itself, its readers, and indeed all ('right-minded'?) British citizens. In so doing, it is making an implicit authority claim rather like the examples of relational modality above – that it has the authority to speak for others. Notice, also, that *Britain* or *the government* could both happily replace (the first) *we*; the newspaper's way of showing its identification with the government and the state is to treat them as equivalent to its composited *we*, i.e. all of the British people. One aspect of this reduction is that it serves corporate ideologies which stress the unity of a people at the expense of recognition of divisions of interest.

Another case where it pays to try to work out relationships which are being implicitly claimed is when the pronoun *you* is used, also in mass communication, where there are many actual and potential addressees whose identity is unknown to the producer. Despite the anonymity of mass-communication audiences, the direct address of members of the audience on an individual basis with *you* is very common indeed. Advertising is a clear example; the heading of a written advertisement for Batchelor's soup, for instance, is *'The cream of the crop, wherever you shop'*. Such simulated personal address has a wide currency in advertising and elsewhere, presumably as an attempt to remedy increasing impersonality. See Chapter 8 for further discussion. *You* is also extensively used as an *indefinite pronoun*, for instance in Mrs Thatcher's political speech – 'you've got to be strong to your own people and other countries have got to know that you stand by your word', is an example. It implies a relationship of solidarity between Mrs Thatcher (the government) and the people in general. See Chapter 7 for more details.

QUESTION 7: WHAT EXPRESSIVE VALUES DO GRAMMATICAL FEATURES HAVE?

I shall limit my comments on expressive values to expressive modality. There is overlap between the modal auxiliaries which mark relational modality and those which mark expressive modality. So we find *may* associated with the meaning of 'possibility' (*the bridge may collapse*) as well as permission, and *must* associated with 'certainty' (*the bridge must collapse under that weight!*) as well as obligation. We also find *can't* ('impossible', e.g.

the bridge can't take that weight); *should* ('probable', e.g. *the bridge should take that weight*); and others.

But, as I said in the last section, modality is not just a matter of modal auxiliaries. Notice for instance the opening of the text on p. 127: *Your library books are overdue*. The verb (*are*) is in the simple present tense form. This is one terminal point of expressive modality, a categorical commitment of the producer to the truth of the proposition; the opposite terminal point would be the negative simple present, *Your library books are not overdue*, an equally categorical commitment to the truth of the negated proposition. The alternative possibilities with modal verbs fall between these categorical extremes: *your library books must/may be overdue*. And the intermediate possibilities include forms which have adverbs, more specifically *modal adverbs* rather than, or as well as, modal auxiliaries: *your library books are probably/are possibly/may possibly be overdue*.

The ideological interest is in the authenticity claims, or claims to knowledge, which are evidenced by modality forms. Newspapers are an interesting case. In news reports, reported happenings are generally represented as categorical truths – facts – without the sort of intermediate modalities I have just illustrated. Look at the opening of the report shown in Text 5.6 written by Gordon Greig, political editor of the *Daily Mail*. The verbs are all in non-modal present tense (*refuses, plans, is preparing, looms*) or perfect (*have been invited*) forms. The prevalence of categorical modalities supports a view of the world as transparent – as if it signalled its own meaning to any observer, without the need for interpretation and representation. 'News' generally disguises the complex and messy processes of information gathering and interpretation which go into its production, and the role therein of ideologies embedded in the established practices and assumptions which interpreters bring to the process of interpretation.

QUESTION 8: HOW ARE (SIMPLE) SENTENCES LINKED TOGETHER?

I focus here on the *connective* (as opposed to *experiential, relational* and *expressive*) values of formal features of text. It has a partially 'internal' character compared with the others, in that it is a matter

Foot refuses offer from No. 10 but...

MAGGIE PLANS THE INVASION

By GORDON GREIG, Political Editor

MRS THATCHER is preparing for the crunch in the Falklands crisis with a landing by commandos and paratroops.

As the prospect of a bloody confrontation looms, Opposition leaders have been invited to discuss the last options with her

Text 5.6 Source: *Daily Mail*, 3 May 1982

of the values formal features have in connecting together parts of texts. But it is also to do with the relationship between texts and contexts: some formal features point outside the text to its situational context, or to its 'intertextual' context, i.e. to previous texts which are related to it (see Ch. 6 pp. 152–55). Also, formal items with connective value often simultaneously have other values, as we shall see.

There are generally formal connections between sentences in a text, which are collectively referred to as *cohesion*. Cohesion can involve vocabulary links between sentences – repetition of words, or use of related words. It can also involve *connectors* which mark various temporal, spatial and logical (in a broad sense) relationships between sentences. And it can involve *reference* – words which refer back to an earlier sentence or, less often, forwards to a later one. I shall call any formal feature of a text which has a cohesive function, which cues a connection between one sentence and another, a *cohesive feature*. The comments which follow on cohesion are very selective, and relate only to connectors (the first two sub-questions) and reference (the third sub-question).

What logical connectors are used?

I focus upon *logical* connectors, because they can cue ideological assumptions. We had one example of this, involving a concessive relation, in the 'problem page' text in Chapter 4 (Text 4.2, p. 82): *I've never been out with anyone even though Mum says I'm quite pretty.* The connector in this case is *even though*, but notice that the sentence can be paraphrased with other connectors: *Mum says I'm quite pretty, but I've never been out with anyone; Although Mum says I'm quite pretty, I've never been out with anyone; Mum says I'm quite pretty. Nevertheless, I've never been out with anyone.* In each case, coherence depends on the assumption that if a young woman (of 13, in this case) is 'quite pretty' (not, notice, if her mum *says* she is quite pretty!), she can expect to have been out with someone.

An example with a relation of result is *They refused to pay the higher rent when an increase was announced. As a result, they were evicted from their apartment.* The assumption in this case is that non-payment of rent may be expected to lead to eviction. *Even though* signals that what would be expected to happen, given the assumption I've referred to, failed to happen, whereas *as a result* signals that the expected happened – that the assumed consequence of not paying rent did indeed come about. What these examples show is that causal or consequential relationships between things which are taken to be commonsensical may be ideological common sense. Such relationships, however, are not always cued by connectors; they can be implied by the mere juxtaposition of sentences.

Are complex sentences characterized by *coordination* or *subordination*?

'Complex' sentences combine simple sentences together in various ways. A distinction is commonly made between *coordination*, where the component simple sentences have equal weight, and *subordination*, where there is a *main clause* and one or more *subordinate clauses* – *clause* is used for a simple sentence operating as part of a complex one. It is generally the case that the main clause is more informationally prominent than subordinate clauses, with the content of subordinate clauses backgrounded. Something to be on the lookout for is ways in which texts commonsensically divide information into relatively prominent and relatively backgrounded (tending to mean relatively important and relatively unimportant) parts. In some cases, the content of subordinate clauses is *presupposed*, taken as already known to or 'given' for all participants. A sentence cited earlier is an example: 'We cannot let our troops lose their edge below decks while Argentine diplomats play blind man's buff round the corridors of the United Nations.' The first clause (up to *decks*) is the main clause, the second (the rest of the sentence) is subordinate. Whereas the main clause contains an assertion, it is not asserted that Argentine diplomats are playing blind man's buff round the corridors of the United Nations, but presupposed. See Chapter 6 (pp. 152–55) for more discussion of presupposition.

What means are used for referring outside and inside the text?

There is quite a range of grammatical devices available for referring in a reduced form to material previously introduced into a text, rather than repeating it whole. The most prominent are the pronouns (*it, he, she, this, that*, etc.) and the definite article (*the*). For example, *she, the* and *it* in the second of these sentences: *A friend of mine wrote a book about India. She tried for two years to get the book published, but kept getting told it wouldn't sell*. The definite article is of particular interest in the present context, because it is extensively used to refer to referents (persons, objects, events) which are not established textually, nor even evident in the situational context of an interaction, but presupposed. Text 5.7 is an example of this, as printed on the packaging of a maternity bra.

This presupposes that there is a woman and a mother 'in you' (the assumed reader), and these two presuppositions are compatible on the basis of an assumption that a woman's 'womanhood' (presumably used here in the narrow sense of her sexual attractiveness to men) and her motherhood are incompatible – until Berlei comes along. Again, see Chapter 6 for more on presupposition.

THE
MATERNITY
BRA
WITH COTTON
by
Berlei

The first bra
to look after the woman
and mother in you

☐ Front fastening for comfort and convenience
☐ Unique non-slip feature
☐ 3-piece cotton cup for comfort and support
☐ Cotton lining for extra absorbency
☐ Stretch straps
☐ 3 placement hook and eye fastening
☐ Available in white only
☐ Sizes 34–40B/C/D/DD/E

Available from
Leading department stores and selected retail outlets.

Text 5.7 Source: Berlei

QUESTION 9: WHAT INTERACTIONAL CONVENTIONS ARE USED?

Formal features at the textual level relate to formal organizational properties of whole texts. Given the broad sense in which 'text' has been used in this book (introduced in Ch. 2), this includes both organizational features of dialogue (e.g. conversations, lessons, interviews) and of monologue (e.g. speeches, news-paper articles). Question 9 relates primarily to dialogue, and Question 10 to both dialogue and monologue. Question 9 is also broadly concerned with higher-level organizational features which have *relational* value, whereas Question 10 is concerned with features which have *experiential* value.

I shall concentrate in Question 9 upon naturalized conventions and their implicit links to power relations, as discussed in the section *Interactional routines and their boundaries* of Chapter 4. We are thus concerned with the relational value of organizational aspects of talk. There have already been a number of relevant examples in the texts of Chapters 2–4: the police interview of Chapter 2 (p. 18), the premature baby unit text and the interview between the headmaster and the youth in Chapter 3 (pp. 44–45, 68–69), and the doctor–patient consultation in the section of Chapter 4 just referred to (p. 100).

What is the turn-taking system?

How is the taking of talking turns managed in dialogue? The answer depends on the nature of the *turn-taking system* that is operative, and this in turn depends on (and is a part of) power relationships between participants. Let us begin with informal conversation between equals. Turn-taking is managed in such conversation by negotiation between the participants on a turn-by-turn basis according to this formula: the person speaking may select the next speaker; if that does not happen, the next speaker may take the turn; if that does not happen, the person speaking may continue. It is assumed that all participants have equal rights at each point in the formula – to select others, 'select themselves', or continue.

Informal conversation between equals has great significance and mobilizing power as an ideal form of social interaction, but its actual occurrence in our class-divided and power-riven society is extremely limited. Where it does occur, its occurrence is itself in need of explanation; it certainly ought not to be taken, as it often is, as a 'norm' for interaction in general.

In dialogue between unequals, turn-taking rights are unequal, as a number of the extracts discussed in earlier chapters have shown. Let us look at a small sample of classroom discourse.

T: Where does it go before it reaches your lungs?
P: Your windpipe, Miss.
T: Down your windpipe . . . Now can anyone remember the other word for windpipe?
P: The trachaea.
T: The trachaea . . . good

Text 5.8 Source: Coulthard M, 1977:94

The turn-taking system is very different from the formula for informal conversation. Pupils take turns only when a question is addressed to the class as a whole or an individual pupil. Pupils cannot normally self-select; teachers, conversely, always self-select because pupils cannot select teachers. And it is not only the taking of turns that is constrained for pupils, it is also the content of the turns they do take: they are essentially limited to giving relevant answers to the teacher's questions. And the criteria for relevance are also the teacher's! Although teachers do a lot of questioning, they can also do many other things in their turns, unlike the pupils. They can give information or issue instructions, for instance, or as in this sample they can give evaluative feedback to the pupil's answers, by repeating an answer (*down your windpipe, the trachaea*) or making an evaluative comment (*good*). Underlying, and reproduced by, the prevalence of such discourse in classrooms are ideologies of social hierarchy and education. One can, however, find classrooms whose discourse practice and ideologies are very different.

Are there ways in which one participant controls the contributions of others?

In Chapter 3, I characterized 'power in discourse' in terms of the more powerful participant putting constraints on the contributions of less powerful participants. There are various devices which are used for doing this, of which I shall mention four:

interruption
enforcing explicitness
controlling topic
formulation

Interruption was illustrated in the premature baby unit text in Chapter 3 (pp. 44–45). Recall that the doctor interrupted the medical student in order to control his contributions: to stop him beginning an examination before washing his hands, to stop him repeating information or giving irrelevant information.

Ambiguity or ambivalence can be a useful device in the hands of less powerful participants for dealing with those with power; but those with power may respond by *enforcing explicitness* – for instance, forcing participants to make their meaning unambiguous by asking things like: *is that a threat? are you accusing me of lying?* Silence is another weapon for the less powerful participant, particularly as a way of being noncommittal about what more powerful participants say; but the latter may again be able to force participants out of silence and into a response by asking *do you understand?* or *do you agree?* or *what do you think?*, for example.

The *topic* or topics of an interaction may be determined and controlled by the more powerful participant. For instance, powerful participants are often in a position (like the teacher) to specify the nature and purposes of an interaction at its beginning, and to disallow contributions which are not (in their view) relevant thereto.

One widely and diversely used device is *formulation*. A formulation is either a rewording of what has been said, by oneself or others, in one turn or a series of turns or indeed a whole episode; or it is a wording of what may be assumed to follow from what has been said, what is implied by what has been said. Formulations are used for such purposes as checking understanding, or reaching an agreed characterization of what has transpired in an interaction. But they are also used for purposes of control, quite extensively for instance in radio interviews, as a way of leading participants into accepting one's own version of what has transpired, and so limiting their options for future contributions.

Here is an example of formulation and its strategic use in discourse. A is recounting events surrounding the breaking of a window.

A: it was broken when I came in for lunch
B: was it
A: so it was being done while I was talking to the kids upstairs sort of thing
B: so it wasn't done by the kids upstairs then .
A: ah. I suppose not

B's second turn formulates A's account – he 'offers' A the conclusion from what the latter said that if he was talking to the kids upstairs while the window was broken, they didn't break it. A appears to feel forced to concede this. Formulation may be the prerogative of the powerful, but that does not mean they always manage to control it. The following is the end of an interview between a headmaster and a youth suspected of misdemeanours:

H: and you deny leaving school during class time ⌈or
Y: ⌊I deny leaving
   school going to that shop taking the money. anything. cos I
   never done that

The headmaster is moving to close the interview by offering the youth a formulation of the latter's response to accusations which have been put to him. However, the headmaster's attempt to formulate misfires, and the youth takes control from him by interrupting him and providing a formulation of his own denials.

QUESTION 10: WHAT LARGER-SCALE STRUCTURES DOES THE TEXT HAVE?

Text 5.10 is an article from my local newspaper. It is an example of how the whole of a text may have structure – may be made up of predictable elements in a predictable order.

Accident (or incident) reports generally involve the main elements we have in this instance, which seem to be: what happened, what caused it, what was done to deal with it, what more immediate effects it had, what longer-term outcomes or consequences it had. The first paragraph gives the immediate effects, followed by an indication of what happened. The second reports what was done to deal with it and further specifies what happened. The third gives more detail on immediate effects, and the fourth refers to long-term consequences. Notice that the order in which elements appear is not particularly logical, and a single element can appear in more than one place. Ordering in newspaper articles is based upon importance or newsworthiness, with the headline and first paragraph in particular giving what are regarded as the most important parts, and the gist, of the story. In this case, the headline highlights what was done to deal with

Firemen tackle blaze

NIGHT shift workers on a coating line at Nairn Coated Products, St Georges Quay, Lancaster had to be evacuated after fire broke out in an oven on Wednesday evening.

Four fire engines attended the incident and firemen wearing breathing apparatus tackled the flames which had started when a break off in an oven caught fire under the infra red element.

The fire caused severe damage to 20 metres of metal trunking, and to the interior of a coating machine and the coating room was smoke logged.

But the department was running again by Thursday morning

Text 5.10 Source: *Lancaster Guardian*, 7 October 1986

the incident, though it also has embedded in it an indication of what happened (*blaze*).

Participants' expectations about the structure of the social interactions they take part in or the texts they read are an important factor in interpretation – and particular elements can be interpreted in accordance with what is expected at the point where they occur, rather than in terms of what they are (see the discussion of 'scripts' in Ch. 6. pp. 158–59). But the significance of global structuring is also longer term: such structures can impose higher levels of routine on social practice in a way which ideologically sets and closes agendas. In the case of newspaper industrial accident reports, for instance, familiarity with the elements I have indicated makes it difficult to see that it is only a matter of naturalized convention that one of the elements is not, let us say, the safety record of the firm concerned. The converse of this is that aspects of events which do not conventionally get separated out as structural elements, will tend to disappear from view and consciousness – this often happens with matters of safety record and precautions in industrial accidents.

REFERENCES

Two general works on vocabulary, word meaning, and meaning relations, are Leech G 1974, and Lyons J 1977. There are discussions of classification, and 'overwording' and 'rewording' (referred to as 'overlexicalization' and 'relexicalization'), in Kress G, Hodge B 1979, and Fowler R *et al.* 1979, which also discuss the relationship between meaning and ideology; for more theoretical discussion of this relationship, see Pecheux M 1982, and Volosinov V 1973. Bolinger D 1980 is helpful on various aspects of meaning, including metaphor and euphemism. A useful study of metaphor is Lakoff G, Johnson M 1980.

Of general value for all aspects of grammar are Quirk R *et al.* 1972, and the more recent and monumental Quirk R *et al.* 1985. The approach to grammar of Halliday M 1985 is particularly fruitful for CLS. On sentence connection, see Halliday M, Hasan R 1976. On presupposition, see Levinson S 1983. There is a lot of material on grammatical analysis within CLS in Fowler R *et al.* 1979, and Kress G, Hodge B 1979. Leech G N 1983 gives an analysis of negation which is suggestive for its intertextual functioning.

Sacks H *et al.* 1974 is a classic study of turn-taking in conversation; see also Schenkein J 1978. Sinclair J, Coulthard M 1975 develops an approach to analysing classroom discourse. Interruption in the particular case of interaction between women and men is discussed in Zimmerman D, West C 1975. On formulation, see Heritage J C, Watson D R 1979. Various aspects of control of discourse by powerful participants are discussed in Stubbs M 1983. See also Thomas J forthcoming. On larger-scale structures of texts see Brown G, Yule G 1983.

The alternative wordings of psychiatric practices reproduced for Question 1 are taken from Edelman M 1974. On 'face', see Brown P, Levinson S 1978.

SIX

Critical discourse analysis in practice: interpretation, explanation, and the position of the analyst

This chapter continues with the presentation of a procedure for critical discourse analysis; Chapter 5 dealt with the stage of description, and we now move on to the stages of interpretation and explanation, which will be discussed in that order. The chapter will conclude with some points about the relationship of the analyst to the discourse she is analysing. Let us begin by briefly returning to the relationship between the three stages, which was sketched out in Chapter 2, as a way of both refreshing readers' memories, and emphasizing the shortcomings of description alone.

In Chapter 5, I claimed that formal features of texts have experiential, relational, expressive or connective value, or some combination of these, and I connected the first three with the three aspects of social practice which (according to Ch. 3) may be constrained by power (contents, relations, and subjects) and their associated structural effects (on knowledge and beliefs, social relationships, and social identities). It is evident, however, that one cannot directly extrapolate from the formal features of a text to these structural effects upon the constitution of a society! The relationship between text and social structures is an indirect, mediated one. It is mediated first of all by the discourse which the text is a part of, because the values of textual features only become real, socially operative, if they are embedded in social interaction, where texts are produced and interpreted against a background of common-sense assumptions (part of MR) which give textual features their values. These discourse processes, and their dependence on background assumptions, are the concern of the second stage of the procedure, *interpretation*.

The relationship is mediated, secondly, by the social context of the discourse, because the discourses in which these values are embedded themselves only become real, socially operative, as parts of institutional and societal processes of struggle; and because the common-sense assumptions of discourse incorporate ideologies which accord with particular power relations. The relationship of discourses to processes of struggle and to power relations is the concern of the third stage of the procedure, *explanation*.

Thus if one's concern is with the social values associated with texts and their elements, and more generally with the social significance of texts, description needs to be complemented with interpretation and explanation. Notice also that neither the dependence of discourse on background assumptions, nor the ideological properties of these assumptions which link them to social struggles and relations of power, are generally obvious to discourse participants. Interpretation and explanation can therefore be seen as two successively applied procedures of unveiling, or demystification.

INTERPRETATION

I use the term *interpretation* both as the name of a stage in the procedure, and for the interpretation of texts by discourse participants. I do so to stress the essential similarity between what the analyst does and what participants do; there are also differences, which are discussed at the end of the chapter. The stage of interpretation is concerned with participants' processes of text production as well as text interpretation, but in this chapter I focus mainly upon the latter. Chapter 7 will include some discussion of production processes.

We saw in Chapter 2 that interpretations are generated through a combination of what is in the text and what is 'in' the interpreter, in the sense of the members' resources (MR) which the latter brings to interpretation. We also saw that, from the point of view of the interpreter of a text, formal features of the text are 'cues' which activate elements of interpreters' MR, and that interpretations are generated through the dialectical interplay of cues and MR. In their role of helping to generate interpretations, we may refer to MR as *interpretative procedures*. MR are often called *background knowledge*, but I think that term is unduly restrictive, missing the point I made in discussing common-sense assumptions in Chapter 4, that many of these assumptions are

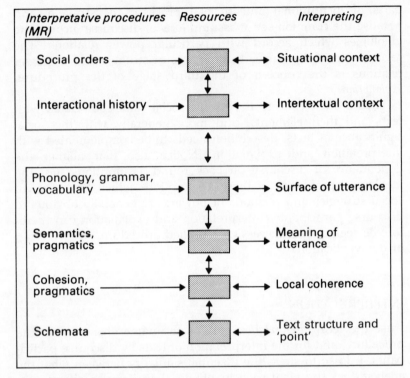

Fig. 6.1 Interpretation

ideological, which makes *knowledge* a misleading term.

Figure 6.1 gives a summary view of the process of interpretation which I shall spend the rest of this section explaining.

In the right-hand column of the diagram, under the heading *Interpreting*, I have listed six major domains of interpretation. The two in the upper section of the diagram relate to the interpretation of context, while those in the lower section relate to four levels of interpretation of text. In the left-hand column (*Interpretative procedures (MR)*) are listed major elements of MR which function as interpretative procedures. Each element of MR is specifically associated with the level of interpretation which occurs on the same line of the diagram. The central column identifies the range of *Resources* which are drawn upon for each of the domains of interpretation on the right. Notice that in each case these resources include more than the interpretative procedure on the left: there are either three or four 'inputs' to each 'box'. Let me spell out what is meant by the entries in the left- and right-hand columns, and then come to these 'boxes'. I begin with the lower section of the diagram, relating to text interpretation, and identify the four levels according to the domains of interpretation listed in the right-hand column.

1. *Surface of utterance.* This first level of text interpretation relates to the process by which interpreters convert strings of sounds or marks on paper into recognizable words, phrases and sentences. To do this, they have to draw upon that aspect of their MR which is often referred to as their 'knowledge of the language', and which I have specified as 'phonology, grammar, vocabulary' in the left-hand column. This level is not of particular relevance here, and I shall say no more about it.

2. *Meaning of utterance.* The second level of interpretation is a matter of assigning meanings to the constituent parts of a text, which I refer to as 'utterances', using that term in a loose sense. In some cases, but not always, utterances will correspond to sentences, or to semantic 'propositions'. Interpreters here draw upon semantic aspects of their MR – representations of the meanings of words, their ability to combine word-meanings and grammatical information and work out implicit meanings to arrive at meanings for whole propositions. They also draw upon pragmatic conventions within their MR, which allow them to determine what *speech act(s)* an utterance is being used to 'perform'. Speech acts are discussed later in this section.

3. *Local coherence.* The third level of interpretation establishes meaning connections between utterances, producing (where feasible) *coherent* interpretations of pairs and sequences of them. Recall the discussion of coherence in Chapter 4. This is not a matter of the 'global' coherence relations which tie together the parts of a whole text – a whole newspaper article or a whole telephone conversation, for example – but of 'local' coherence relations within a particular part of a text. Global coherence comes into the picture at the next level. At the third level, interpreters draw upon that aspect of their 'knowledge of language' which has to do with *cohesion*, which was discussed under Question 8 in Chapter 5. But coherence

cannot be reduced to formal cohesion: interpreters can infer coherence relations between utterances even in the absence of formal cohesive cues, on the basis of implicit assumptions which Chapter 4 (pp. 84–86) suggested are often of an ideological character. These inferential processes are generally regarded as a matter of pragmatics, and so 'pragmatics' is identified in Fig. 6.1 as an interpretative procedure for this level of interpretation as well as the previous one.

4. *Text structure and 'point'*. Interpretation of *text structure* at level four is a matter of working out how a whole text hangs together, a text's global coherence as I put it above. This involves matching the text with one of a repertoire of *schemata*, or representations of characteristic patterns of organization associated with different types of discourse. Once an interpreter has decided she is involved in a telephone conversation, for example, she knows she can expect particular things to happen in a particular order (greetings, establishing a conversational topic, changing topics, closing off the conversation, farewells). The 'point' of a text is a summary interpretation of the text as a whole which interpreters arrive at, and which is what tends to be stored in long-term memory so as to be available for recall. The experiential aspect of the point of a text is its overall *topic*; I prefer 'point' to 'topic' as a general term here because there are also relational and expressive aspects of the point of a text. There are discussions of point and of schemata and related notions below.

Let us turn now to the upper section of the diagram, which relates (as I said above) to the interpretation of context. I am assuming that interpretation is interpretation of *context* as well as text, and I shall explain and justify this assumption later. Participants arrive at interpretations of *situational context* partly on the basis of external cues – features of the physical situation, properties of participants, what has previously been said; but also partly on the basis of aspects of their MR in terms of which they interpret these cues – specifically, representations of societal and institutional social orders which allow them to ascribe the situations they are actually in to particular situation types. How participants interpret the situation determines which discourse types are drawn upon, and this in turn affects the nature of the interpretative procedures which are drawn upon in textual interpretation. But we also need to refer to *intertextual context*: participants in any discourse operate on the basis of assumptions about which previous (series of) discourses the current one is connected to, and their assumptions determine what can be taken as given in the sense of part of common experience, what can be alluded to, disagreed with, and so on.

Now let us come to the 'boxes' in the central column in Fig. 6.1. The figure represents the 'contents' of each box as a combination of the various 'inputs' (identified by the arrows) which feed into it. Notice firstly that linking each box with the domain of interpretation identified to its right is a double-headed arrow. What this means is that, at a given point in the interpretation of a text, previous interpretations constitute one part of the 'resources' for interpretation. This applies for each of the domains of interpretation.

Notice, secondly, that the boxes in the central column are also linked vertically with double-headed arrows. What this means is that each domain of interpretation draws upon interpretations in the other domains as part of its 'resources'. This interdependence is I think in part obvious for the four levels of text interpretation: for instance, to interpret the global coherence and 'point' of a text, you draw upon interpretations of the local coherence of parts of it; and to arrive at these, you draw upon interpretations of utterance meanings; and to arrive at these, you draw upon interpretations of the surface forms of utterances. But there is also interdependence in the opposite direction. For instance, interpreters make guesses early in the process of interpreting a text about its textual structure and 'point', and these guesses are likely to influence the meanings that are attached to individual utterances, and the local coherence relations set up between them. We may capture this by saying that interpretations have the important property of being 'top-down' (higher-level interpretations shape lower-level) as well as 'bottom-up'.

There is a similar situation with the relationship between interpretations of context and interpretations of text: interpreters quickly decide what the context is, and this decision can affect the interpretation of text; but the interpretation of context is partly based upon, and can change in the course of, the interpretation of text.

The picture of interpretation which emerges, then, is a rather complex one. For the rest of this section, I shall discuss in rather more detail some aspects of what is represented in Fig. 6.1 which are of particular interest in the context of this book, under the following headings: situational context and discourse type; intertextual context and presupposition; speech acts; schemata, and the related notions of script and frame; topic and point.

Situational context and discourse type

Discussion of this issue will be based upon Fig. 6.2, which represents schematically how interpreters arrive at interpretations

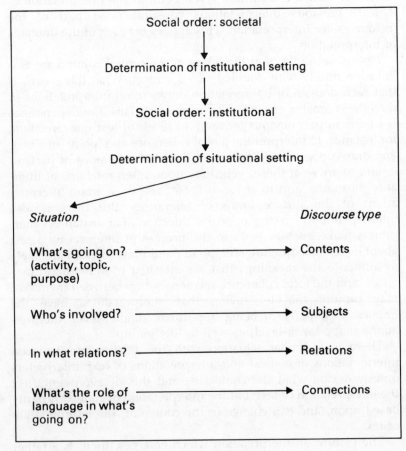

Social order: societal

↓

Determination of institutional setting

↓

Social order: institutional

↓

Determination of situational setting

Situation   *Discourse type*

What's going on? ─────────────→ Contents
(activity, topic,
purpose)

Who's involved? ─────────────→ Subjects

In what relations? ─────────────→ Relations

What's the role of ─────────────→ Connections
language in what's
going on?

Fig. 6.2 Situational context and discourse type

of the situational context, and the way in which this determines decisions about which discourse type is the 'appropriate' one to draw upon. I assume here for simplicity that only one discourse type is drawn upon in each interaction, though as I said earlier this is not actually so; Chapter 7 contains an extended discussion of how an interaction can draw upon two or more discourse types.

Let us look at the lower half of the diagram first. On the left-hand side, I have given four questions which relate to four main dimensions of the situation: what's going on, who's involved, what relationships are at issue, and what's the role of language in what's going on? We can use the police interview text from Chapter 2, partly reproduced below, to illustrate these dimensions.

(1) P: Did you get a look at the one in the car?
(2) W: I saw his face, yeah.
(3) P: What sort of age was he?
(4) W: About 45. He was wearing a . . .
(5) P: And how tall?
(6) W: Six foot one.
(7) P: Six foot one. Hair?
(8) W: Dark and curly

1. *'What's going on?'* I have subdivided 'what's going on' into *activity, topic, purpose*: one could certainly make finer discriminations, but these will suffice for our purposes. The first, activity, is the most general; it allows us to identify a situation in terms of one of a set of *activity types*, or distinctive categories of activity, which are recognized as distinct within a particular social order in a particular institution, and which have larger-scale textual structures of the sort referred to under Question 10 of Chapter 5. For instance, in police work, activity types would include making an arrest, entering a report, interviewing a witness, examining a suspect, and so forth. In this case, the activity type is interviewing a witness. The activity type is likely to constrain the set of possible *topics*, though this does not mean topics can be mechanically predicted given the activity type. The topic here is the description of an alleged offender. Similarly, activity types are also associated with particular institutionally recognized *purposes*. In this case the

overriding purpose is the elicitation and documentation (recall that P is filling in a form during this interview) of information and accounts about the alleged crime.

2. *'Who's involved?'* The questions of 'who's involved' and 'in what relations' are obviously closely connected, though analytically separable. In the case of the former, one is trying to specify which *subject positions* are set up; the set of subject positions differs according to the type of situation. It is important to note that subject positions are multi-dimensional. Firstly, one dimension derives from the activity type; in this case, it is an interview, and interviews have subject positions for an interviewer (or more than one) and an interviewee. Secondly, the institution ascribes social identities to the subjects who function within it; in our example, we have a 'policeman' and a 'member of the public', who is furthermore a 'witness', and a likely victim. Thirdly, different situations have different speaking and listening positions associated with them – speaker, addressee, hearer, overhearer, spokesperson, and so forth. In our example, we have speaker and addressee roles alternating between P and W.

3. *'In what relations?'* When it comes to the question of relations, we look at subject positions more dynamically, in terms of what relationships of power, social distance, and so forth are set up and enacted in the situation. In this case, one would be concerned with the nature of relationships between members of the police and members of 'the public' – noting for instance that 'processing' W in terms of 'procedure' seems to be more pressing for the police interviewer than empathizing with W as someone who has just witnessed a violent crime.

4. *'What's the role of language?'* Language is being used in an instrumental way as a part of a wider institutional and bureaucratic objective – it is being used to elicit information from W which is needed for filling in an official form which will be part of the documentation of the case. The role of language in this sense not only determines its genre – an interview of this type is an obvious way of obtaining the necessary information – but also its channel, whether spoken or written language is used.

Sometimes bureaucratic information of this sort is extracted through written language – people are asked to fill in the forms themselves. The fact that this is not so in this case, that the form-filling exercise is complicated by an interview, is indicative of the degree of control which the police exercise over all aspects of the case: information from w is only officially valid in a form which is mediated, and checked, by the police.

On the right-hand side of the lower part of Fig. 6.2, I have listed four main dimensions of a discourse type, in our sense of a set of underlying conventions belonging to some particular order of discourse. The top three of these will be familiar: a discourse type embodies certain constraints on contents, subjects and relations, or on the experiential, expressive and relational meanings which it makes possible. What the diagram shows is that these dimensions of the discourse type which is conventionally associated with a particular type of situation are determined by the dimensions of situation I have just been referring to: contents by what is going on, subjects by who's involved, and relations by the relationships between subjects. In addition, there is a fourth dimension, *connections*, determined by the role of language in what's going on: connections includes both ways in which texts are tied to the situational contexts in which they occur and ways in which connections are made between parts of a text (including those we have referred to as 'sentence cohesion'), both of which are variable between discourse types.

This situationally dependent determination of which discourse is to be drawn upon for producing and interpreting in the course of interaction, in turn controls elements of MR involved in the levels of text interpretation shown in Fig. 6.1. We can think of a discourse type as a *meaning potential* in the terminology of the linguist Michael Halliday: a particular constrained configuration of possible experiential, expressive and relational, and connective meanings. And some of the elements of MR drawn upon as interpretative principles will be particular to this discourse type, and to the realization of this meaning potential: vocabulary, semantic relations, pragmatic conventions, as well as schemata, frames and scripts.

Let us now look at the top of Fig. 6.2. The first point to make here is that the analysis of a situation in terms of the four dimensions of situation suggested above *is* a matter of interpretation.

Observable features of the physical situation, and text which has already occurred, do not themselves determine the situational context, though they are important cues which help the interpreter to interpret it. These cues are 'read' in conjunction with, and in the light of, an element of the interpreter's MR: the *social orders* that she brings to interpretation, that is the particular representations of how 'social space' is organized that the interpreter has in her MR. A social order is a sort of typology of social situation types, and interpreting is a matter of assigning an actual situation to a particular type. Recall the earlier discussion of social orders in Chapter 2.

We can think of this as happening in two stages. In the first, represented by the top two lines of the diagram, the interpreter arrives at a determination of the institutional setting, of which institutional domain the interaction is happening within, on the basis of a societal social order in her MR. That is, a societal social order divides total social space into so many institutional spaces, and any actual situation must first be placed institutionally in terms of this division. In the second stage, represented by the third and fourth lines of the diagram, the interpreter arrives at a determination of the situational setting, of which situation type the interaction is happening within, on the basis of the institutional social order selected in stage 1. Each institutional social order divides institutional space into so many situation types, and each actual situation is typified in terms of (or at least in relation to) a category from this typology.

I said in Chapter 2 that one dimension of a social order, be it societal or institutional, is an *order of discourse*. Correspondingly, in typifying a situation in terms of a given social order, one is also typifying it in terms of a particular discourse type from the associated order of discourse. I have represented this double process of typification in Fig. 6.2 as if the situation were typified first, then the discourse type: although it is analytically helpful to think in these terms, the two are really simultaneous. Figure 6.2 also gives the impression that values for each of the four dimensions of situation are determined independently, and that each dimension then independently selects values for the dimension of discourse type corresponding to it. Again, it is helpful analytically to see things in this way, but an institutional social order sets up as recognized situation types a relatively small number of conventional combinations of values for situational dimensions; and each situation type can be thought of partly in terms of a discourse type, which is a conventionalized combination of values for the four dimensions of discourse types.

Chapter 2 argued that social orders and orders of discourse are relative to particular ideologies and to particular power relations. One consequence of this is that situations may be differently interpreted if different social orders are being drawn upon as interpretative procedures by different participants. Such differences are relatively familiar cross-culturally, and they are likely to underlie cases of cross-cultural miscommunication or communication breakdown (see Ch. 3, p. 48). But they also occur within a culture between different ideological positions. This means that we cannot simply take the context for granted, or assume that it is transparently available to all participants, when we appeal to the role of context in text interpretation or production. We need in each case to establish what interpretation(s) of situational context participants are working with, and whether there is or is not a single shared interpretation. We need also to be conscious of how a more powerful participant's interpretation can be imposed on other participants.

Another consequence is that ideologies and the power relations which underlie them have a deep and pervasive influence upon discourse interpretation and production, for they are embedded in the interpretative procedures – the social orders – which underlie the highest level of interpretative decision on which others are dependent – *what situation am I in?* This influence is underlined by recent research into the nature of discourse processing, which has shown situational context to be a more significant determinant of interpretation than it had been thought to be. It is not the case, for instance, that interpretation consists first in computing 'literal meanings' for the sentences of a text, and then modifying those meanings in the light of context, as has often been assumed. Rather, interpreters operate from the start with assumptions (which are open to later modification) about the context, which influence the way in which linguistic features of a text are themselves processed, so that a text is always interpreted with some context in mind. This means that the values which particular features of a text have, depend on the interpreter's typification of the situational context.

The implications of this radical dependence of interpretation on situational context can be somewhat alarming for linguists who have been used to seeing meaning as a purely linguistic property of linguistic forms themselves. An understandable reaction is to try to delimit context – to somehow constrain the vastness of context. It follows from what I have just been saying, however, that the situational context for each and every discourse includes the system of social and power relationships at the highest, societal, level. Just as even a single sentence has traditionally been seen to imply a whole language, so a single discourse implies a whole society. This is so because the basic classificatory and typifying schemes for social practice and discourse upon which all else depends – what I have been calling social orders and orders of discourse – are shaped by the societal and institutional matrices of that single discourse.

Intertextual context and presupposition

Discourses and the texts which occur within them have histories, they belong to historical series, and the interpretation of intertextual context is a matter of deciding which series a text belongs to, and therefore what can be taken as common ground for participants, or *presupposed*. As in the case of situational context, discourse participants may arrive at roughly the same interpretation or different ones, and the interpretation of the more powerful participant may be imposed upon others. So having power may mean being able to determine presuppositions.

Presuppositions are not properties of texts, they are an aspect of text producers' interpretations of intertextual context. It is to underline this point that I have delayed discussing them until now, rather than including them in Chapter 5 in the description stage. But presuppositions are cued in texts, by quite a considerable range of formal features. Two important ones referred to under Question 8 in Chapter 5 are the definite article, and subordinate clauses. Others are *wh*–questions and *that*-clauses after certain verbs and adjectives (*regret, realize, point out, aware, angry,* etc.). There are a variety of cues in the following extract, which is taken from a report in a women's magazine on the wedding of Sarah Ferguson and Prince Andrew, written by Brenda McDougall:

Wasn't it a lovely day?

The sun came out, the colourful crowds gathered, and at the centre of it all were Sarah and Andrew, spilling their happiness in every direction and making it a day to remember – for them and for us.

Along with half the world, probably, I saw that enchanting TV interview the night before the wedding, and was struck by the completeness of their relationship. How they complement each other – in humour, in delight in each other's personalities, and in commitment to the future. Sarah obviously realises the demands of the role she has taken on as Navy wife and Royal duchess, yet still retains her own career. Surely that must be unique in Royal history, but how in tune with contemporary life and relationships.

Text 6.1 Source: *Women's Weekly*, 9 August 1987

Among the presuppositions of this extract are: it was a lovely day, the crowds were colourful, they are happy, that TV interview was enchanting, their relationship is complete, they complement each other, they delight in each other's personalities, they are committed to the future, the role Sarah has taken on is demanding, she has her own career. The passage is exceptional in the amount of presupposition: because of the nature of the topic and the numbers who watched the wedding on television, it is inevitably telling at least most people what they already know – giving back to people snippets of what are assumed to be antecedent texts they have already experienced as viewers or listeners or readers.

Or rather, it is purporting to tell people what they already know: with media texts such as this one, there is no way that the writer can know what actual readers' intertextual experiences are, so the writer must construct an 'ideal reader' with particular intertextual experiences. And there is of course no guarantee that the texts which are assumed to be within the experience of the audience have actually ever existed outside the head of the producer! Producers in mass communication thus have a rather effective means of manipulating audiences through attributing to their experience things which they want to get them to accept.

Because the propositions concerned are not made explicit, it is sometimes difficult for people to identify them and, if they wish to, reject them.

So presuppositions can be, let us say, *sincere* or *manipulative*. But presuppositions can also have *ideological* functions, when what they assume has the character of 'common sense in the service of power', in the terms of Chapter 4. An example is expressions like *the Soviet threat*, which become frequently repeated formulae in newspaper reports, for instance, and can cumulatively help to naturalize highly contentious propositions which are presupposed – in this case, that there is a threat (to Britain, Europe, 'the West') from the Soviet Union. Such presuppositions do not evoke specific texts or textual series, but are rather attributed to readers' textual experience in a vague way: while presuppositions are sometimes drawn from particular texts, in other cases they make a general appeal to 'background knowledge'.

In addition to simply presupposing elements of intertextual context, text producers can contest or challenge them. A significant means of doing so is *negation*, illustrated in Text 6.2, which is an article from a teenage magazine.

NO amount of make-up and hair stuff will turn you into a glamorous chick if your gnashers aren't in good condition. It's nothing to be proud of if you haven't been to the dentist for the past five years — you're only asking for trouble. Treatment isn't the equivalent of a week of listening to Nana Mouskouri albums, and your dentist isn't there to give you nightmares and inflict unnecessary pain on you. Regular check-ups are the best idea — prevention is always better than cure! If you haven't been to your dentist for eons, pluck up the courage and make an appointment — it'll be worth it! The British Dental Health Foundation have produced a series of well-helpful booklets on dental care. Including information on crowns, gum disease, oral hygiene, sugar and selecting a dentist, they're worth a look. For free copies of the leaflets, send an SAE to the British Dental Health Foundation, 88 Gurnards Avenue, Unit 2, Fishermead, Milton Keynes, Bucks.

Text 6.2 Source: *Blue Jeans* No. 488, 24 May 1986

This extract is made up of a series of assertions most of which are negative. But what is the motivation for all these negative assertions when the writer could have made the same points positively? The writer is evidently using negatives as a way of implicitly taking issue with the corresponding positive assertions (*treatment is the equivalent of a week of listening to Nana Mouskouri albums*, etc.). But that would be a rather peculiar thing to do unless those positive assertions had in fact been asserted, and unless their assertion were somehow connected with this discourse. What the writer in fact seems to be assuming is that these assertions are to be found in antecedent texts which are within readers' experience. As with presupposition, negation can be sincere, manipulative, or ideological.

This extract is a sort of 'dialogue' between the text producer and (the producers of) other texts which are adjudged to be part of the intertextual context. Presupposition gives a similar dialogic quality to texts, though of a less dynamic sort. Since texts always exist in intertextual relations with other texts, it is arguable that they are always 'dialogic', a property which is sometimes referred to under the general heading of *intertextuality*.

The concept of intertextual context requires us to view discourses and texts from a historical perspective, in contrast with the more usual position in language studies which would regard a text as analysable without reference to other texts, in abstraction from its historical context. The next two chapters of the book are premised upon such a historical perspective. Chapter 7 is centred around a view of the text as produced through the producer drawing upon a mixture of two or more discourse types – two or more conventions, traditions – as a means of making creative use of the resources of the past to meet the changing communicative needs of the present. Chapter 8 takes in a longer time-scale, being concerned with how transitions between historical periods are reflected in, and partly constituted by, transformations in orders of discourse.

Speech acts

Speech acts are a central aspect of *pragmatics*, which is concerned with the meanings which participants in a discourse ascribe to elements of a text on the basis of their MR and their interpretations of context, part of the second level of text interpretation in Fig. 6.1. The pragmatic properties (meanings) of a text are therefore not formal, and do not belong in the description stage of the procedure of Chapter 5, but rather here.

I have referred to speech acts at a number of points in earlier chapters without explaining what I mean by this term. In characterizing part of a text as a speech act, one is characterizing what the producer is doing by virtue of producing it – making a statement, making a promise, threatening, warning, asking a question, giving an order, and so on. The producer can be simultaneously doing a number of things, and so a single element can have multiple speech act values. Speech act values cannot be assigned simply on the basis of formal features of an utterance; in assigning values, interpreters also take account of the textual context of an utterance (what precedes and follows it in the text), the situational and intertextual context, and elements of MR.

For example, writers on classroom discourse have pointed out that a declarative sentence or a grammatical question on the part of a teacher is likely to be assigned the speech act value of command by pupils if it refers to some action or activity which they have an obligation to perform. Examples would be *the door's still open* or *did you shut the door*. The classrooms these writers are describing are very traditional in terms of teacher–pupil relations; indirect, 'hinting' commands of this sort imply a categorical power relationship. Perhaps in more liberal classrooms where ideologically different discourse types are operative, such hinted commands would not occur, and these sentences could therefore not (or not as easily) be interpreted as commands. Certainly the same sentences in further or higher education are less likely to be interpreted in this way. The main point is that in order to determine the speech act values or 'forces' of these examples, we need to know what sort of situational context they occur in, and therefore which discourse types are operative. Their form alone tells us very little.

I have just referred to *indirect* commands. Speech acts can be given relatively direct expression (*Shut the door!* as a command, for instance), or relatively indirect expression, with various degrees of indirectness. Discourse types differ in their conventions for the directness of expression of speech acts, and these differences are broadly connected with the way in which social relations are coded in them. Indirect commands or requests, for instance, may occur as in the example above where power relations are so clear that it is not necessary for the teacher to be direct. Conversely, they may occur where the person being requested to do something is more powerful than the person asking, or is a stranger who one would not normally ask such things of, so that indirectness is a way of trying to mitigate an imposition. These alternative values associated with indirectness underline, again, that the assignment of speech act values is relative to situational context and discourse type.

Let us take as a further example the first two turns (question and answer) of the now familiar police interview in Chapter 2:

P: Did you get a look at the one in the car?
W: I saw his face, yeah.

P's question is rather direct. Nevertheless, a value can be attributed to it only by referring it to the system of options from which it represents a choice in the operative discourse type – in this case the discourse of police–witness information-gathering interviews. In this case, it is an unmarked choice in the system of options associated with 'impositive' speech acts – unmarked in the sense that it is neither especially blunt nor especially mitigated. The same direct form of question might be marked as blunt in a different discourse type – for example in a university seminar. The way in which W answers the question is again dependent on the discourse type. There are indefinitely many ways in which this question might have been answered, but most are precluded here. The answer might have been, for instance, *Oh lord that's a difficult one . Now let me think . I'm sure I got a glimpse of his face, yes.* Such an answer certainly could have occurred, maybe as a rather effective way of challenging the normative expectations of this discourse type! But what is expected here is the sort of answer that actually occurs – one that just gives the information asked for.

The conventions for speech acts which form part of a discourse type embody ideological representations of subjects and their social relationships. For example, asymmetries of rights and obligations between subjects (a police interviewer and a witness, say) may be embedded in asymmetrical rights to ask questions, request action, complain, and asymmetrical obligations, to answer, act, and explain one's actions. Or again, conventions governing the degree of (in)directness for the expression of a speech act may vary for different subjects, in line with assumptions about the ways in which and degrees to which they should be polite to other subjects, avoid imposing upon them, and so on.

In sum, it is worth while asking of any discourse sample or type, who uses which speech acts, and in which forms.

Frames, scripts, and schemata

Schemata are a part of MR constituting interpretative procedures for the fourth level of text interpretation in Fig. 6.1, and frames and scripts are closely related notions, which is why I am including them in this discussion. They constitute a family of types of mental representation of aspects of the world, and share the property of mental representations in general of being ideologically variable. Use of these three terms is not standardized, and one finds them used in various senses. Figure 6.3 summarizes a way of differentiating the three notions which fits in with the contents–relations–subjects distinction I have been using throughout.

Schema	Contents: activity
Frame	Contents: topic
Script	Subjects/relations

Fig. 6.3 Frames, scripts and schemata

A *schema* (plural *schemata*) is a representation of a particular type of activity (what I referred to above as an *activity type*) in terms of predictable elements in a predictable sequence. It is a mental representation of the 'larger-scale textual structures' which were discussed under Question 10 of Chapter 5. Recall the example there of a newspaper accident report, which I suggested is made up of: cause of accident, how it was dealt with, consequent damage or injury, longer-term outcomes. Or the example of a telephone conversation, which I used above. Schemata are mental typifications of such structures which operate as interpretative procedures.

Whereas schemata represent modes of social behaviour, *frames* represent the entities that populate the (natural and social) world. A frame is a representation of whatever can figure as a topic, or 'subject matter', or 'referent' within an activity. I have already used the term in the section *Implicit assumptions, coherence and inferencing* of Chapter 4, referring to frames for 'a woman' which were activated by textual cues in a text. Frames can represent types of person or other animate beings (a woman, a teacher, a politician, a dog, etc.), or inanimate objects (a house, a computer, etc.), or processes (running, attacking, dying, etc.), or abstract concepts (democracy, love, etc.). They can also represent complex processes or series of events which involve combinations of such entities: an air crash, a car factory (car production), a thunderstorm.

While frames represent the entities which can be evoked or referred to in the activities represented by schemata, *scripts* represent the subjects who are involved in these activities, and their relationships. They typify the ways in which specific classes of subject behave in social activities, and how members of specific classes of subjects behave towards each other – how they conduct relationships. For instance, people have scripts for a doctor, for a patient, and for how a doctor and a patient can be expected to interact.

There are overlaps between scripts and frames (there is a close connection between the script for a class of subject and the frame for the corresponding class of animate being, for instance), and between schemata and frames (frames for complex processes are not far from schemata, for instance). This is to be expected, because the three terms identify three very broad dimensions of a highly complex network of mental representations. Notice also that there are interdependencies between the three, in the sense that a particular schema will predict particular topics and subject matters, and particular subject positions and relationships, and therefore particular frames and scripts. Nevertheless, the three do vary independently to some extent, and it therefore does make sense to distinguish them in analysis. Although I have assigned a specific role as interpretative procedures only to schemata in Fig. 6.1, frames and scripts also function as interpretative procedures, for instance in arriving at interpretations of topic and point (see the next section for details). They all do so in accordance with the dialectical relationship between textual cues and MR which I have stressed throughout: textual cues evoke schemata, frames, or scripts, and these set up expectations which colour the way in which subsequent textual cues are interpreted.

Topic and point

How people interpret the point of a text is of considerable significance in terms of the effect of a text, for it is the point that is
generally retained in memory, recalled, and intertextually alluded
to or reported in other texts. The experiential or 'content' aspect
of point is what is familiarly known as *topic*, but point cannot be
reduced to topic because there are also relational and expressive
dimensions of point. Consider as an example of this the *Daily
Mail* text (*The paras' new leader*) of Chapter 3 (Text 3.4, p. 53). The
topic of this text can be represented as a proposition: the wife of
the new CO of the 2nd Parachute Battalion says her husband will
do the job well. However, there is another, expressive dimension
to the point of this text to do with the woman herself: as I said
in my comments on it in Chapter 3, the text implicitly conveys
the meaning that Jenny Keeble is a 'good wife' and admirable
person, through the expressive values of attributes attached to
her.

How does the text implicitly convey this meaning? I think it
very clearly relies upon the interpreter's MR to do so: the
meaning that Jenny Keeble is a 'good wife' is not explicitly
expressed in the text, and it is only because interpreters have in
their heads a mental representation of what a 'good wife' is stereotypically supposed to be that they are able to recognize attributes thereof which occur in the text and so infer the meaning.
In the terms of the preceding section, interpreters make use of
a *script* for 'the good wife'. In fact, schemata and frames as well
as scripts can be regarded as playing a role in the interpretation
of point: they act as stereotypical patterns against which we can
match endlessly diverse texts, and once we identify a text as an
instance of a pattern, we happily dispense with the mass of its
detail and reduce it to the skeletal shape of the familiar pattern
for purposes of longer-term memory and recall. We can do this
for textual units of varying extent: a paragraph, a chapter, a
conversation, a book, or a lecture series.

If it is the point of a text that it has longer-term effects on the
interpreter, then it is important to be conscious of the social
origins of the cognitive apparatus that the interpreter relies upon
to interpret the point. Schemata, scripts and frames are as I said
earlier ideologically variable, like MR generally, and it is schemata, etc., which bear the ideological imprint of socially dominant
power-holders that are likely to be a naturalized resource for all.

In this way, thoroughly routine ways of appropriating and internalizing texts can be indirectly constrained by unequal relations of power. But this begins to take us into the stage of explanation, which is the concern of the second part of this chapter.

Conclusion

Before summarizing what I have been saying in the section on interpretation, in the form of a set of questions, I ought briefly to contrast the process of participant interpretation (which I have focused on so far) with the process of production, and refer to the possibility of differences between discourse participants in respect of their MR.

The process of production is really parallel to the process of interpretation, except that the interpretative procedures associated with the four levels of text interpretation in Fig. 6.1 are drawn upon to *produce* surface structures of utterances, utterance meanings, locally coherent groups of utterances, and globally coherent texts, rather than to interpret them. In the case of context interpretation, there is no difference: both producers and interpreters generate interpretations of the situational and intertextual contexts of the discourse. The production and interpretation processes are parallel in another way which I have not so far referred to: producers must assume that their interpreters or likely interpreters are equipped with particular interpretative procedures, and conversely interpreters must assume that the producers of the texts they are interpreting are so equipped. This very often amounts to reciprocal assumptions – assumptions that one's interlocutor has the same interpretative procedures available as oneself.

However, this is often not the case. Participants may, as I said earlier, arrive at different interpretations of situational (as well as intertextual) context. Correspondingly, they may draw upon different interpretative procedures at the four levels of text interpretation in Fig. 6.1, and so particular textual features may be ascribed different values by different participants. Moreover, interpretations of context, and so also interpretative procedures, may shift during the course of an interaction for any or all participants. These considerations underline the importance of being sensitive to variations between participants and in time in respect of interpretation. We need also to be sensitive to the

possibility that, when there is such diversity between participants, a participant with power may attempt to impose her own
interpretation of context, and interpretative procedures upon less
powerful participants – recall the discussion of situational power
in Chapter 3 (the *Power in discourse* section).

Let me now summarize what has been said about interpretation in the form of three questions which can be asked about a
particular discourse, and which readers may find useful to refer
to in doing their own analyses.

1. *Context*: what interpretation(s) are participants giving to the
   situational and intertextual contexts?

2. *Discourse type(s)*: what discourse type(s) are being drawn upon
   (hence what rules, systems or principles of phonology,
   grammar, sentence cohesion, vocabulary, semantics and pragmatics; and what schemata, frames and scripts)?

3. *Difference and change*: are answers to questions 1 and 2 different
   for different participants? And do they change during the
   course of the interaction?

The stage of interpretation corrects delusions of autonomy on
the part of subjects in discourse. It makes explicit what for
participants is generally implicit: the dependence of discourse
practice on the unexplicated common-sense assumptions of MR
and discourse type. What it does not do on its own, however,
is explicate the relations of power and domination and the ideologies which are built into these assumptions, and which make
ordinary discourse practice a site of social struggle. For this, we
need the stage of explanation.

EXPLANATION

We can make the transition from the stage of interpretation to the
stage of explanation by noting that, when aspects of MR are
drawn upon as interpretative procedures in the production and
interpretation of texts, they are thereby reproduced; recall the
discussion of reproduction in Chapter 2 (the section *Dialectic of
structures and practices*). Reproduction is for participants a generally unintended and unconscious side-effect, so to speak, of
production and interpretation. Reproduction connects the stages

of interpretation and explanation, because whereas the former is concerned with how MR are drawn upon in processing discourse, the latter is concerned with the social constitution and change of MR, including of course their reproduction in discourse practice.

The objective of the stage of explanation is to portray a discourse as part of a social process, as a social practice, showing how it is determined by social structures, and what reproductive effects discourses can cumulatively have on those structures, sustaining them or changing them. These social determinations and effects are 'mediated' by MR: that is, social structures shape MR, which in turn shape discourses; and discourses sustain or change MR, which in turn sustain or change structures. Given the orientation of this book, the social structures which are in focus are relations of power, and the social processes and practices which are in focus are processes and practices of social struggle. So explanation is a matter of seeing a discourse as part of processes of social struggle, within a matrix of relations of power.

We can think of explanation as having two dimensions, depending on whether the emphasis is upon process or structure – upon processes of struggle or upon relations of power. On the one hand, we can see discourses as parts of social struggles, and contextualize them in terms of these broader (non-discoursal) struggles, and the effects of these struggles on structures. This puts the emphasis on the social effects of discourse, on creativity, and on the future. On the other hand, we can show what power relationships determine discourses; these relationships are themselves the outcome of struggles, and are established (and, ideally, naturalized) by those with power. This puts the emphasis on the social determination of discourse, and on the past – on the results of past struggles. Both social effects of discourse and social determinants of discourse should be investigated at three levels of social organization: the societal level, the institutional level, and the situational level. This is represented in Fig. 6.4.

We can take it as a working assumption that any discourse will have determinants and effects at all three levels, though the 'societal' and 'institutional' levels will be clearly distinct only for more institutional types of discourse, and that any discourse is therefore shaped by institutional and societal power relations, and contributes (if minutely) to institutional and societal struggles.

Let me try to clarify what this contribution to struggles means,

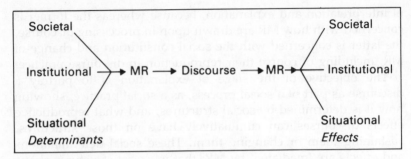

Fig. 6.4 Explanation

and what it does not mean. It does not mean that every discourse manifests conflict – social struggle, as we saw in Chapter 2, does not necessarily take the form of overt struggle or conflict. Even a discourse in which participants apparently arrive at (virtually) the same interpretations of the situation, and draw upon the same MR (interpretative procedures) and discourse types, can be seen as an effect of power relations and as a contribution to social struggle. For example, a perfectly ordinary and harmonious conversation between two married people, by virtue of its perfectly ordinary unequal division of conversational 'labour' between the woman and the man, both manifests patriarchal social relations within the institution of the family and the society as a whole, and makes a tiny contribution, on the conservative side, to struggles over the position of women in the family and in society.

In terms of the three levels of social organization in Fig. 6.4, what I am suggesting is that there are different ways of seeing the same discourse according to whether we are focusing upon it as situational, institutional, or societal practice. We are not necessarily or even normally looking at different features of the discourse at these different levels; rather, we are often looking at the same features from different perspectives, as if we were changing the filters on a camera lens. It has been noticed, for example, that in perfectly ordinary domestic conversation between women and men, women react more to what men say and show more involvement, understanding and appreciation (with markers like *mmhm, yeah, no, really, oh*) than men do when women are speaking. This feature can be seen firstly in situational terms as showing the 'supportive' position of particular women in particular domestic relationships; but it can also be seen in institutional and societal terms as one of a number of features which show a tendency for women to be cast as supporting players in interactions, while men get the star parts.

In terms of effects, a discourse may reproduce its own social determinants and the MR which it draws upon with virtually no change, or it may to a greater or lesser degree contribute to their transformation. We can see these contrasting possibilities in terms of contrasting relationships of producers (and interpreters) to MR. In the former case, the producer is in a *normative* relation to her MR, in the sense that she is acting in accordance with them in a rather direct way. In the latter case, the producer is in a *creative* relation to her MR, in the sense that she is drawing upon them and combining them in creative ways, and thus transforming them. In so far as particular directions of creative use and adaptation of MR come to be systematic, they may bring about long-term transformations of MR and, thereby, of the social relations which underlie them.

Broadly speaking, the choice between these contrasting relations of participants to MR depends on the nature of the situation. Normative relations to MR are associated with situations which are unproblematic for participants, whereas creative relations to MR are characteristic of situations which are problematic. A situation is unproblematic if participants can easily and harmoniously interpret it as an instance of a familiar situation type – if what is going on, who's involved, and the relations between those involved, are clear and 'according to type'. In such cases, MR constitute appropriate norms (discourse types, interpretative procedures) which can simply be followed. Conversely, if these things are not clear, MR do not provide clear-cut norms. There is a mismatch between the concrete situation and familiar situation types, which requires participants to draw upon the resources which their MR provide in creative ways in order to cope with the problematic properties of the situation. Such situations constitute moments of crisis for participants, and they typically arise when social struggle becomes overt, and when MR and the power relations which underlie them – the temporarily stabilized results of past struggles – therefore themselves come into crisis. Chapter 7 gives an extended example of a problematic, creative situation of crisis of this sort.

Exploration of the determinants and effects of discourse at the institutional and societal levels in particular can easily lead one into detailed sociological analysis. Since we are looking at discourse as social practice, this is hardly surprising. However, there are usually practical limitations which prevent someone doing critical discourse analysis from going too far in that direction. There is no rule of thumb determining how far one should extend one's analysis into sociological aspects of the institution and the society. If one is embarking upon a detailed research project, a great deal of sociological analysis might be necessary, and it might make sense for a researcher whose main interests are in language to collaborate with a sociologist. In less ambitious circumstances, even quite a general account of the institution and the society in terms of social groupings and relationships may provide enough of a social matrix for the discourse.

The stage of explanation involves a specific perspective on MR: they are seen specifically as ideologies. That is, the assumptions about culture, social relationships, and social identities which are incorporated in MR, are seen as determined by particular power relations in the society or institution, and in terms of their contribution to struggles to sustain or change these power relations – they are seen ideologically.

Let me now summarize what has been said about explanation in the form of three questions which (like the three questions for interpretation on page 162) can be asked of a particular discourse under investigation.

1. *Social determinants*: what power relations at situational, institutional and societal levels help shape this discourse?

2. *Ideologies*: what elements of MR which are drawn upon have an ideological character?

3. *Effects*: how is this discourse positioned in relation to struggles at the situational, institutional and societal levels? Are these struggles overt or covert? Is the discourse normative with respect to MR or creative? Does it contribute to sustaining existing power relations, or transforming them?

CONCLUSION: POSITION OF ANALYST

This concludes the presentation of the three-stage procedure which has taken up the last two chapters. To round it off, let us consider the position of the analyst in the stages of interpretation and explanation, starting with the former. How is the analyst to gain access to the discourse processes of production and interpretation? These processes take place in people's heads, and it is therefore not possible to observe them as one might observe processes in the physical world. The only access that the analyst has to them is in fact through her capacity to herself engage in the discourse processes she is investigating. In other words, the analyst must draw upon her own MR (interpretative procedures) in order to explain how participants draw upon theirs. The analysis of discourse processes is necessarily an 'insider's' or a 'member's' task – which is why I have called the resources drawn upon by both participant and analyst members 'members' resources' (MR).

But if analysts are drawing upon their own MR to explicate how those of participants operate in discourse, then it is important that they be sensitive to what resources they are themselves relying upon to do analysis. At this stage of the procedure, it is only really self-consciousness that distinguishes the analyst from the participants she is analysing. The analyst is doing the same as the participant interpreter, but unlike the participant interpreter the analyst is concerned to explicate *what* she is doing. For the critical analyst, moreover, the aim is to eliminate even that difference: to develop self-consciousness about the rootedness of discourse in common-sense assumptions of MR. See Chapter 9 for more details.

The position of the analyst in explanation is more easily distinguishable from that of the participant in that the 'resources' the analyst draws upon here are derived from a social theory – recall that I outlined key elements of my resources in this respect in Chapter 2. However, self-consciousness is just as important if one is to avoid importing untheorized assumptions about society, or acting as if explanation could be theory-independent or theory-neutral. Participants do have, to varying degrees, their own rationalizations of discoursal practice in terms of assumptions about society, but such rationalizations cannot be taken at face value. Again, for the critical analyst, the aim is to bridge the gap between analyst and participant through the widespread development of rational understanding of, and theories of, society. See Chapter 9.

REFERENCES

On the distinction between description, interpretation, and explanation, see Fairclough N L 1985 and Candlin C N 1986; on interpretation see Jameson F 1981, Thompson J B 1984, and van Dijk T forthcoming; and on interpretative procedures see Cicourel A 1973. Levinson S 1983 is a thorough introduction to pragmatics, with chapters on speech acts, implication ('implicature') and presupposition. Leech G N 1983 is an account of the author's own approach to pragmatics, which includes relevant discussion of the pragmatics of negative sentences. See also Searle J 1969 on speech acts. Schank R, Abelson R 1977 is a major study of schemata and related notions. See also Tannen D 1979. There is a great deal of sociolinguistics literature on analysing situational context. Downes W 1984 is a recent introduction to sociolinguistics, and Hymes D 1962 is a classic paper. Halliday M A K, Hasan R 1985 is written from the perspective of systemic linguistics. On the radical dependence of interpretation on situational context, see Garrod S 1986. Giddens A 1976 includes a general sociological account of problems relating to the position of the analyst in social analysis. The example of speech acts in classroom discourse on p. 156 is from Sinclair J, Coulthard M 1975.

SEVEN

Creativity and struggle in discourse: the discourse of Thatcherism

One objective of this chapter is to fill something of a gap which I left in the procedure of Chapters 5 and 6: I said relatively little there about processes of text production. Another closely related objective is to develop the conception of the *subject* in discourse which I have introduced in Chapters 2 and 4 (see pp. 38–40 and 102–106). I presented the subject there as having the apparently paradoxical properties of being socially determined, and yet capable of individual creativity; obliged to act discoursally in preconstituted subject positions, yet capable of creatively transforming discourse conventions. I shall argue that social determination and individual creativity are not the opposites they appear to be.

A third objective is to provide an opportunity for us to work with the procedure introduced in Chapters 5 and 6 on an extended example. Most of this chapter will be taken up with a case study on the discourse of Thatcherism, that is, the political discourse associated with the so-called Thatcherite trend in British Conservatism. We shall be working with an extract from a radio interview with Mrs Thatcher herself. This part of the chapter will be organized around a series of questions about the interview. As in previous chapters, I hope that readers will work through these questions themselves before reading my suggested answers.

PRODUCING TEXTS

First of all, then, let us look at the connections between text production, and the social determination and creativity of the subject. I want to focus in this section upon one motivation, not necessarily or even normally conscious, that people have for producing texts: the resolution of problems of various sorts in their own relationship to the world and to others. We can categorize such problems with the now familiar distinction between contents, relations, and subjects. The position of the producer may be problematized in any of these respects.

The position of the producer may be problematized as to *contents* where some discrepancy arises between the producer's common-sense (ideological) representations of the world, and the world itself. This may happen because of changes in the world, for instance, or when the producer's representations come into contact with other incompatible representations. A familiar case of the former type is where a newspaper, say, tries to deal with some event which appears to conflict with its normal way of representing that 'part' of the world – say a newspaper which consistently supports the police come thick or thin needs to deal with large-scale serious injuries to members of 'the public' in the course of an industrial picket.

The producer's position may be problematized in terms of *relations*, in the sense of the social relations between producer and interpreter(s) (addressee, audience). An example might be an interaction in any of a range of types of situational context, where producer and addressee are of different sexes. Mixed-sex interaction is widely problematic these days because of the increasingly contested relative social positions of women and men.

The position of the producer may be problematized in terms of *subjects*, either in terms of the subject position or social identity of the producer, or in terms of the subject position or social identity of the interpreter(s). Examples of the former can be found in education wherever the precise nature of the subject position of 'teacher' is in doubt – when for example the pupils or students are narrowing the gap between themselves and their teachers in terms of attaining the status of adults, or attaining knowledge or qualifications commensurate with the teacher's. The latter case is specifically to do with situations in which the subject position of the interpreter(s) is a problem for the producer. This may be so, for instance, for a politician who is trying to either maintain or create commonality of ideology or allegiance among (the sections of a population represented in) an audience – the case study later in the chapter will give us an example of this.

These three types of problems in the position of the producer are not purely of a discoursal nature, but I have presented them in such a way as to indicate their discoursal aspects. These discoursal dimensions of producers' problems can be seen as a consequence of discourse conventions becoming destabilized – or, in the terminology I introduced in Chapter 2 (p. 39), the 'de-structuring' of orders of discourse, in the sense that a relatively stable relationship between discourse types in an order of discourse comes to be disrupted. In other words, producers experience problems because the familiar ways of doing things are no longer straightforwardly available. There are, as we shall see below, social reasons for the de-structuring of orders of discourse.

If problems are the consequence of de-structuring, resolving them requires some restructuring: a strategy for dealing with the problematization of one's position is to be creative, to put together familiar discourse types in novel combinations as a means of finding new ways of doing things to replace the now-problematic old ones. There may be evidence of restructuring in the formal features a text: formal features constitute traces of the production process, and where this involves combining diverse discourse types, we might expect diversity in the traces. We can put this in the terms of Chapter 5: formal features have experiential, relational, and expressive values, and an indication of creative restructuring is where we find formal features which clash on one or more of these dimensions of value.

Sometimes the traces of the different discourse types drawn upon are relatively easily separable in the text. But if producers are to successfully resolve problems through restructuring, the texts they produce will need to be what we might call 'seamless', in the sense that the traces of different discourse types are not easily separable, and a harmonization of values is achieved between them. This is likely to need time: texts generated from a particular restructuring of discourse types may progressively come to be seamless, as the novel combination of discourse types comes to be naturalized. In this way, restructurings which are effected by producers in particular discourses in response to particular experiences of problematization, come to be restructurings of the order of discourse. One outcome may be that what starts as a new combination of discourse types ends up being a discourse type in its own right. Advertising is a case in point: its importation of features of face-to-face spoken interaction, such as the direct form of address with *you*, is now so well naturalized that what was originally a mix of 'public' and face-to-face discourse types is now arguably a discourse type in its own right. See Chapter 8 for further discussion of advertising.

I have so far been focusing upon the individual producer's experience of problems, and attempts to resolve them. This has been within the domain of interpretation, in terms of the procedure. But interpretation needs complementing with the stage of explanation: although the de-structuring and restructuring of orders of discourse affect individuals and involve individual creativity, their main determinants and effects lie outside the individual, in the struggles between social groupings. What are experienced as individual problems can be interpreted socially as indicators of the de-structuring of orders of discourse which occur in the course of social struggles – see Chapter 3 (pp. 68–69) on discourse as a *stake* in as well as a *site* of social struggle. And what are experienced as individual attempts to resolve problems can be interpreted as moves in social struggles towards the restructuring of orders of discourse.

What, then, of the relationship we started with in this section, between text production, and the subject as socially determined and yet creative? What I have been drawing attention to is *the social nature of individual creativity*: the creativity of the subject is socially determined, in the sense that creativity flourishes in particular social circumstances, when social struggles are constantly de-structuring orders of discourse; and the creativity of the subject is socially constitutive, in the sense that individual creative acts cumulatively establish restructured orders of discourse. Thus the social and the individual, the determined and the creative, are not paradoxically opposed to one another, but facets of a dialectical process of social fixation and transformation.

CASE STUDY

The text we shall be working on is an extended extract from a much longer interview between Margaret Thatcher (MT) and Michael Charlton (MC), which took place on BBC Radio 3 on 17 December 1985.

(1) MC: Prime Minister you were at Oxford in the nineteen
           forties and after the war Britain would embark on a
           period of relative prosperity for all the like of which it
           had hardly known but today there are three and a
(5)   quarter million unemployed and e:m

Britain's economic performance by one measurement
has fallen to the rank of that of Italy now can you
imagine yourself back at the University today what
must seem to be the chances in Britain and the
(10)   prospects for all now
   MT: they are very different worlds you're talking about
               because the first thing that struck me very forcibly as
               you were speaking of those days was that now we do
               enjoy a standard of living which was undreamed of
(15)   then and I can remember Rab Butler saying after we
               returned to power in about 1951–52 that if we played
               our cards right the standard of living within twenty
               five years would be twice as high as it was then and
               em he was just about right and it was remarkable
(20)   because it was something that we had never thought
               of now I don't think now one would necessarily think
               wholly in material terms indeed I think it's wrong to
               think in material terms because really the kind of
               country you want is made up by the strength of its
(25)   people and I think we're returning to my vision of
               Britain as a younger person and I was always brought
               up with the idea look Britain is a country whose
               people think for themselves act for themselves can act
               on their own initiative they don't have to be told
(30)   don't like to be pushed around are self-reliant and
               then over and above that they're always responsible
               for their families and something else it was a kind of
               em I think it was Barry who said do as you would be
               done by e: you act to others as you'd like them to act
(35)   towards you and so you do something for the
               community now I think if you were looking at
               another country you would say what makes a country
               strong it is its people do they run their industries well
               are their human relations good e: do they respect law
(40)   and order are their families strong all of those kind of
               things
               ⌈and you know it's just way beyond economics
   MC: ⌊but you know people still   people still ask
               though e: where is she going now General de Gaulle
(45)   had a vision of France e: a certain idea of France as he
               put it e: you have fought three major battles in this

country the Falkland Islands e:m against the miners
and local councils and against public expenditure and
people I think would like to hear what this vision you
(50)   have of Britain is it must be a powerful one what is it
that inspires your action

MT: I wonder if I perhaps I can answer best by saying how
I see what government should do and if government
really believes in people what people should do I
(55)   believe that government should be very strong to do
those things which only government can do it has to
be strong to have defence because the kind of Britain I
see would always defend its freedom and always be a
reliable ally so you've got to be strong to your own
(60)   people and other countries have got to know that you
stand by your word then you turn to internal security
and yes you HAVE got to be strong on law and order
and do the things that only governments can do but
there it's part government and part people because
(65)   you CAN'T have law and order observed unless it's
in partnership with people then you have to be strong
to uphold the value of the currency and only
governments can do that by sound finance and then
you have to create the framework for a good
(70)   education system and social security and at that point
you have to say over to people people are inventive
creative and so you expect PEOPLE to create thriving
industries thriving services yes you expect people
each and everyone from whatever their background
(75)   to have a chance to rise to whatever level their own
abilities can take them yes you expect people of all
sorts of background and almost whatever their
income level to be able to have a chance of owning
some property tremendously important the
(80)   ownership of property of a house gives you some
independence gives you a stake in the future you're
concerned about your children

MC: but could you sum this vision up
MT: (   ) you said my vision
(85)   please let me just go on and then that isn't enough
if you're interested in the future yes you will
probably save you'll probably want a little bit of
independent income of your own and so constantly

	thinking about the future so it's very much a Britain
(90)	whose people are independent of government but
	aware that the government has to be strong to do
	those things which only governments can do
MC:	but can you sum it up in a in a in a phrase or two the
	aim is to achieve what or to restore what in Britain
(95)	when clearly risking a lot and winning in a place like
	the Falkland Islands is just as important in your
	philosophy ⎡ for Britain as as
MT:	⎣ I think
	restoring sound money reducing the money supply in
(100)	the Bank of England
MT:	but of course it showed that we were reliable in the
	defence of freedom and when part of Britain we: was
	invaded of course we went we believed in defence of
	freedom we were reliable I think if I could try to sum
(105)	it up in a phrase and that's always I suppose most
	difficult of all I would say really restoring the very
	best of the British character to its former
	preeminence.
MT:	but this has meant something called Thatcherism now
(110)	is that a description you accept as something quite
	distinct from traditional conservatism in this country
MT:	no it is traditional conservatism
MC:	but it's radical and populist and therefore not
(115)	conservative
MT:	it is radical because at the time when I took over we
	needed to be radical e: it is populist I wouldn't call it
	populist I would say that many of the things which
	I've said strike a chord in the hearts of ordinary
(120)	people why because they're British because their
	character IS independent because they DON'T like to
	be shoved around coz they ARE prepared to take
	responsibility because they DO expect to be loyal to
	their friends and loyal allies that's why you call it
(125)	populist. I say it strikes a chord in the hearts of
	people I know because it struck a chord in my heart
	many many years ago

Text 7.1 Source: Interview between Michael Charlton and
Margaret Thatcher, BBC Radio 3, 17 Disember 1985

Case study: the analysis

As I indicated at the beginning of this chapter, this section will be organized around a series of questions, and I recommend readers to work through these questions themselves before looking at my suggested answers. There are six questions. The first four are to do with the description stage of the procedure outlined earlier. In accordance with the focus of this chapter, they are specifically concerned with textual features considered as traces of the process of production. In the case of questions 1–3, these are traces of the restructuring of discourse types with respect to relations between the interviewee (Mrs Thatcher) and the audience (question 1), the subject position of the female political leader (question 2), and the subject positions of the addressees in the radio audience (question 3). I have not assigned a question to contents, representations of the world, because it is less interesting than relations and subjects in this case. Question 4 is concerned with traces of struggle in the text. Question 5 is concerned with the procedural stage of interpretation, and with the processes of production and interpretation within it. And question 6 is concerned with the stage of explanation.

'Thatcherism'

Before we start working on the questions, let me briefly contextualize the extract and the topic of the case study, the discourse of Thatcherism, by sketching out the political context of Thatcherism. In so doing, I shall be pre-empting the explanation stage of procedure, and therefore pre-empting the answer to question 6. But, as I said in Chapter 5, there is no reason why the procedure should be applied in one order rather than another. Indeed, it is often helpful to come back to a stage one has already applied in the light of what emerges from applying the other stages. The view of Thatcherism I shall present owes most to the political analysis associated with the Communist Party journal *Marxism Today*.

Britain has been afflicted for decades with a process of relative decline, as an industrial nation, and as a world power. Successive Conservative and Labour governments have been unable to halt or reverse this process despite temporary successes. Since the onset of world capitalist recession at the beginning of the 1970s, it has intensified, and Britain has suffered from a prolonged crisis, not only economic, but also a general social crisis which is manifested in many ways – intensified industrial struggle, urban decay, crises in welfare services, an upsurge of racism, a widespread crisis in relations between women and men, and so forth. The Conservative (1970–74) and Labour (1974–79) administrations of the 1970s were both ineffectual in dealing with this crisis, and both ended up in disarray – the miners' strike and the 3-day week for Edward Heath, the 'winter of discontent' for James Callaghan.

Thatcherism is a radical response from the right to these deep-seated problems and political failures. It is radical in the sense that it has broken with the 'postwar consensus', the political settlement following the Second World War which both main parties had hitherto respected, and whose main elements were commitments to full employment and the 'welfare state'. It therefore rejected post-war Conservatism, and especially the Conservatism associated with Heath, as decisively as it rejected social democratic Labourism. It set out to swing the political spectrum and the limits of acceptable political action decisively to the right.

To do so, it not only had to generate new policies, it also had to try to reconstruct the political map, and reconstitute its own political base. Thatcherism has been characterized as an 'authoritarian populism', a designation which tries to capture the new mix of political elements that it has attempted to put together. The first of these elements is an ('authoritarian') commitment to strengthening the state in certain respects (defence, 'law and order', control over money supply, control of trade unions, etc.) which gives continuity with traditional Conservatism. The second element, which originates in neo-liberalism, centres around a commitment to a 'free market' unencumbered by state 'interference', and entails 'rolling back' the state in other respects – notably in respect of its direct involvement in the economy through the nationalized industries. The third element is the 'populism': there is a direct appeal to 'ordinary people' which actually constructs 'the people' as a political entity in a nationalistic, anti-'state interference', anti-union, pro-family, pro-property and share-owning, and so forth, image.

This novel articulation of political elements is partly brought about in the novel restructurings of Thatcherite discourse. In their struggle with political opponents in their own party as well as outside it, the Thatcherites have problematized and de-structured the political discourse of their opponents, and attempted to impose their own restructuring. In our text, these processes are best represented in the constitution of a subject position for 'the people' (and more specifically the section thereof who make up the radio audience) as a political subject (question 3). They are also represented to an extent in the constitution of relations between Mrs Thatcher and her audience, and more generally between a political leader and 'the people', though the de-structuring of earlier (remote and authoritarian) relations is a problem which successive leaders have had to deal with.

The Thatcherites have also been faced with an articulatory problem not of their own making: how to establish a subject position for a woman political leader in a social context characterized by institutionalized sexism (question 2). Mrs Thatcher's own attempts are to some extent evident in the text, though they also require reference to features which are not represented – the way she sounds, and the way she looks. Finally, part of the radical nature of Thatcherism is a relatively aggressive political style which does not back away from attacking political opponents; this is reflected, though only to a very limited extent, in argumentative allusion to the intertextual context of the text (question 4).

Relations: Mrs Thatcher and 'the people'

An interview is an interaction between, usually, two people in a face-to-face setting, with interviewer and interviewee alternating (under the orchestration of the former) between the positions of speaker and addressee. However, when an interview takes place on radio or television, these relations become more complex, because both participants' contributions are likely to be affected by the audience, or *hearers*. Given the diverse and indeterminable composition of mass-media audiences, the speaker necessarily has to postulate, and set up a subject position for, a typified 'ideal' hearer, and question 3 will be particularly concerned with the nature of the subject position set up by Mrs Thatcher.

For the moment, it will be sufficient to say that the ideal hearer is assumed by Mrs Thatcher to be an 'ordinary person', a member of 'the people'. What we are concerned with here is what relationship Mrs Thatcher places herself in with 'the ordinary person' as represented by the radio audience. This is not just a matter of Mrs Thatcher and her audience; what we are concerned with is the particular configuration of discourse types underlying relations between political leaders and 'the people' in the discourse of Thatcherism. Notice that the hearer does not figure explicitly in the text at all; a subject position for the hearer is constituted indirectly through the way in which Mrs Thatcher represents the experience, beliefs, and aspirations of all of 'the people', and therefore by implication of the audience as well.

Here, then, is the first question, followed by my answer. I suggest that readers should focus their attention in gathering textual 'evidence' for their answers on the pronouns *we* and *you* (refer to question 6 in Ch. 5); on *relational* values of vocabulary items – note in particular differences between the interviewer's questions and Mrs Thatcher's answers and what these differences might imply in terms of Mrs Thatcher's control over the direction of the interview (see question 2 in Ch. 5); and on the relational implications of the assertions Mrs Thatcher makes about 'the people' (and therefore the audience) in, for example, lines (27)–(32).

Question 1: What relational values do textual features have? Are there inconsistencies in relational values which could indicate a new articulation of discourse types?

1. *We.* Mrs Thatcher (henceforth MT) uses the pronoun *we* mainly in lines (13)–(25) and (101)–(104), both inclusively and exclusively (see Ch. 5 p. 127 for the distinction). The inclusive use (e.g. *now we do enjoy a standard of living which was undreamed of then*) is relationally significant in that it represents MT, her audience, and everyone else as in the same boat. It assimilates the leader to 'the people'. Even in this case, however, it is not clear who exactly is being claimed to have this 'undreamed of' standard of living: when *we* refers to a collective like 'the British people', claims can be made about the collective which do not necessarily hold for any particular member of it – if *we* are better off, it doesn't follow that I am! Claiming that a collective has a certain standard of living when it is in fact characterized by gross disparities might be regarded as somewhat mystificatory.

This imprecision in terms of who is being referred to is even more marked in other cases. It is not clear, for instance, in lines (101)–(104) whether *we* is being used exclusively to refer to a collective (the state, the government) which excludes those addressed, or whether it is being used inclusively to refer to the whole 'people' like the previous example. This ambivalence effectively allows what the government was, believed and did to be put across as what 'the people' was, believed, did. Although the relational value is, again, to represent everyone as being in the same boat, the direction of assimilation is reversed: it assimilates 'the people' to the leader, or the leadership (the government). There is only one case of unambiguously exclusive *we*, in line (16), referring to MT's political party.

2. *You.* The pronoun *you* is used mainly as an indefinite pronoun, referring to people in general. It occurs most in lines (34)–(37), and (59)–(88). The relational value of *you* is partly to do with the significance of choosing it rather than the indefinite pronoun *one*. Readers might like to try replacing *you* with *one* to see how it changes the relational value (e.g. lines (80)–(82), *a house gives one some independence gives one a stake in the future one's concerned about one's children*). Firstly, *one* undermines the meaning of 'people in general' because people in general don't use the word – it is, roughly, a middle-class pronoun; it is therefore difficult to make an effective claim to 'ordinary people' about the common experience of 'ordinary' people using *one*. *You*, on the other hand, is used to register solidarity and commonality of experience in working-class speech. Secondly, *one* is sometimes used as a delicate way of saying *I*; the example I have just given could be interpreted in that way, as a delicate way of stating a self-centred perception of interests.

You, as I have been suggesting, claims solidarity, and by using it MT is able to pass off her practices, perceptions and precepts as those of 'the people' in general, and by implication claim for herself the status of one of 'the people'. It also, in the process, allows distinctions of perspective to be fudged. In lines (59)–(88), for example, it is instructive to see which of the following expressions can most easily be substituted for *you: the government, I, the ordinary person.* Lines (59)–(71) are mainly about the perspective of government, lines (72)–(77) could be interpreted as dressing up what MT and other Thatcherites think as if it were common belief (notice that *I expect* substitutes quite easily for *you expect* in lines (72), (73)–(74) and (76), and lines (80)–(88) are actually about 'the ordinary (middle-class!) person'. By reducing the concerns of (her sort of) government, the political credos of a political faction, and the aspirations of the affluent 'ordinary person' to the status of common experience, MT is also helping to constitute a subject position from which these do constitute a coherent set. This takes us on to the concerns of question 3.

3. *Relational values of vocabulary items*. It appears that MT's selection of vocabulary is in part oriented to the hearers, the audience, rather than the interviewer, and where this is so, she selects items which mark, again, her solidarity with 'the people'. In lines (29)–(36), the cliché *don't have to be told* as well as *pushed around*, and the euphemistic *do something for* (the community) fall into this category. The first two are expressions of casual conversation, while the third evokes for me middle-class members of voluntary organizations; one would not expect any of them if this discussion between two politically sophisticated intellectuals were private.

It is instructive to compare MC's questions and MT's answers in terms of vocabulary, because the differences indicate a relationally significant feature at the *textual* level. In lines (49)–(51), MC asks MT to be specific about her *vision* and what *inspires* her action. MT in her answer does not use expressions like these or, generally, the vocabulary of self-analysis and introspection. Looked at textually, MC seems to be asking for MT to be self-revelatory, but MT answers with a sketch of the Thatcherite view of the responsibilities and limits of the state. So MT's answer to the question is relatively non-compliant. Why? Perhaps because self-analysis (and its vocabulary) would in her judgement (and I think in fact) alienate some of the 'ordinary people' she is trying to show solidarity with.

There is another example in lines (114)–(120). MC appears to be asking MT to engage in a rather abstract debate on politics, which MT does not do. As a part of her non-compliance, her answer shifts the meaning of *radial* from its semi-technical political sense to an 'ordinary language' sense (*we needed to be radical* means much the same as *we needed to take decisive action*). She also rejects *populist*, no doubt partly on ideological grounds (the word belongs to a left analysis of Thatcherism), but partly perhaps because of its intellectualism. Notice that it is replaced by an expression (*strikes a chord in the hearts of ordinary people*) whose selection is a good example of populism: it conveys a sort of nationalistic sentimentality which is anathema to most intellectuals but a well-established strand in the outlook of some 'ordinary people'.

In both these cases, MT's answers steer the interview away from directions which MC seems to be trying to go in, but which would be problematic for MT in terms of her claims to solidarity with 'ordinary people'.

4. *Mrs Thatcher's assertions about 'the people'*. Finally, the assertions that MT makes about 'the people', in lines (27)–(32), for example. What is significant about these assertions in terms of MT's relationship to the audience and, as a political leader, to 'the people', is that she implicitly claims the authority to tell people what they are like – or, since she is

herself a part of 'the people', the right to articulate on its behalf its own self-perceptions. This has the effect of distancing MT and 'the people', marking her off as having a special authority, being the leader. This is certainly in marked contrast to the use of *you* and the vocabulary items I have referred to. But what about *we*? Although as I said above *we* puts everyone in the same boat and assimilates the leader to the people or vice versa, it does not have the solidarity value of *you*: in referring to *we*, MT again speaks in the role of leader, on behalf of 'the people'.

In summary, then, these textual features have contrasting values of solidarity and authority, which may suggest (see question 5) a new articulation of discourse types. Notice that all of these features could be interpreted in relation to subject positions under the rubrics of questions 2 and 3, and similarly the material discussed below in connection with these questions fills out what has been said so far about relations. This is not surprising: although the distinction between relations and subjects is analytically useful, there is no sharp dividing line in reality between social relations and social identities – indeed, a modification in one entails a modification in the other.

Subject position: woman political leader

The few women who achieve positions of prominence in industry, the professions, politics, or generally anywhere outside the home, are faced with a double-bind, 'heads I win, tails you lose', situation. This has been neatly summed up as 'damned if they behave like men, and damned if they don't'. They are damned if they behave like men, in the sense that masculine behaviour opens a woman to the slur, highly damaging in our society, of being 'unfeminine'. They are damned if they don't, in the sense that those in positions of prominence are accepted only if they conduct themselves in the way in which people in such positions always have. Since positions of prominence have traditionally gone with a very few exceptions (e.g. hospital matron, primary school headmistress) massively to men, this means in a masculine way.

MT has faced this dilemma in a particularly acute form because the sort of radical right politics that she has committed herself to puts particular emphasis on the need for tough, resolute, uncompromising and aggressive political leadership. All the adjectives

I have just used conventionally refer to the behaviour of men, and any woman whose behaviour has these qualities risks the 'unfeminine' jibe. Yet it is my impression that MT has managed to structure for herself a subject position as the woman political leader, which has allowed her to be quite widely perceived as having all these qualities without being unfeminine.

As I indicated earlier, this is partly a matter of how she sounds and how she looks, and it is a significant fact that she has taken a great deal of advice on both during the course of her career, and put in a great deal of work on changing both. I am suggesting that we look at her appearance in answering question 2. As to the way she sounds, she has, with professional tuition, lowered the pitch of her voice and reduced the speed at which she speaks. One motivation for doing so is that her voice used to be regarded as 'shrill'; 'shrillness' is very much (according to stereotypes) a feminine voice quality associated with being overly emotional. Apart from not sounding 'shrill', she now sounds more 'statesmanlike' and, according to some people, her husky voice quality is 'sexy'.

I suggest that for this question readers focus upon these features of the text: modality, especially the relational modality of obligation (*must, have got to,* etc.) and expressive modality (categorical truth, certainty, probability, possibility), focusing on lines (52)–(92) (see questions 6 and 7 in Ch. 5); turn-taking, specifically line (84) (cf. question 9, Ch. 5); features of the text which express 'toughness'; MT's assertions about 'the people', one example of which (lines (27)–(32)) was looked at under question 1; and MT's appearance – her hair, her clothes, her jewelry, etc. – in photographs of her you have seen.

Question 2: What values do textual features have in terms of the subject position of the producer? Are there inconsistencies which might indicate a novel articulation of discourse types?

1. *Modality.* The modalities which predominate in lines (52)–(92) are the relational meaning of 'obligation' expressed by the modal auxiliaries *have to, have got to, shoud,* and the expressive modality of categorical truth expressed by the present tense. There are some others I refer to below. For the moment, notice that both types of modality place MT in an authoritative position, with respect both to what must be done (by governments) and to what is the case.

It is significant that MT uses *have (got) to* where she might have used *must*. While *must* conveys the personal authority of the speaker, *have (got) to* conveys obligation based upon some external compulsion, which may for instance be the rules of an institution. MT's use of the latter implies that the obligation is not just based upon her say-so, but in some unspecified way based in the nature of government, as if the claims she is making about government were matters of fact rather than opinion. This impression of factuality is reinforced in lines (90)–(92): the proposition in a *that*- clause following *aware* is presupposed, so MT is now taking as a matter of given fact what she has just put forward as an opinion. The categorical present tense is best illustrated in lines (71)–(82). Notice that there is another authoritative expressive modal meaning in line (65) – impossibility (*can't*).

There are other modal meanings which are not authoritative. MT begins her answer to MC's question with an expressive modal meaning of possibility, which is moreover very tentatively worded (*I wonder if I perhaps I can answer*, as opposed to, say, *maybe I can answer*). This gives an impression of self-effacement which is in marked contrast with the predominantly authoritative modality; there is another expression with a rather similar value in (105)–(106), *that's always I suppose most difficult of all*. Then there is the expressive modal meaning of probability in lines (86)–(87). MT shifts from categorical truth to probability as she shifts from owning a home, part of general but by no means universal experience, to having savings and independent income, very much a minority situation. The step back from categorical meaning gives the impression of a discrete concession to the sensitivity of this for many people who have no hope of 'independent income', and that impression is reinforced by the minimizer *a little bit*. Thus there is some inconsistency in the values of modal features, between authoritativeness and self-effacement/discretion.

2. *Turn-taking*. The turn-taking feature in line (84) which I alluded to above is MC's attempt to interrupt MT and bring her back to the question he originally put to her and which, as I said above, she is answering rather non-compliantly. What is of interest is MT's rejection of MC's attempt to control the interview, and the way, polite but firm, in which it is worded (*please let me just go on*). MT generally treats what she regards as undue attempts to control her contributions in interviews in this way.

3. *'Toughness'*. Such turn-taking is one expression of MT's toughness and determination. Another is the use of *look* in line (27); beginning an utterance with *look* marks it as putting somebody in their place, or forcefully correcting their misapprehensions. Although MT purports to be quoting some unidentified mentor in this case, she makes quite a

lot of use of *look* on her own account; later in the same interview, MT quotes herself as *writing an article saying look if democracy is just going to be a public auction at election times it won't last.*

4. *MT's assertions about 'the people'*. I have already discussed the significance of MT's claim to the right to tell 'the people' about themselves, and it obviously fits in with other elements of the authoritative/tough side of MT's subject position. Notice just how much of this there is in the extract, and MT's overt reference to her authority in line (126) – *I know.*

5. *MT's appearance*. Finally, MT's appearance. MT has all the trappings of a certain middle-class smart adult femininity. Her hair is always carefully groomed, as if she had just emerged from the hairdresser. She favours smart two-piece suits. She wears brooches, necklaces and earrings. She generally carries a handbag.

Subject position: 'the people'

Any political party or political tendency needs to have a social base, some section or sections of a population whom it can claim to represent and can look to for support; it is commonplace for parties to project this social base onto the whole population, claiming that 'the people' have the properties of their own supporters. However, social bases do not necessarily exist ready-made; they (and by implication 'the people') often have to be constituted by welding together diverse social groupings into a coherent political constituency. This is particularly so in Britain for the Conservative Party, which has always depended on a constituency which included a substantial minority of the working class as well as the capitalist and 'middle' classes. And it is particularly true when there is a new tendency such as the Thatcherites, who cannot rely entirely upon a previously constructed constituency. But it is true also of the Labour Party, which regards itself as needing middle-class support to win elections.

Part of what is involved is the (re)structuring of a subject position for the people who are the targets of political discourse, especially mass audiences. In the case of the extract we are looking at, it is more specifically a subject position for the 'hearer', the radio audience as assumed representatives of 'the people'. What is involved is essentially a matter of projecting onto the audience a configuration of assumptions, beliefs, and values which accord with the mix of political elements which constitutes what I referred to above as the 'authoritarian populism' of Thatcherite politics. This is done indirectly, however, as I said above: MT makes many claims in the text about 'the people', which by implication position the audience as representatives of 'the people'.

For question 3, I suggest that we concentrate upon *coordination*. I introduced that term in Chapter 5 (question 8) for the case where simple sentences are combined with equal weight in a complex sentence, generally linked with *and, but* or *or*. In fact various grammatical elements can be coordinated apart from simple sentences – noun phrases and subordinate clauses, for instance. Let us focus upon elements linked by *and* or *but* in lines (58)–(59), (59)–(61), (67)–(69), (89)–(92). More prominent, though, are various *lists* in the text, whose elements can be regarded as coordinate, but which are not explicitly linked together – lists of assertions, lists of questions, lists of noun phrases, lists of *because*-clauses, in line (28)–(36), (38)–(41), (72)–(73), (79)–(80), (80)–(82), (103)–(104), (120)–(124).

Question 3: What values do textual features have with respect to the subject positions of members of the audience? Are there inconsistencies which might indicate a novel restructuring of discourse types?

Some of the coordinate structures in the text explicitly attribute properties to 'the British people' – those of lines (28)–(36), (89)–(92), (120)–(124). MT adds to these throughout the interview, but let me just quote one additional short extract: *it's not British we don't like being pushed around we're not going to ask the union bosses union bosses aren't there to be bosses over their people they're there to respond to the people.* Two other structures, the questions of lines (38)–(41) and the assertions of lines (80)–(82), list desirable qualities for a people, which I think we can take as implicitly contributing to the characterization of the audience subject position.

If we take all of these together, MT's construal of 'the people' can be summed up as follows: self-reliant, independent in thought and action, independent of government, responsible for their families, use resources wisely for the sake of their children, dislike being 'pushed around' (e.g. by 'union bosses', or – by implication – an interfering state), supportive of strong government (in certain respects), respect law and order, in favour of the family, involved in charitable works in the community, personally and politically loyal, economically efficient.

Of course, there are less charitable formulations one might think of, for example: self-centred and individualistic, authoritarian with respect to 'law and order' and state oppression generally, the family, trade unions, and the welfare state, chauvinistic, . . . and so forth! What is evident in either version, however, is the conjunction of the neo-liberal element of individual self-reliance and the reduction of welfare support for individuals and families, and more traditional conservative elements such as support for a strong state when it comes to law and order or international relations, and support for the traditional conception of the family.

Let us now turn to other structures not referred to so far. The example in lines (58)–(59) attributes two properties to Britain – *defend its freedom* and *be a reliable ally*. Britain is personified here (people can literally have these properties, but not states), which makes it easy to read these attributes as applying again to 'the people', especially since the second of them is echoed in *loyal allies* in line (124). The example in lines (103)–(104) applies the same pair of attributes to *we*, which as I noted above can be taken as referring either to the government or to 'the people' as a whole. Since by this stage we recognize these attributes as those of 'the people', it makes it easier to interpret *we* as referring to 'the people'.

In other cases, we find a coordination of wordings which may reflect MT's sensitivity to the diversity of the audience she is trying to weld into a single constituency. Perhaps the best example is in lines (79)–(80), *the ownership of property of a house*. For some of MT's constituency, owning property means something much more glamorous than having a mortgage, but for the majority it could never be much more than that. Another case is in lines (67)–(69), where *uphold the value of the currency* is an expression which is accessible to all of the audience, whereas *sound finance* is a semi-technical expression belonging to Thatcherite economic theory which only those 'in the know' would pick up. A rather different example is that in lines (59)–(61), where the second part of the coordination personifies governmental matters in terms of interpersonal relations (*stand by your word*) perhaps as a way of getting the point across to certain parts of the audience. One thinks here of Mrs Thatcher's well-known analogies between the national economy and domestic housekeeping. The final example is quite different: the coordination of *thriving industries thriving services* in lines (72)–(73) is a small instance of ideological creativity whose interpretation requires of the audience the implicit assumption that services can be evaluated according to criteria of success analogous to those which apply to industries – a truly Thatcherite assumption. This example in fact is a matter of contents, of representation of the world.

Finally, a note on the significance of MT's use of lists. Where one has lists, one has things placed in connection, but without any indication of the precise nature of the connection. This means that the interpreter has to 'do the work', in the sense of inferring connections which are left implicit. In so far as MT's lists are doing ideological 'work' upon her audience, therefore, members of the audience are being drawn into doing some of this work on themselves!

Struggle: the intertextual context

As I said earlier, Thatcherism does not draw back from attacking political opponents, though in the text we are looking at there are no overt references at all to opponents. There are, however, a small number of covert allusions to them, which we can regard in accordance with Chapter 6 (pp. 154–55) as allusions to oppositional texts in the intertextual context. In answering this question, focus upon the two negative sentences in lines (29)–(30), the emphatic and contrastive assertions (marked with capital letters on emphasized words) of lines (62)–(63), (65), (72)–(73), (120)–(124).

Question 4: What traces are there in the features of the text of struggle between the producer and her opponents?

1. *Negative sentences*. Negative assertions evoke and reject corresponding positive assertions in the intertextual context. But the picture is rather more complicated than this suggests in the case of the negative assertions of lines (29)–(30), because it is hardly credible to attribute the positive assertions *they do have to be told* and *they do like to be (are willing to be) pushed around* to MT's political opponents. The point is that in alluding to opposition texts in the intertextual context, producers standardly reformulate them, substituting for the wording of their opponents an ideologically contrastive wording of their own. In this case, for instance, MT is alluding to and arguing against positive assertions which are more likely to be worded as something like *people need guidance* or *people are quite willing to accept guidance (from welfare agencies)*.

2. *Emphatic assertion*. This is really the converse of negation: it evokes and rejects a corresponding negative assertion. In the example in lines (62)–(63), for example (*yes, you HAVE got to be strong on law and order*), a negative assertion like *you don't need to make a big issue of law and order* (allowing for MT's reformulation as above) is attributed to the intertextual context. Similarly in line (65). In lines (120)–(124), however, contrastive assertion works rather differently: it is a way of

reiterating assertions which MT has made earlier in the extract. The one instance of contrastive assertion is in lines (72)–(73): *people* carries emphasis, with the effect that this is interpreted as 'you expect people and not X to create thriving industries thriving services'. It is left to the audience to determine the identity of X on the basis of their social knowledge, as well as the immediate context in which MT is opposing *people* to *government*. I assume X is governments, and that MT is here reflecting the policies of her political opponents that government ought to exercise direct control over the economy, as well as services. The coordination of *thriving industries thriving services*, which I have remarked on above, is quite subtle here in attributing to the opposition a commitment to government responsibility for services construed as having the same success criteria as industries.

Interpretation

We now need to try to partially reconstruct MT's production process in order to show how problems arise and how she tries to resolve them. Ideally, we ought also to reconstruct the interpretative processes of members of the audience, because otherwise we have no way of knowing whether MT's resolutions 'work' for the audience. But I shall just make one or two comments on this at the end, given that we have not included information on the audience in the case study. We would also ideally supplement the information we have available for interpreting MT's production process – with her own rationalizations of the textual choices she made, for example.

I shall make the simplifying assumption below that the ways in which MT attempts to resolve problems, and associated novel combinations of discourse types, are specific to and new to the particular discourse from which the extract is taken. In fact, this is certainly not the case. MT is drawing upon combinations of discourse types which have become conventional for her, which do not need to be recreated anew in each discourse. We may think of these as accumulated 'capital' from all her previous creative restructuring 'work'. My simplifying assumption will thus make this particular discourse appear to be much more innovatory than it is.

Question 5: What problems arise for MT in the process of production through mismatches between her resources, and her analysis of the situation? And what novel combinations of discourse types does she generate in trying to resolve them?

Let us begin with the interpretation of the situational context, using the framework of Chapter 6 (pp. 146–52). The interpretation I suggest seems on the evidence of the text to be that which MT is operating with. In terms of 'what's going on', the activity type is a broadcast political interview; notice that this gives it a dual institutional status, in politics and in broadcasting. In terms of 'who's involved' and 'in what relations', the subject positions for participants are: (i) speaker, addressee, and hearers (speaking and listening positions associated with the situation); (ii) interviewer, interviewee, and 'onlookers' (positions associated with the activity type). Since there is dual institutional status, we have (iii) two sets of identities ascribed to participants by institutions: those of broadcasting – media personality, journalist, audience; and those of politics – political leader, journalist, members of 'the public'. Other relevant aspects of the participants are that MT is a woman speaking to a male interviewer before a mixed audience, and that the audience is likely to be socially and politically diverse – though within limits given that this is a Radio 3 interview.

I would assume that, so far, the interviewer's (MC's) interpretation would not differ much from MT's. But they are likely to interpret purposes and topics (aspects of 'what's going on') rather differently. For MC, the institutional matrix for the discourse is broadcasting, and politics has a subsidiary status, as a topic; the hearers are primarily a radio audience, and MT is primarily a 'personality'. Correspondingly, the purpose of the programme (and indeed of the series it belongs to) is seen as giving the audience access to the views of an important public figure.

MT on the face of it accepts all this. But at a covert level, she is virtually bound as a politician to see the institutional matrix for the discourse as politics, to see broadcasting as a vehicle for politics, to see the hearers as primarily members of 'the public', and herself as primarily a political leader. Consequently, MT has beneath her superficial acceptance of MC's definition of purposes, an unacknowledged (though widely understood) *strategic* purpose, to make a politically favourable impact on the members of 'the public' in the audience. This strategic purpose leads MT not to 'be herself' and try to relate to the audience as she assumes it to be, but to *construct* an image of herself, of her audience, and of their relationship, which accords with her strategic purpose.

I am focusing on the situational context rather than the intertextual context, but let us think of the latter for a moment. MT has to assess the intertextual experience of both the interviewer and her audience in order to determine what can be left unsaid, and what texts can be alluded to. Her assessment of the audience seems to be decisive; she avoids assuming intertextual experience which the interviewer would have but many of the audience would not. An example is the textual traces of struggle discussed in connection with question 4.

Let us now turn to mismatches between elements of this analysis, and MT's resources, and how she appears to attempt to resolve them. I shall follow the order of questions 1–3 above, discussing in turn relations, MT's subject position, and the subject position for the audience.

In the case of relations, I shall assume to simplify matters that MT's resources include discourse types which embody assumptions about social relationships between political leaders and 'the public' that roughly correspond to those that Churchill, Attlee or Eden among post-war British Prime Ministers would have had. Summed up as a recipe for political leadership, they amount to 'keep your distance and assert your authority'. In fact, Prime Ministers since the war have increasingly experienced the problematization of this remote and authoritarian relationship, for reasons I refer to under question 6. In this example, we can see this as arising immediately from a mismatch between these resources and the analysis of participant relations which MT is trying to impose upon the context for strategic purposes. Different politicians have produced various versions of the sort of strategy of problem resolution that MT adopts – combining relational elements of conversational discourse which express solidarity (*you*, etc.) with relational elements of a more traditional political discourse type which express authority (speaking on behalf of 'the people'). The recipe changes to 'claim solidarity but assert your authority'. There is a risk that in claiming solidarity, one will be unable to sustain authority, which makes this a problematic mix to achieve. It is particularly problematic for MT because of the traditional exclusion of women from authority positions. This leads us to the next mismatch.

In the case of MT's subject position, there is a mismatch between the resources which politicians have had available (I exclude changes in resources which MT herself had contributed to bringing about before this interview), including assumptions embedded in discourse types that the subject position of a political leader was a male position, and not only the obvious fact that MT is a woman, but also the image of herself which MT wishes to project into the context for strategic reasons. Notice that the problem in this case is not a matter of the de-structuring of a previous structure of discourse types for a woman leader – there has never been such a structure. MT's strategy of problem resolution can be summed up as the recipe 'be authoritative, decisive and tough, yet do not compromise your femininity'. This sounds contradictory, because the three adjectives in the first part are all associated with masculinity. What MT has done is to combine authoritative expressive elements of a traditional male political discourse type (e.g. the authoritative modality); 'tough' expressive elements (*look*, rejection of interviewer control over her turns) from other male discourse types; and 'feminine' expressive elements most obviously from a visual 'discourse' of fashion, but also the nonauthoritative modality features – the values of self-effacement and discretion which I ascribed to these are stereotypically feminine. Although MT is remarkably successful in constructing a feminine leader position, it is anything but a *feminist* position. See question 6 for discussion.

Finally, the subject position for those members of 'the public' who make up the audience. The mismatch in this case is between the assumptions one would find in the discourse of more traditional forms of Conservatism about 'the public', and 'the public' which MT's particular political commitments and objectives lead her to construct. MT's strategy is, as we have seen, to combine elements of traditional Conservative discourse (patriotism, commitment to family, etc.), with a 'neo-liberal' discourse (against state 'interference', etc.). Further properties of her construction of 'the people' follow from what has been said about relations and about MT's subject position: 'the people' accepts leaders who are tough and decisive, and accepts that these leaders have the right to claim solidarity with 'the people' and articulate their desires, hopes, fears, and so on. This is a populist projection of 'the people', a further element in MT's novel restructuring.

Explanation

In accordance with the concerns of the stage of explanation as presented in Chapter 6, we now need to look at MT's discourse as an element in social processes at the institutional and societal levels, and to show how it is ideologically determined by, and ideologically determinative of, power relations and power struggle at these levels. I shall split Question 6 into two parts, corresponding to the two levels: social institution, and society.

Question 6a: What institutional processes does this discourse belong to, and how is it ideologically determined and ideologically determinative?

The institutional matrix of this discourse is actually rather complex, because 'politics' actually cuts across a number of institutions: political parties, political institutions (e.g. Parliament), governmental institutions (e.g. state bureaucracies), and of course the media. An interesting question is the trajectory which Thatcherite discourse has followed across institutional boundaries. In the present example, the immediate institutional matrix is the media, broadcasting, though as I suggested above, MT does not allow herself to be constrained by that matrix.

The institutional processes which this discourse belongs to are, generally, the struggle between political parties (in the media and other institutions) for political support and political (governmental) power, and, more specifically, the struggle of the Thatcherite 'new right' for ascendancy in the Conservative Party; then governmental power; then the building of a new political consensus. Recall the general discussion of Thatcherism above. The discourse of Thatcherism of which we have a sample has been an important factor in this struggle, and perhaps a good example of the capacity of discourse to affect power relations and the outcome of struggles, through its shaping and determining effect on ideologies. I shall focus at this level on ways in which the discourse of MT is ideologically determinative and creative, and discuss ways in which it is ideologically determined under question 6b.

MT's discourse can be regarded as potentially ideologically determinative with respect to social relationships in so far as it effects a particular articulation of authority and solidarity in relations between MT as a political leader and 'the public'. In fact, however, as I suggested above, it is rather artificial to isolate MT's contribution or the contribution of Thatcherism, in that they form part of a wider reconstitution of the leader/'public' relation which has involved all the main political parties. In part, the dramatic growth in the importance of the media as an institutional site for political struggle explains this: it would be difficult to maintain a remote and paternalistic relation given the overwhelming commitment of the media to egalitarian relationships between media workers and 'performers' and audiences. But there are I think deeper societal reasons which I touch on below. Versions of the solidarity/authority mix are now conventional for political leaders, but their effects in terms especially of solidarity upon the actual social relationship between politicians and the rest of the population cannot be taken for granted. The solidarity of the politicians is with constructed and fictional 'publics'; they do not claim solidarity with all the diverse sections of the actual 'public', nor one imagines would such a claim be reciprocated! There is a spurious and imaginary quality about this 'solidarity' which I return to under question 6b.

MT's ideological impact in respect of the social identities of the woman political leader and of 'the public' is more specifically due to her own creations. MT has brought to the institutions of politics a new sort of leader who combines traditional properties of authoritativeness with a tough and aggressive style, and with being a woman. In so far as she has established a tough and aggressive style of leadership, she has strengthened the position of the new right in British politics. To what extent she has strengthened the position of women is a more open question; no doubt women will find it easier to hold leading political positions thanks to the ground MT has broken, but within severe limits – see question 6b for discussion. As to the social identity of 'the public', MT and the Thatcherites certainly appear to an extent to have produced a social base for the competitive individualism which they advocate.

Now question 6b, and a shift from the institutional level to the societal level:

Question 6b: What societal processes does this discourse belong to, and how is it ideologically determined and ideologically determinative?

I shall comment upon this discourse as a part of two societal processes: class struggle between the capitalist class (or the dominant bloc it constitutes) and the working class and its allies; and the struggle between women and men. Here I shall focus not just upon the ideologically determinative aspects of the discourse as I did under question 6a, but on the way in which the ideologically determinative elements interact with the ideologically determined elements. This will bring us back to the dialectical relationship between the social determination of the subject and the creativity of the subject from which we started at the beginning of the chapter.

Let us begin with social relationships. In our capitalist society, the dominant bloc exercises economic and political domination over the working class and other intermediate strata of the population, as I argued in Chapter 2 (see *Class and power in capitalist society*, pp. 31–36). Consequently, the relationship of power-holders in public life to the mass of the population is a controlling and authoritative one. In politics, as in other domains, those who aspire to power – the parties which seek governmental power – have sought to ameliorate to varying degrees the condition of the working class but not to challenge class domination. The authority element in political leadership, as in leadership in other domains, is thus determined by class relations.

Why, then, have political leaders affected solidarity with 'the people'? Essentially, I think, in response to changes in the balance of power between the capitalist class and its dominant bloc and the rest of society. The twentieth century has witnessed a gradual, though not always smooth, increase in the capacity of the working class and its allies to determine the course of events within capitalism – through the growth of the trade unions, through political representation in Parliament and government via the Labour Party, and so forth. Correspondingly, there has emerged a 'partnership' ideology which has tried to portray capitalist society as controlled by the 'partnership' between capitalists and workers. Surface markers of social inequality

have disappeared *en masse* from many institutions, of which politics is
only one.

The 'solidarity' of political leaders with 'the public' is particularly
closely related to a more general phenomenon of the mass media and
other social domains – *synthetic personalization*, a concept I introduced
in Chapter 3 (p. 60) and which I shall have more to say about in
Chapter 8. Synthetic personalization simulates solidarity: it seems that
the more 'mass' the media become, and therefore the less in touch
with individuals or particular groupings in their audiences, the more
media workers and 'personalities' (including politicians) purport to
relate to members of their audience as individuals who share large
areas of common ground. This form of 'solidarity' functions as a
strategy of containment: it represents a concession to the strength of
the working class and its allies on the one hand, but constitutes a veil
of equality beneath which the real inequalities of capitalist society can
carry on, on the other. Thus the ideologically creative and
determinative element is contained within the ideologically
determining element. This is the relationship which, I shall suggest,
exists right across Thatcherite discourse.

Turning to the social identity of a woman political leader, we can
again see a strategy of containment at work beneath the advance in the
position of women which MT's construction achieves on the surface.
After MT, there are powerful women. But in being powerful, MT
projects a style of womanhood which is essentially patriarchal, and
which reproduces patriarchal society in the process of appearing to
break through it. Paradoxically, then, what looks like a gain for
women is a defeat for feminism. As in the case of social relationships,
there is an element of concession in MT's achievement: a concession to
the growing strength of women in the economy, the professions, and
public life. But it is, again, a double-edged concession, which contains
the advance of women within patriarchal limits. Similar things could
be said about the limits within which women are advancing into
relatively more powerful positions in industry, the professions, the
police, and so forth.

The case with the social identity which MT sets up for 'the public' is
somewhat different, in that what is involved is not a concession in any
sense. However, it is still the case that the apparent ideological
creativity is contained within parameters set down by the longer-term
power relations within which MT is operating. More traditional
Conservative constructions of 'the public' stress some elements which
appear in MT's but not others. They stress in particular commitments
such as nation and family as definitive of 'the public'. In the context of
class power in a capitalist society, however, what is decisive is not so
much precisely how 'the public' is defined, as ensuring that people are

not defined in terms of their social class. In this respect, the Thatcherite 'public' is a mere local variant of other versions. And there are affinities between politics and various other institutional domains in which some mass 'public' is constituted – for instance, the 'consumers' of advertising, where again social class, position in processes of economic production, and so forth, never figure.

CONCLUSION

I have suggested immediately above that MT's discourse is characterized by a relationship of containment between what is ideologically creative and what is ideologically determining, the former developing only within limits set down by the latter. This is a particular illustration of the general claim that I made at the beginning of this chapter about the relationship between individual creativity and social determination. Individual creativity, in discourse and more generally, is never the wilful and extra-social business it is commonly portrayed as being; there are always particular social circumstances which enable it, and constrain it, and which may even (as in this case) partially vitiate it.

REFERENCES

I have drawn extensively for this chapter on Kress G 1985, which contains a helpful discussion of relationships between the subject, creativity, and social determination in discourse. The work of Foucault, especially Foucault M 1972, is a general backdrop to this chapter. Two interesting approaches to political discourse are those of Faye and Laclau and Mouffe – see Faye J P 1972 and Thompson J B 1984, Ch. 6, on the former and Laclau E, Mouffe C 1985. On Thatcherism see the periodical *Marxism Today*, and the collection of papers taken from it edited by Hall and Jacques (Hall S, Jacques M 1983). On the discourse of Thatcherism see Harding S 1983. Candlin C N, Lucas J L 1986 gives a suggestive analysis of the creative combination of discourse types in the discourse of family planning counselling.

EIGHT

Discourse in social change

CLS (critical language study) should direct its attention to discoursal dimensions of major social tendencies, in order to determine what part discourse has in the inception, development and consolidation of social change. This implies concentrating our attention upon changes in the societal order of discourse during a particular period. In this chapter, I hope to make a modest beginning, by looking at the relationship between certain social tendencies and certain tendencies in orders of discourse in contemporary capitalism. Readers will recall that I briefly discussed this relationship in Chapter 2 (pp. 35–36). Although I shall be referring to Britain, both social tendencies and discoursal tendencies seem to have parallels in other similar societies.

TENDENCIES IN SOCIETY AND DISCOURSE: A SUMMARY

At the centre of Jürgen Habermas's analysis of contemporary capitalism is the claim that it is characterized by a degree of 'colonization' of people's lives by 'systems' that has reached crisis proportions. The 'systems' are money and power – or the economy, and the state and institutions. On the one hand, in the form of *consumerism*, the economy and the commodity market have a massive and unremitting influence upon various aspects of life, most obviously through the medium of television and in advertising. On the other hand, unprecedented state and institutional control (specifically by 'public' institutions) is exercised over individuals through various forms of bureaucracy.

What I want to suggest is that those forms of 'colonization' of people's lives are partly constituted by 'colonizations' in the societal order of discourse. A societal order of discourse is a particular structuring of constituent institutional orders of discourse, and (as we saw in Chapter 7) given structurings may be de-structured in the course of social struggle. The social tendencies identified by Habermas can be seen as imposed in struggle by the dominant bloc, and as involving the de-structuring of previous societal orders of discourse. Many readers will I am sure be conscious of this process, and specifically of the way in which discourses of consumerism and bureaucracy have 'colonized' other discourse types, or expanded at their expense. Readers will find it useful to have examples of their own in mind as they read through this chapter.

We can think of these restructurings in terms of changes in salient relationships between discourse types within the societal order of discourse. Discourse types of consumerism, most notably the discourse of *advertising*, and discourse types of bureaucracy, such as the discourse of interviewing, have come to be particularly salient or prominent within the order of discourse. This means not only that they have a high profile – that people are aware of their importance – but also that they constitute models which are widely drawn upon. They are both types of what we might call, following Habermas, *strategic* discourse, discourse oriented to instrumental goals, to getting results. Strategic discourse is broadly contrastive with *communicative* discourse, which is oriented to reaching understanding between participants. And their salience is therefore interpretable as a general colonization of communicative discourse by strategic discourse in the societal order of discourse. (Notice that this is a special and unusually narrow sense of 'communicative'.)

These impingements of the economy and the state upon life have resulted in problems and crises of social identity for many people which have been experienced and dealt with individually, rather than through forms of social struggle. A great many people now seek some form of 'help' with their 'personal problems', be it in the casual form of 'problem' columns or articles in magazines, or through various forms of therapy or counselling. The discourses of therapy, counselling, and so forth have correspondingly come to be a further socially salient group within the societal order of discourse. As in the case of consumerist and bureaucratic discourse types, they are a 'colonizing' centre within the order of discourse.

In what follows, I shall discuss these aspects of the societal order of discourse in turn, under the headings:

Advertising and consumerism

Discourse technologies and bureaucracy

The discourse of therapy

And, to avoid any impression that the tendencies which I have identified above are the only ones in contemporary capitalism, which they are not, I conclude the chapter with a brief discussion of other, in one sense contrary, tendencies in society and discourse.

ADVERTISING AND CONSUMERISM

I begin this section with a discussion of 'consumerism', and then go on to look at the British Code of Advertising Practice as a way of identifying the ideological 'work' of advertisements. Three dimensions of the ideological work of advertising discourse are then discussed in turn: the relationship it constructs between the producer/advertiser and the consumer, the way it builds an 'image' for the product, and the way it constructs subject positions for consumers. These dimensions constitute respectively the constraining of relations, contents and subjects, in the terms I have used throughout the book. I then discuss the relationship between verbal and visual elements in advertising, and the increasing salience of visual images. Finally, I come to what I referred to above as the 'colonizing' tendencies of advertising discourse.

Consumerism

Consumerism is a property of modern capitalism which involves a shift in ideological focus from economic production to economic consumption, and an unprecedented level of impingement by the economy on people's lives. Let us briefly trace the emergence of consumerism before looking at its contemporary impact.

Consumerism grew out of sets of economic, technological and cultural conditions which have mostly developed since the early decades of the twentieth century; although we can identify consumerist tendencies in the earlier part of this period, in the 1920s for instance, consumerism has grown in salience through the period as these three types of conditions have developed. And, indeed, it has helped to feed its own growth by contributing to these developments, particularly in the cultural sphere.

The economic conditions relate, firstly, to the stage of development of capitalist commodity production. Consumerism is a product of mature capitalism when productive capacity is such that an apparently endless variety of commodities can be produced in apparently unlimited quantities. The second aspect of the economic conditions is the position of the workforce: consumerism is dependent on wage levels which leave a substantial section of the population with a significant residue after meeting subsistence costs, and on a reduction in working hours which creates significant amounts of leisure time.

The technological conditions are, firstly, a modern press, which was already in place at the beginning of the century; but secondly, the development of film, radio, and television. It is with the emergence of television not only as a technology but as a cultural institution which has absorbed a high proportion of the leisure time of a high proportion of the population, that consumerism has really 'taken off'.

The third set of conditions, and the one which is in focus here, is cultural. Capitalism, in the processes of industrialization and urbanization, has fractured traditional cultural ties associated with the extended family, the local or regional or ethnic community, religion, and so forth. In certain circumstances, these traditional ties have been replaced by ties generated by people in their new urban and industrial environments, notably ties of class.

But this has not always happened, and even where such ties have existed, they have in many cases been undermined, by de-industrialization for example. Many readers will be familiar with the ways in which people experience loss or lack of a community: rootlessness, the loss of a sense of reality, uncertainty about one's own social identity, and so forth. For many people, these are perceived as purely *individual* experiences. This cutting off of people from cultural communities which could provide them with senses of identity, values, purposes, is what underlies the growth of, broadly, therapeutic practice and discourse, as I argue later.

Of more immediate concern is the way in which capital, through the mediation of the advertisers, has been able to purport to fill these gaps. Advertising is of course the most visible practice, and discourse, of consumerism, and its most immediately striking characteristic is its sheer scale. We are all exposed to massive daily injections of advertising. Readers might like to work out how many advertisements they see or hear each day, on TV, radio, in newspapers and magazines, on hoardings, coming through the letter box, in shops and shopping centres, and so forth. It is on the basis of sheer quantity that advertising is able to achieve its most significant qualitative effects: the constitution of cultural communities to replace those which capitalism has destroyed, and which provide people with needs and values. Or *displace* rather than replace: ersatz communities are offered as alternatives to real ones. These communities have been called *consumption communities*. The unprecedented degree of impingement of the economy on people's lives, which I referred to above, consists in this. The next question is, how?

Ideology and the British Code of Advertising Practice

I shall approach the question of how advertising constructs consumption communities indirectly, by way of a discussion of some extracts from the British Code of Advertising Practice, a voluntary code of practice administered by the Advertising Standards Authority, which applies to printed material and cinema. The Advertising Standards Authority is financed by the advertising industry, though it claims to be independent. A rather similar compulsory code applies to radio and television, administered by the Independent Broadcasting Authority.

Here are three short extracts from the abridged version of the Code:

1. All advertisements should be legal, decent, honest and truthful.

2. The Code's rules on truthful presentation place no constraint upon the free expression of opinion, including subjective assessments of the quality or desirability of products, provided always that
   — it is clear what is being expressed is opinion;
   — there is no likelihood of the opinion or the way it is expressed misleading consumers about any matter in respect of which objective assessment, upon a generally accepted basis, is practicable.

3. No advertisement should cause children to believe that they will be inferior to other children, or unpopular with them, if they do not buy a particular product, or have it bought for them.

The main point that I want to make is that the Code is directed at controlling more surface-level features of advertising which relate to its nature as strategic and more particularly persuasive communication, in the sense of being oriented to selling things (see further below), but ignores what I suggest is the societally more important *ideological* work of advertising. For the short answer to the question of how advertising constructs consumption communities is, 'through ideology'

1 above sums up a central part of the Code, and 2 is part of the more detailed specification of 'truthful' advertising. It shows the Code working with a sharp differentiation between matters of fact, which are open to objective assessment, and matters of opinion, which are subjective. In the case of matters of fact, advertisements are required to substantiate claims with proper evidence. The options of 'fact' or 'opinion' are the only ones available in the Code when an advertisement is evaluated in terms of its relationship to truth.

But this is based upon a very superficial view of the relationship of discourse to truth, in the sense that it takes account only of explicit claims and evaluations. What about *implicit assumptions*, where discourse takes truth for granted? Implicit assumptions are a necessary part of all discourse, and, as we saw in Chapter 4, typically of an ideological nature. The Code manages, in ignoring the implicit side of truth in discourse, to overlook ideology. This oversight is, I think, strikingly evident in 3: it is my impression that advertisements do cause children to have the beliefs referred to on a significant scale, not by openly alluding to detrimental peer-group consequences for the child who fails to buy a particular toy (let us say), but implicitly, by ideology.

In the sections below, I shall spell out in some detail how advertisements work ideologically. Let me summarize what I shall be saying:

1. *Building relations.* Advertising discourse embodies an ideological representation of the relationship between the producer/advertiser of the product being advertised and the audience, which facilitates the main ideological 'work'.

2. *Building images.* Advertisements get their audiences to draw upon ideological elements in their MR in order to establish an 'image' for the product being advertised.

3. *Building the consumer.* Advertisements, using the 'images' which audiences 'help' them to generate for products as vehicles, construct subject positions for 'consumers' as members of consumption communities; this, as I suggested earlier, is the major ideological work of advertising.

An example

We shall be working with the example shown in Text 8.1 throughout the rest of the discussion of advertising.

Building relations

The Miele advertisement, like advertisements in general, is 'public' discourse in the sense that it has a mass and indeterminable audience. It also has a complex and indeterminable (from the point of view of the audience) producer, made up in part of the team who produce the magazine it is taken from (*Radio Times*), in part of the advertising agency team which designed it, and in part of the manufacturer of the washing machine who is trying to sell it. And it is 'one-way' discourse in the sense that the producer and interpreter roles do not alternate – the advertiser is the producer, and the audience are interpreters. Advertisements, of course, share these properties with the discourse of the mass media in general.

Both the mass and indeterminate nature of the audience, and the complex and indeterminate nature of the producer, present the advertiser with a challenge. For it will be individual members of the audience who will read the advertisement and (perhaps!) buy the product, and so somehow the advertiser needs to direct an appeal, presupposing a determinate appealer, to individual audience members. Both producer and audience need to be *personalized*, but because of the actual conditions of production and interpretation of advertising discourse, this has to be *synthetic personalization* – recall the introduction of this term in Chapter 3 (p. 60).

Text 8.1 Source: Miele Company Ltd

Look, with attention to textual features, at how the synthetic personalization of the audience member and the producer are achieved in this advertisement.

In part, the synthetic personalization of the audience member is a matter of the position which is constructed for the consumer, which is discussed below. But it is also in part a matter of the personalized relationship between producer and consumer, as evidenced in textual features which are widespread in advertising discourse – direct address of audience members with *you*, and imperative sentences (e.g. *think of it as a load off your mind*).

The synthetic personalization of the producer is partly achieved through the fact that individual audience members *are* directly addressed: that implies an individual addresser. The addresser is not specifically identified; this text differs from others which have the 'corporate' *we* to identify the addresser as spokesperson for the company which produces the commodity. However, the addresser is individualized through the expressive values of textual elements she (purportedly!) selects. Notice for instance the structure of the sentences in the body of the text (i.e. excluding headings): the familiar advertising elements (appeal to readers, account of the commodity and its benefits, invitation to readers to follow up the advertisement) including a lot of claims about the machine are concisely packed into mainly short, snappy sentences. It is the syntax of concise, no-nonsense, to-the-point efficiency, and the constructed addresser is individualized in terms of these properties. So, as I argue below, are both the machine and the consumer: the addresser speaks to the audience member in her own voice, about a commodity which chimes with both.

Building images

Advertisements get their audiences to draw upon ideological elements in their MR in order to establish an 'image' for the product being advertised. How does this work in the case of the Miele advertisement?

It works I think through cues in the advertising text, both verbal and visual, evoking a frame for a 'modern' lifestyle, roughly that associated with younger and more dynamic fractions of the middle class, which is then used to 'interpret' the product as part of this lifestyle. The visual cues are the elegant, unfussy and spotless decor of the room, which bespeaks an efficient and sophisticated household, and the defocused garden scene on the right, with (one assumes) the woman and man of the household enjoying the fruits of their efficiency. The verbal cues are the many expressions for the priorities of the 'modern' lifstyle – ease, efficiency, economy, beauty: *a load off your mind, easy to use, economical, efficient, reliable, durable,* and so forth.

The product image is produced by association, so to speak: by being associated with the elegant and efficient 'modern' lifestyle, the washing machine becomes a part of it. Its properties as a physical object, as a piece of engineering, are enhanced in the process of image-building, in that it comes to have cultural properties in addition to its physical properties. This process of enhancement is crucial for modern commodities, especially when several products with more or less the same material properties are in competition for a particular market.

But in what sense is this an ideological process? It is ideological because the frame it evokes, for what I have referred to as a 'modern' lifestyle, is an ideological construct which is both used as a vehicle for the generation of the product image, and produced and reproduced in its own right in the process. The frame packages together social subjects in particular sorts of relationship, activities, settings, values, and so on, in a powerful prescription for how one should live, or at least what one should acknowledge to be the best way to live, in the modern world, together with the myth that this lifestyle is open to everyone. It is ideological because the keynote values of this lifestyle overlap with the preoccupations of contemporary capitalism – with maximal *efficiency* as a target not only in economic activities (where it has long been familiar) but in all the details of a person's 'private' (but no longer so private!) life. By leading people to acknowledge and pursue this lifestyle (see below), advertising is helping to legitimize contemporary capitalism.

Building the consumer

I said above that the major ideological work of advertising was constructing subject positions for consumers as members of consumption communities, and that this work used the images which members of the audience generate for products as vehicles. Let us now see how this works for the Miele advertisement.

Characterize the subject position that is set up in the Miele advertisement for the reader. What sort of community would the ideal occupier of this subject position belong to? How does the reader's image of the product contribute to positioning the reader as a consumer subject?

The answer to this question follows closely upon the answer to the last one. The subject position set up for the reader is defined precisely in terms of acceptance as naturalized common sense of the ideological frame which one needs to interpret the advertisement and assign an image to the product. The ideal occupier of this subject position belongs to a community whose needs and values and tastes are those embedded in this frame. It is a community which is preoccupied with the easification of life at the least possible cost. That is, it is a community of *consumers*, for these preoccupations are ascribed generally to consumers. It is a community which requires its easified environment to have practical and aesthetic properties such as those represented here – functionality, ease of maintenance, unfussy elegance – and which has a particular idea of leisure, alluded to in the garden scene. That is, it is a community with very particular tastes.

But in what sense can one talk of advertisements *building* the consumer, or the consumption community? Advertising has made people into consumers, i.e. has brought about a change in the way people are, in the sense that it has provided the most coherent and persistent models for consumer needs, values, tastes and behaviour. It has done this by addressing people as if they were all commonsensically already fully fledged consumers. The general point is that if people are obliged day-in day-out to occupy the subject position of consumer, there is a good chance that they will become consumers. What may begin as a sort of game, a suspicious experimentation for audience members, is likely through the sheer weight of habit to end up being for real.

What applies to consumers applies also to specific consumption communities. Advertising can show people lifestyles (and patterns of spending) which they might not otherwise meet, but also invite them to 'join', and to come to see their chosen consumption community (for it is claimed to be merely a matter of choice), with its rapid transformations, as one of their primary memberships. In the process, other memberships are likely to be diminished; the great loser has arguably been communities of production – the social classes, and particular fractions and sections of social classes (such as craft communities, or trade unions).

Verbal and visual elements in advertising

The combination of verbal and visual elements to constitute texts is becoming increasingly important in our society, and advertising is at the forefront of it. Television as a medium produces only such composite texts, but advertisements in printed materials also give ever greater emphasis to them. And the visual element is progressively becoming the more important in advertising. The salience of the image has been taken to be one of the main characteristics of contemporary 'postmodern' culture.

This tendency accords with what I have been saying about the ideological processes of advertising. On the one hand, visual images underline the reliance of the image-building process upon the audience: where visual images are juxtaposed the interpreter *has to* make the connection, whereas in language connections can be made for the interpreter, though as we have seen they are often not. On the other hand, the building of 'consumption communities' is more easily achieved through primarily visual means, because the visual medium lends itself more easily to the production of 'simulacra' in Plato's sense: identical copies for which no original has ever existed. To put the point more plainly, visual images allow advertising to more easily create worlds which consumers may be led to inhabit, because of the strength of the ideology expressed in the saying that 'the camera doesn't lie'

> Look at the Miele advertisement in the light of these comments. How do the visual and verbal elements interact in the building of an image and of a consumer and consumption community?

Colonizing tendencies in advertising discourse

There is an immediate sense in which we can conceive of advertising as a colonizer: the dramatic increase in the volume of advertising in the past three decades, in the extent to which people are exposed to advertising on a daily basis, and in the 'penetration' of advertising into non-economic aspects of life, notably its penetration into the home through television. The family and family life have been penetrated by the economy and by the dominant class forces within the economy, and these colonizers have had some effect in restructuring family life as well as other aspects of non-economic life.

But we can also trace more concrete colonizing trends whereby other discourse types are influenced by advertising discourse. Text

As caring professionals, your family doctor, dentist, pharmacist, optician, district nurse, health visitor and midwife are concerned to make the service they provide even better.

Collectively, the services they offer are known as Primary Health Care. And each and every day over a million of us use them.

We spend over £5,000 million a year on these services.

Yet they have never been comprehensively reviewed in all their forty year history. Until now. The Government has put forward a discussion paper called 'Primary Health Care' to act as an agenda for public debate.

Basically, its objective is to raise standards and make services more responsive to the changing needs of the people who pay for them.

You.

To find out exactly what's being proposed, fill in the coupon for a leaflet or write to us.

It's your Health Service and we need your views on how to make it even better.

To: Primary Health Care, Curzon House, 20-24 Lonsdale Road, London, NW6 6RD.

Please send me the leaflet 'Primary Health Care'.

Name _____

Address _____

Primary Health Care

WW 1   ISSUED BY THE ✓ DEPARTMENT OF HEALTH AND SOCIAL SECURITY

Text 8.2 Source: Department of Health and Social Security

8.2 is an example from the discourse of public information – official communications from public authorities to 'the public'. This text clearly uses a familiar advertising format, yet there is no obvious product being advertised, and on the face of it this looks like simply the giving of information and soliciting of opinion –

not advertising at all. However, in a sense there is a 'product' whose image readers are called upon to build: the source of information and solicitor of opinion, which is (if one reads the small print in the bottom right-hand corner) the Department of Health and Social Security (the Health Service).

> What advertising features does this text have, in respect of building relations, a 'product' image, and a subject position for the 'consumer' ('the public')?

> The text has synthetic personalization of audience members (*you*, imperatives, *Please send me the leaflet*), and the producer is personalized with exclusive 'corporate' *we* – in the last sentence (*It's your Health Service and we need your views*) – though inclusive *we* (*a million of us use them*) is also used. An image is built for the Health Service through cues which evoke in the reader a frame for 'the doctor' in the picture which accompanies the text: it consists of a picture of a stethoscope with a snatch of 'doctor talk' printed over it (*We'd like a second opinion*). From this frame, values of professionalism, a high sense of responsibility, and so forth, which are ideological attributes of doctors, are transferred to the Health Service. The subject position set up for the reader is that of a member of a 'public' that is concerned and informed, that will want to know what is proposed, and that will be able to contribute a worth-while 'second opinion'. The image of the Health Service is further enhanced through the postulation of such a public as a public authority which respects 'the public'.

We can connect back at this point to the concern in Chapter 7 with the de-structuring and restructuring of orders of discourse. This text can be analysed as a mixture of features which partly draw upon an advertising discourse type, and partly draw upon a traditional discourse type of public information. This mixture can be seen as indicating a rearticulation of the order of discourse of health administration (and public administration more generally) as an effect of the colonization of that order of discourse by advertising. It also brings together what I identified at the beginning of the chapter as two main colonizing discourse types, showing an interpenetration of consumerism and bureaucracy, and the latter feeding off the former. See p. 221 below for a further example.

In the light of this example, it is possible to see how the discourse types of politics, and specifically the discourse of Thatcherism which we were looking at in Chapter 7, have come to be colonized and shaped by advertising. Margaret Thatcher, as we saw, builds a relationship with 'the public' based in part upon synthetic personalization, provides carefully managed cues for her audience to construct an image for a woman political leader, and constructs 'the public' as a community of political consumption, so to speak, which real people are induced to join. As in the case of the Health Service advertisement, the producer and the commodity coincide: Mrs Thatcher is trying to sell herself. Party politics, in becoming increasingly conducted through one-way public discourse in the media, with advertising as its model, is increasingly retreating from two-way, face-to-face discourse. Door-to-door canvassing, political debate and argument, and political meetings, are decreasingly significant elements of the discourse of politics. Under the impact of the generalization of the economic relationship of consumption, party politics is losing its base in people's lives. People's involvement in politics is less and less as citizens, and more and more as consumers; and their bases of participation are less and less the real communities they belong to, and more and more the political equivalents of consumption communities, which political leaders construct for them. Of course, the process is reversible, and there are counterveiling tendencies – see the section *Other tendencies* below.

DISCOURSE TECHNOLOGIES AND BUREAUCRACY

In this section, I develop the suggestion made at the beginning of this chapter that state control through bureaucracy has had major effects on orders of discourse. I discuss first of all the social tendency towards increased control over people through various forms of bureaucracy, and then turn to an examination of what I shall call *discourse technologies* – types of discourse which involve the more or less self-conscious application of social scientific knowledge for purposes of bureaucratic control. The argument will be that the effect of bureaucracy on orders of discourse is via the 'colonizing' spread of discourse technologies. I then give an example of the application of social scientific research to discourse technologies, so-called *social skills training*, and refer to one discourse technology (which I have referred to earlier in different terms), the interview. There is then an example involving two discourse technologies, the public information document, and the official form.

Bureaucracy

According to the sociologist Max Weber, a bureaucracy is 'a hierarchical organization designed rationally to coordinate the work of many individuals in the pursuit of large-scale administrative tasks and organizational goals'. 'Rationally' is to be understood in this definition in a restricted, strictly instrumental sense: rationality is the systematic matching of means to the ends of whatever bureaucratic institution or organization is involved. And the references to 'hierarchy' and 'coordination' in the definition underline the element of control in this means–ends rationality, both internal control from above within the bureaucracy, and control by the bureaucracy of the people. From the perspective of bureaucratic rationality, people are often objects to be ordered, checked, registered, shifted, and so forth.

The modern state which has grown up with capitalist society has entailed a considerable expansion of bureaucracy, which has brought more and more aspects of people's lives into the control of the state. This process of expansion and incursion has been especially evident since the inception of the 'welfare state'. The welfare state was set up in response to bitter experience of the effect of the unconstrained market in the depression of the 1920s and 1930s. The state was to protect people against the ravages of the market. The welfare state has indeed vastly improved the conditions of life of the majority of the people, though its achievements are now under threat. But it has been a two-edged process: the welfare state has been administered through bureaucracies which have thereby intensified their incursion into, and therefore state control over, people's lives. Given the conception of the state which I sketched out in Chapter 2, this ultimately means control by the capitalist class and the dominant bloc over people's lives. This bureaucratic, intrusive aspect of the welfare state has led to a widespread perception of the state as interfering and insensitive to people's needs, a perception which Thatcherism has exploited, as we saw in Chapter 7.

Discourse technologies

I defined discourse technologies above as types of discourse which involve the more or less self-conscious application of social scientific knowledge for purposes of bureaucratic control. What I have in mind are types of discourse such as interviews, official forms, questionnaires, tests and examinations, official records, medical examinations, lessons, which are themselves the object of social scientific investigation, and where the results of this investigation are fed back into the discourse technologies, helping to shape and modify them. Discourse technologies fall within the more general category of strategic discourse, discourse oriented to instrumental goals and results.

Discourse technologies are a specifically modern phenomenon, as are the social sciences which feed them. They represent a fairly generalized effect of bureaucracy and the modern state upon the societal order of discourse. Although their origins can be traced in specific institutions, they have come to have a transinstitutional status which allows them to be drawn into – to colonize – a whole variety of institutions, and articulated with other discoursal elements in a whole variety of ways. They correspond to what some people have called *genres*, though I find the term insufficiently specific for what I have in mind.

Discourse technologies have been associated with a quite fundamental change in the societal order of discourse in the modern period: the shaping of discourse to an unprecedented degree in accordance with self-conscious calculations of the relationship of means to ends, in accordance with instrumental bureaucratic rationality, which are based upon *knowledge about discourse itself*. This knowledge is provided by those sections of the social sciences which specialize in the study of discourse and language. It is one instance of a more general phenomenon of the modern period: the interpenetration of power and knowledge, and the massive dependence of power upon knowledge. It underscores the importance of critical discourse analysis being complemented by critical analysis of the sciences of language and discourse, as I argued in Chapter 1.

Social skills training

One of the routes by which the results of social scientific research have passed into discoursal practice is through *social skills training* (SST for short), which has developed out of social psychological research into social skills.

This research is based upon an instrumental view of social practice as the pursuit of goals which harmonizes with that of bureaucratic rationality as I have described it above. Larger units of practice, and discourse, such as an interview, are assumed to be composed of sequences of smaller units which are produced through the automatic application of skills which are selected on the basis of their contribution to the achievement of goals. It is assumed that these skills can be isolated and described, and that inadequacies in social practice can be overcome by training people to draw upon these skills.

SST has been widely implemented. It has been used to train mental patients, and others judged to be socially 'inadequate' or 'incompetent'. It has been used for training social workers, health workers, counsellors, therapists, and doctors to deal more effectively with their clients or patients. And it has been used for training industrial managers and salespeople to manage and sell more effectively, and for training public officials in bureaucratic institutions to combat impersonal and alienating images of these institutions which reduce their legitimacy and effectiveness.

The 'social skills' view of social practice tends to reduce practice generally and discourse particularly to a dimension of what we have been calling their 'contents' – instrumental goals or purposes. What we have referred to as relational and subjective/expressive dimensions of discourse are not given any independent or authentic status of their own. Rather, they tend to be reduced to the status of dependent variables, and to be seen as available for manipulation in the course of the constant endeavour to make discourse/practice maximally effective in the achievement of instrumental goals. Successful models set up for emulation in SST are regularly manipulative in this sense, and SST arguably thus contributes to strengthening the manipulation of relations and subjects in practice.

Let us take a specific example. The following is part of a recommended strategy for the conduct of a 'personnel interview', for instance a disciplinary interview in the workplace, or in a school, which 'can make it a pleasanter and more effective occasion'. It comes from a book by the well-known social psychologist Michael Argyle:

2. The supervisor (S) establishes rapport with the client (C), who may be very nervous about the interview. This will be easier if S maintains good day-to-day contacts with C. They may chat briefly about common interests, so that status barriers are reduced, and C is ready to talk freely.

3. It may be necessary for S to explain that there is a problem – C has been persistently late so that production has fallen, C has been getting very low marks, etc. This should be done by stating objective facts, not by passing judgement, and should be done in a manner that is pleasant rather than cross.

4. S now invites C to say what he thinks about the situation, what he thinks the reason for it is. This may involve a certain amount of probing for fuller information, if C is reluctant to open up. S is sympathetic, and shows that he wants to understand C's position. S may ask C whether he thinks the situation is satisfactory; in an appraisal interview he can ask C to evaluate his own performance. C may produce new information, which explains the cause of the trouble, and suggests how it can be tackled; the interview could then end at this point.

[5 and 6 omitted.]

7. . . . if further interviews become necessary, sterner means of influence may have to be resorted to. Most Ss are in a position to control material sanctions, such as bonuses, promotions, and finally dismissal. S will not usually want to sack C – what he wants is to keep him but make him behave differently. The possible use of such sanctions should first be mentioned reluctantly as a rather remote possibility – for example by the quite objective statement, 'There are several other people who would like this job', or, 'I may have to tell the people who pay your grant about your progress'.

8. The interview should end with a review of what has been agreed, the constructive steps that have been decided upon, when S and C will meet again to discuss progress, and so on. The meeting should end on as friendly a note as possible.

(M Argyle 1978: 243–5)

In what ways do these recommendations suggest the manipulation of relational and subjective dimensions of discourse for instrumental reasons?

Through urging Ss to simulate a particular subject position and a particular relationship with Cs, Ss are urged to simulate solidarity and equality with Cs (paragraph 2), as well as sympathy (paragraph 4), and to simulate a pleasant (paragraph 3) and friendly (paragraph 8) manner as well as reluctance (paragraph 7) to take drastic action. The justification for these simulations, quoted above, is that they are likely to make the interview more 'pleasant and effective'. I take 'effective' to refer to the instrumental goal of resolving disciplinary problems.

These recommendations are also interesting in what they implicitly assume. They assume that Ss have the right to total control over the contents, relations and subjects of interviews, and the capacity to implement the suggested manipulations of relations and subjects at will without fear of challenge. Conversely, they assume that Cs are totally powerless. Consequently there is a certain irony about such recommendations: the very act of formulating recommendations directed at one participant who is assumed to be able to carry them out and impose them upon the other at will, excludes the involvement of the other participant on something approaching an equal basis which the recommendations are suggesting.

Perhaps this is just part of the deeper irony of discipline being exercised in an interview rather than, say, in a bawling out. The interview has colonized the disciplinary apparatus, making the disciplinary process appear to be something else. This is the basic simulation, of which the further simulations referred to above can be seen as refinements. At this level, the disciplinary process is transformed by being merged with common-sense assumptions underlying the interview: that both parties have something to contribute to the process (in tune with the modern tendency to achieve discipline through self-discipline); that the interviewer/discipliner has (given a prima facie disciplinary infringement) the right to probe into various aspects of the behaviour and motivations of the interviewee/disciplinee; that the latter has the obligation to cooperate therein; and so forth.

There are many different types of interview, which can be regarded as being produced through the articulation of the interview as a discourse technology with various different institutional orders of discourse. We should therefore not regard the recommendations above as applying straightforwardly to all interviews – Argyle actually gives separate attention to two other types, the selection interview (i.e. for selecting people for jobs), and the social survey interview.

But there are common trends in the influence of social research on interviews of these and other types. For instance, Argyle mentions the establishment of 'rapport' and the equalization of the relationship between interviewer and interviewee in all cases. These entail, as we have seen in the case of the personnel interview, the manipulation of relational and subjective aspects of discourse through simulation. These properties of interviews are akin to what we have been referring to as *synthetic personalization* earlier in this chapter. I suggest that we might use this term to refer to all phenomena in strategic discourse, whether in its consumerist or bureaucratic varieties, where relational and subjective values are manipulated for instrumental reasons. This may be a matter of constructing fictitious individual persons, for instance as the addresser and addressee in an advertisement, or of manipulating the subject positions of, or the relationships between, actual individual persons (in the direction of equality, solidarity, intimacy or whatever), as in interviews. Synthetic personalization is a major strand in the systemic restructuring of the societal order of discourse I am concerned with in this chapter.

In addition to SST for interviewers, SST for interviewees is increasingly common. For instance, a pamphlet recently issued by the Department of Employment offers help with 'job-getting skills' to unemployed people. There seems to be a widespread delusion (or in some cases, an attempt to delude) that if more people were trained in getting jobs, there would be more jobs – or to put it differently, that people's failure to get jobs is due to their own inadequacies, including for instance their inability to 'interview well', rather than to those of the social system.

However, training of this sort may constitute what I refer to in the final chapter as *empowerment* – developing people's capacity to explore the full range of what is possible within the given order of discourse, without actually changing it. There is a great deal to be said for empowerment, as I argue in the next chapter, as a means of giving confidence and a sense of their own potential to dominated social groupings. But I feel that there is something of a dilemma.

Not only are some of the applications of SST dubious in terms of social scientific ethics – particularly those which may improve the skills of people who dominate or manipulate others to achieve their particular instrumental goals. It may also be that the reduction of social practice and discourse to 'skills' is in itself bound to have a debilitating effect on communicative discourse, in the sense of discourse which has no underlying instrumental goals for any participant, but is genuinely undertaken in a cooperative spirit in order to arrive at understanding and common ground. It is likely to have this debilitating effect, because as synthetic personalization becomes increasingly widespread, it may be difficult to prevent even the most genuine of relational and subjective practices being open to synthetic interpretation. When we are surrounded by synthetic intimacy, friendship, equality and sympathy, could that not affect our ability to confidently recognize the real article?

Public information and official forms

The transmission of information to 'the public' by bureaucratic organizations, and the solicitation of information from members of 'the public' through official forms, are discourse technologies which are often paired together in welfare contexts. Bureaucracies produce information leaflets which describe the various available welfare benefits and identify those who qualify for them, and these leaflets may incorporate or be distributed alongside forms which those so identified are required to complete in order to apply for benefits. These two technologies, as well as the interview, exemplify the striking increase which has taken place in the communicative demands which the society makes of the mass of its dominated members.

The properties of such leaflets and official forms have been the basis for permanent and pervasive controversy during the welfare state era, as part of a sort of guerilla warfare waged 'publicly' but also 'privately', in the conversational encounters of everyday life, against bureaucracy. A central complaint has been that such material is inaccessible to a substantial proportion of the people supposedly addressed by it, because of indigestibility of format and layout, complexity of syntax, technicality of vocabulary, and so forth. This complaint has been linked to the low level of uptake of benefits: many people who qualify do not apply.

Official leaflets and forms have undergone substantial trans-formations on the basis of social scientific advice on how to meet these complaints. Texts 8.3 and 8.4 are recent examples which illustrate rather well the effort which has gone into making such documents accessible. The texts are, respectively, the main part

Family Income Supplement

If you work and have children,
you should know about
Family Income Supplement – FIS for short.
FIS means more money for families on low earnings.

Who can get it?

You can claim if you are
single, married or living with
someone as if you are
husband and wife – it doesn't
matter which one of you is
working.

You can get FIS if you work
for an employer or if you are
self-employed.

And these things free

Free school meals

Free milk and vitamins

Free prescriptions

Free dental treatment

Free glasses

Free hospital travel for treatment

More money

How much money you get
depends on your income, how
many children you have and
how old they are. The less
you earn, the more FIS you
get. A family with one child
under 11 could get from 20p to
£25.30. With two or more
children it could be more.

FIS is paid at the same
amount every week for a year.
And it's tax free.

Claim FIS if you can answer YES to these three questions –

1 Do you have any children under 19?

You can get FIS for any children
under 16, or under 19 if they still
attend courses up to and
including A levels.

You can claim for children you support and who normally live with
you, even if they are not your own.
You can't get FIS if all your
children are 16 or over and have
left school.

2 Do you or your partner work full time?

By full time work we mean at
least 30 hours a week by you or

your partner, or 24 hours a week
if you are bringing up children
on your own.

3 Is your total weekly income less than £86.95 plus...

£11.65 for each child under 11
£12.65 for each child 11–15
£13.65 for each child 16 or over?

For example, if you have one
child aged 8 and one aged 14
you may be able to get FIS if
your total weekly income is less
than £111.25 (£86.95 + £11.65 +
£12.65).

To work out your total weekly
income: Add up your and your
partner's earnings before tax,
national insurance and other
deductions have been taken off.

Then add any other money from

things like benefits or maintenance payments. Don't include
child benefit, one parent benefit,
your children's income (other than
maintenance payments) or
any help you get with rent and
rates – these don't count.

This is only a rough guide. It's
worth claiming even if you think
your income is a bit too high to
qualify for FIS.

These income limits apply for
claims made from 29 July 1986. If
you already get FIS, these limits
will only apply to you when you
make a new claim at the end of
your FIS year.

How to claim

You do not have to go to a social
security office to claim. FIS
claims are dealt with by post.
Fill in the claim form and send
it to:
**FIS
Freepost
Blackpool FY2 0YA**
Telephone: 0253-52311

What you put on the form is
private and confidential

Claim as soon
as you can,
or you may
lose money.

Text 8.3 Source: Department of Health and Social Security

For DHSS use						
Exp. date				NT		

Family Income Supplement   **FIS**

Please give details for yourself **and your partner**. Your partner is your husband or wife or the person you live with as if you are married to them. If you are a one-parent family, tell us about you and your children. Please write clearly in CAPITALS. There is a space at the end for you to give extra information.

1 START HERE ▰▰▰▰

	MAN ▰▰▰	**WOMAN** ▰▰▰
Title	Mr	Mrs/Miss/Ms
Surname		
Other names		
Date of birth	/ /	/ /
National Insurance (NI) number	Letters Numbers Letter	Letters Numbers Letter
Address and Postcode		

Do you have a FIS book now?

Tick ✓ No or Yes

No ☐ If you ticked No, please answer this question
have you had FIS in the last 4 weeks? no ☐ yes ☐

Yes ☐ If you ticked Yes, please answer this question
what is the number on the cover of the book?......................

At which Post Office would you like to get FIS? – give address.

Is your (and your partner's) permanent home in the UK? **No** ☐ **Yes** ☐

Are you a one-parent family? **No** ☐ **Yes** ☐

If you are claiming FIS as a couple but your partner lives at a different address, please explain why.

Please give details of the children who you want to claim FIS for. Generally that means children under 19 who live with you. You cannot include
- children who are 16 or over if they have left school.
- children who you do not provide for.
- children who the Council gives you a boarding allowance for.

You can include
- children who are not your own, so long as you provide for them.
- children who normally live with you but are in a home or at boarding school.

Surname	Other names	Age	Date of birth

If you (or your partner) are pregnant, when is the baby due?   /   /

Now go on to section 2 on the next page

Text 8.4 Source: Department of Health and Social Security

of an information leaflet on Family Income Supplement (FIS) produced by the Department of Health and Social Security (DHSS), and the first page of a four-page application form for FIS. The application form was distributed with (inside) the leaflet.

What bureaucratic objective(s) or purpose(s) do the texts serve, and how are these reflected in textual features?

The main bureaucratic objective in the case of the leaflet would seem to be the 'recruitment' of qualified applicants for FIS; most of the many conditional clauses (*if*-clauses) in the text are there to specify the precise section of the population which qualifies (e.g. *If you work and have children, you should know about Family Income Supplement*). The main objective in the case of the form is presumably to elicit accurately and in an easily processable form the information necessary to assess applications for FIS; this is reflected in various ways in the 'easification' of the text – relatively simple sentences, non-technical vocabulary, and many properties of layout including the choice of character style, variations in colour, in character size and boldness and between upper and lower case, the highlighting of blocs for answers to go in, and the provision of 'multiple choice' boxes for answers. Some of these features are clearer than others in the reproduction of the form. The leaflet is also characterized by 'easification', presumably to ensure maximally effective 'recruitment' of applicants; again, this is reflected in sentence grammar, vocabulary, and various aspects of layout.

Easification is a manipulation of aspects of the contents of the text, but in this as in many other cases of easification in bureaucratic discourse, it is accompanied by manipulation of relations and of subjects, by synthetic personalization. In the part of the leaflet headed *And these things free*, for example, the producer (DHSS) appears to occupy the subject position of advertiser, and constructs for the reader the subject position of consumer. This illustrates that the two sides of the impingement of the system on people's lives which I have distinguished, the economic/consumerist and the bureaucratic/discourse technological, are not autonomous, but on the contrary increasingly overlap. In particular, the powerful consumer subject position constructed in advertising can be made use of for bureaucratic purposes. Notice also that advertising shares with the discourse technologies the property of being fed by social scientific research; indeed, it probably makes sense to widen the notion of discourse technologies to include advertising.

More generally, there is direct address of the reader and questions and imperatives are directed to her. A common dimension of synthetic personalization is simulated equalization, as we saw above in connection with interviews, and in this case, there seems to be some attempt to put the producer on an equal footing with the reader through choices of expression which the majority of readers might themselves make: easification of vocabulary and grammar also tends simultaneously to be equalization. This is by no means consistently carried through (for instance, *partner* has a limited usage to refer to the person one lives with), but there are quite a number of examples. For instance, *can get* rather than, say, *qualifies for* in the headline *Who can get it?*, or *living with someone* rather than *cohabiting with someone* – though ordinary usage makes do without the specification *as if you are husband and wife*.

Such equalizing features are articulated with counterveiling properties of these discourse technologies which place the producer firmly in the authoritative position. Members of 'the public' engage upon the activity of form-filling, for instance, very much on the terms of the bureaucratic organization: it is assumed that the latter has the right to ask for all sorts of personal details and that the former is obliged to provide them, that the latter exercises absolute control over valid and invalid contents and forms of answer, and so on. Easification can underline the powerlessness of the applicant; I feel that this is the case with the 'traffic rules' in the form (*START HERE, Now go on to section 2 on the next page*) and with the way in which the form is designed to exclude any answers more complex than 'yes' or 'no' in some cases, and any answers beyond a normative length in others. I think that in general, synthetic personalization may strengthen the position of the bureaucracy and the state by disguising its instrumental and manipulative relationship to the mass of the people beneath a façade of a personal and equal relationship – but only so long as people do not see through it!

THE DISCOURSE OF THERAPY

I suggested at the beginning of the chapter that, under the impact of the impingement of the economy and the state on ever more aspects of life, a great many people experience problems and 'crises of identity', which they perceive as their individual 'personal' problems, and for which they seek 'help' from one source or another. There is a whole range of 'helping' organizations which people turn to, ranging from professional psychiatry to voluntary organizations such as the Samaritans.

These organizations have generated a considerable variety of therapies and counselling techniques. The first point to make about them is that they are further examples of discourse technologies; they share with other discourse technologies the property of being applied forms of social scientific knowledge. Unlike the types of discourse technology I discussed above, however, they are not in a direct relationship with bureaucratic rationality. It will be helpful therefore to distinguish them as *therapeutic technologies* from *disciplinary technologies*. However, I argue later that they do nevertheless have a significant relationship to bureaucratic rationality.

The following is an extract from a therapeutic interview (cl: Client; t: Therapist):

(1) cl: It all comes pretty vague. But you know I keep, keep having the thought occur to me that this whole process for me is kind of like examining pieces of a jig-saw puzzle. It seems to me I, I'm in the process now of examining the individual pieces which really don't have too much meaning. Probably handling them, not even beginning to think of a pattern. That keeps coming to me. And it's interesting to me because I, I really don't like jig-saw puzzles. They've always irritated me. But that's my feeling. And I mean I pick up little pieces (*T gestures throughout this conversation to illustrate CL's statements*) with absolutely no meaning except I mean the, the feeling that you get from simply handling them without seeing them as a pattern, but just from the touch, I probably feel, well it is going to fit someplace here.

(2) t: And that at the moment that, that's the process, just getting the feel and the shape and the configuration of the different pieces with a little bit of background feeling of, yeah they'll probably fit somewhere, but most of the attention's focused right on, 'What does this feel like? And what's its texture?'

(3) cl: That's right. There's almost something physical in it. A, ə
—

(4) t: You can't quite describe it without using your hands. A real, almost a sensuous sense in —

(5) cl: That's right. Again it's, it's a feeling of being very objective, and yet I've never been quite so close to myself.

(6) T: Almost at one and the same time standing off and looking at yourself and yet somehow being closer to yourself that way than —

(7) CL: M-hm. And yet for the first time in months I am not thinking about my problems. I'm not actually, I'm not working on them.

(8) T: I get the impression you don't sort of sit down to work on 'my problems'. It isn't that feeling at all.

(9) CL: That's right. That's right. I suppose what I, what I mean actually is that I'm not sitting down to put this puzzle together as, as something, I've got to see the picture. It, it may be that, it may be that I am actually enjoying this feeling process. Or I'm certainly learning something.

(10) T: At least there's a sense of the immediate goal of getting that feel as being the thing, not that you're doing this in order to see a picture, but that it's a, a satisfaction of really getting acquainted with each piece. Is that —

(11) CL: That's it. That's it. And it still becomes that sort of sensuousness, that touching. It's quite interesting. Sometimes not entirely pleasant, I'm sure, but —

(12) T: A rather different sort of experience.

(13) CL: Yes. Quite.

Text 8.5 Source: Rogers C, 1967: 77–78

Look at the relationship between the therapist's (T's) contributions and the client's (CL's). Consider in particular to what extent T's contributions judge or try to control CL's, or show rapport with CL.

I think the short answer is that T's contributions do not on the face of it at least judge or try to control CL's, and that T does show rapport with CL. Take turn (2). Notice first of all how the syntactic form of this turn makes it a continuation of CL's preceding turn: that turn ended with *I probably feel* followed by a noun clause functioning as object of *feel*, and turn (2) is structured as another noun clause (beginning with *that at the moment*) which is coordinated with that of turn (1). Notice also that T echoes CL's use of self-directed direct speech (compare *well it is going to fit someplace here*, and *yeah they'll probably fit somewhere*). These formal relationships between turns (1) and (2) are indicative of their functional relationship: turn (2) is a reformulation of the end of turn (1) which paraphrases it closely. This pattern is repeated throughout the extract, and in each case CL accepts T's reformulation of what she has said – *That's right* in turn (3), for example. T shows rapport by producing acceptable reformulations of CL's contributions.

According to a recent overview, most definitions of counselling regard it as 'a person-to-person form of communication marked by the development of a subtle emotional understanding often described technically as "rapport" or "empathy"; that is centred upon one or more problems of the client; and that is free from authoritarian judgements and coercive pressures by the counsellor'. Where the roots of the problem are seen as internal rather than external, the aim is generally to deal with it by achieving behavioural changes on the basis of the client coming to understand things about herself which she had not previously been aware of.

The 'helping skills' of the counsellor which facilitate this process are the object of self-conscious reflection and control. One standing issue is the extent to which the counsellor's responses to the client ought to go beyond paraphrasing reformulations. The prominent psychotherapist Carl Rogers describes the role of the therapist in this way: 'He does not merely repeat his client's words, concepts or feelings. Rather, he seeks for the meaning implicit in the present inner experiencing toward which the client's words or concepts point.' If the counsellor is offering such interpretations to the client, however, the line between helping the client to formulate her own meanings and leading the client to accept the therapist's must be somewhat blurred.

Therapy and counselling offer help to individuals suffering from socially generated ills. This is made clear in the overview quoted earlier:

> A new area of specialisation seems to be emerging, gathering form slowly from the many diverse occupational roles with which it is associated, and in response to a deeply felt social need for individual guidance and support amid the maelstrom of social and economic change, the increasing geographical mobility of the population, and the partial collapse of community life in highly urbanised areas. . . . it is deeply humanitarian throughout its diverse forms, and . . . is part of an essential counterpoise to the totalitarian trends also very evident throughout the pattern of modern industrial and cultural change.

To the extent, however, that therapy and counselling assume that the effects of social ills can be remedied on the basis of the hidden potentials of individuals, they can be regarded as ideological practices, which may be in competition with practices of political mobilization based upon the contrary assumption that social ills can be remedied only through social change. Indeed,

Michel Foucault argues that the 'confession', which can be regarded as including therapy and counselling, has become a vital ingredient of social control.

The way in which counselling has rapidly colonized many institutional orders of discourse, including those of work, education, social work, general medicine, vocational guidance, law, and religion, does indeed raise questions about its relationship to social control. Here for example is an extract from a discussion of counselling in education:

> In a strongly authoritarian school, in which all members of the community from the headmaster downwards are constantly giving orders to those over whom they have formal authority; there is little scope for any but the most paternalistic 'pastoral care' and the most amateurish kind of counselling; and there is little chance of inculcating any real understanding of shared responsibility, individual self-discipline and a concern and respect for other people as people. In a school that is genuinely aiming at the optimum personal development of all individuals, the head's responsibility must no longer be thought of as lessening the responsibility of the staff, nor can the responsibility of the staff be allowed to diminish that of the pupils.

From this contrast between two types of school, one might reasonably conclude that counselling is being suggested as a technology within a new mechanism for achieving and legitimizing social order in schools, a sort of corporate individualism which views schools as partnerships for the benefit of all individuals involved. One finds parallel corporate ideologies elsewhere, including industry. Counselling in such cases is arguably as much a disciplinary technology as a therapeutic technology. Its spread could be seen to correspond to changes in strategies for achieving discipline, which place the onus on the individual to discipline herself.

To conclude this section, let us look at an example of counselling in one of the colonized orders of discourse. The following is an extract from an employment counselling session, more specifically from the 'mid-career' counselling of a successful business woman who is having difficulties with her boss and is in the process of trying to shift jobs. The extract is taken from a radio programme which was actually structured around a discussion between the programme producer (P) and the counsellor (C), with extracts from counselling sessions being used to illustrate points in the discussion (CL: client). The text begins with such an extract, but the last two turns bring us back to the producer–counsellor discussion. (A spaced dot indicates a short pause, a dash a longer pause.)

(1) CL: the other thing that's difficult is if I don't succeed in getting this job I think the real difficulty will actually be at . staying where I am . I mean if I don't get it I'm almost tempted to resign . become unemployed .

(2) C: well there's e . have you talked to your husband about this

(3) CL: e:m . in passing yes . I've threatened it on more than one occasion . we could . afford it . for a short period . because of an inheritance . literally I mean just just pure coincidence e:m . in normal circumstances no .
    C: mhm

(4) C: well then . that's your call . it would be sad because it is much easier to get a job (CL: mhm) from a job . so . if you have the chance or the opportunity . to . stay . and . grit your teeth then that would be very good . and have you considered that by handling . the emotional stress . and the hassle from . ignoring and . almost being crucified (by) the other people that you actually grow and mature as a person —

(5) CL: I recognize that as an objective statement but I'm not sure if I recognize it when it becomes subjective .

(6) P: are you telling her there Michael that suffering's good for you .

(7) C: e:m good question I'm not sure how to handle that myself e: good question

Text 8.6 Source: 'Employment Counselling', BBC Radio 4, 7 December 1986

Turn (2) is immediately striking because of the sexist assumptions which underlie the counsellor immediately evoking the husband as a control on rash actions. But the question I want to focus on is how counselling, when it colonizes orders of discourse such as those associated with work, squares its own therapeutic, person-oriented and individualistic ground rules with institutional goals.

Notice the producer's question in turn (6). What *is* the counsellor telling the client, or rather presupposing, in (4)? And is the presupposition of a therapeutic nature, or a disciplinary nature associated with work, or both?

What is presupposed here is the whole of *by handling . . . grow and mature as a person*. The presupposition actually merges the specific case ('you individually will grow as a person because of this experience'), which is referred to in the subordinate clause, and the universal common-sense assumption which makes sense of the specific case ('someone who handles emotional stress, etc., grows and matures as a person'), which the main clause (*you actually grow and mature as a person*) partly articulates. The equation of success in dealing with emotional crises and personal growth and maturation is part of the common sense of counselling. What is interesting here is that this proposition is flexible enough to include the stress and hassle arising from work. Stress and hassle, and the associated families of illnesses, are increasingly familiar aspects of people's working lives as those still in employment are subjected to ever greater pressure to increase their productivity. They are, of course, in no sense necessary (still less desirable) accompaniments of work. If employment counselling is attributing to these a positive role in 'personal growth', it would seem to be helping to legitimize them.

OTHER TENDENCIES

The tendencies in society and in discourse which I have discussed in this chapter by no means account for everything that is going on socially and discoursally in contemporary capitalism. To underline this, let me conclude the chapter by referring briefly to tendencies which are in a sense contrary to those I have discussed, in that they are indicative of increased fragmentation rather than increased integration.

I have referred to one way in which people have reacted to the increasing impingement of the economy and the state upon their lives: through seeking individual solutions to their disorientation, loss of identity, and so forth, in the various forms of therapy, counselling, and 'helping' services. But people have also, to varying degrees, reacted collectively, through forms of struggle. It is a well-known feature of the contemporary political situation that there is a plethora of organizations and movements which traditional channels of political action, via the political parties, the trades unions, the churches, etc., have been unable to contain (though there is a view that alliance with these more traditional channels, and with each other, is the only route to pushing back the system). The very diversity of these *new social movements*, as I shall call them, reflects the scale of the system's impingement upon life, and the many aspects of life that it has put under pressure.

Any listing of the new social movements reflects their bewildering variety, for the movements are often quite incomparable in such matters as the size and nature of their social base, the breadth of the issue(s) they are concerned with, the (in)directness of their relationship to impingements by the system, and so on. A list might include: the women's movement, ecological and antinuclear groups, national movements, alternative lifestyle groups, the black movement and ethnic groups, the gay liberation movement, the peace movement, animal liberation groups, and so on.

Just as the integrating tendencies discussed earlier are manifested in colonizing integrations in the societal order of discourse, so these tendencies to fragmentation are manifested in a proliferation of types of discourse, and particularly in a fragmentation of oppositional political discourse. The newspaper extract in Text 8.7, for example, represents a feminist discourse; it is the opening of an article in a feminist newspaper.

Focus upon the vocabulary of this text, and in particular on how the feminist discourse type upon which it draws words the rapes and forms of protest action against them, and responses to this action.

The wording of the rapes shows a vocabulary feature characteristic of the text as a whole: compound expressions which are vocabulary items in feminist wordings: *male violence, crimes against women* and *rape survivors*. Notice that such vocabulary items belong to a distinctively feminist classification of the persons and events of the feminist domain of political action: *male violence* is not just something which happens, but a key phenomenon (and target) of the domain. Notice also that there is a wording for a category of person that goes unworded in other discourse types, the *rape survivor* (*rape victim* is not equivalent – it can refer to someone who does *not* survive a rape); the choice of wording is politically significant, not only suggesting that rapists sometimes kill their victims, but also focusing upon rape as a disaster

Misogynist hysteria unleashed over Molesworth rapes

Three women were raped at Molesworth peace camp over the past 12 months, as reported in *Outwrite no. 50.* The four known rapists have been and still remain, active in peace circles. Meanwhile, sections of the peace movement agonies, with little apparent success, over how to effectively deal with male violence and feminist anger. In addition, the demand made by the rape survivors and their supporters that Molesworth peace camp be closed altogether, in recognition of the crimes against women committed there, crimes which have gone ignored, trivialised and even disbelieved, remains unmet.

Predictably, the response of some male pacifists exposes rampant misogyny. An examination of some of the letters published in recent issues of *Peace News* speak for themselves. Opinions range the spectrum of typical patriarchal reaction — disbelief at the occurrence of the rapes; likening the efforts of the women to close the peace camp to those of Tory MPs and bailiffs; condemnations of the 'violence' of the women for taking direct action at Molesworth in protest; accusations that the women are dividing the peace movement, and so on.

Almost all objectors withdraw support from *Peace News* for what they describe as its biased, ignorant and offensive stance on the issue. The stance in question is *PN*'s support for the women demanding the closure of the camp. However, *PN*'s non-editorial stand on this would seem to be contradicted by their decision to publish offensive, anti-woman statements in their letters pages. *PN* comments, that they see their role as *'seeking to change these views* (misinformed and misogynist views on rape) *by allowing open debate whilst making our own positions clear in editorial statements.'* They go on to claim that suppression of such views would alienate rather than bring about changes, a position that is at once questionable and potentially dangerous. The protesting women are angry, declaring that *PN* has violated its own anti-sexist policy.

Still, it is clear that these virulent attacks on the women, disguised as moral outrage, reveal fear at women's anger. The causes

of the anger, ie. the rapes of the women by individual men, seem to have been forgotten and buried as accusing fingers point at the women who, in their anger, destroyed some property at the camp and spray painted bunkers and caravans. After all, violence against property must be punished, while violence against women, the commonest crime of all, continues to go unnoticed.

What is being displayed is the paucity of understanding of issues surrounding rape and male violence against women and women's anger. Can non-violent strategies work effectively against individual acts of male violence against women? The failure of the peace movement to work out effective strategies, strategies that permit *expression* of anger rather than containment of it, is emerging.

Perhaps the most offensive letter published in *Peace News 17th October,* is the drivel delivered by Keith Ollett who protests that 'Molesworth is becoming the scapegoat for all rapes against all wimmin throughout time', and goes on to whine about the women who want to close the camp and who 'are trying to enforce that with with *violence'* (our italics). '. . .*Instead of diminishing, the violence and anger of the women is growing. It seems that venting their rage and grief, rather than helping them and healing them, is damaging these angry wimmin even more. Instead of dispersing in destruction, they are drawing strength from that destruction, a dreadful, fearful strength. . . are the angry wimmin acknowledging the vigilantes,*

the lynch mobs, the bailiffs they are becoming?' Fear reigns, is the man trembling?

This self-opinionated bigot then suggests that both peace and feminist movements take a long very hard look at what they are doing, and also, that male violence must be dealt with. But how? No strategies are offered. Must we conclude that communally sipping camomile tea by the camp fire is the true expression of harmonious fraternal relations?

The rape survivors, and supporters, themselves are undeterred, and continue their campaign, addressing meetings, forcing the issue and getting an inevitably mixed response of abuse (they have been compared to the NF!) and support. CND groups are being asked to stop supporting Molesworth peace camp, which continues to function as a mixed camp, and a proposal is to be put to CND National conference in mid-November asking that groups withdraw support. CND office has expressed its deep concern and has claimed that since it doesn't set up peace camps, it is not empowered to close them, but *'condemns unequivocally all violence'.* The outcome remains to be seen. That the issue is now being debated and is even on the agenda of the CND National conference is a victory in itself. But only partial, considering the overwhelming reaction that the women had to battle with, and the fact that the rapists remain free.

Shaila

Contact the rape survivors and supporters at: Kari, c/o Box MW, 3 Fletchers Terrace, Cambridge

Text 8.7 Source: *Outwrite* No. 52, November 1986

and an outrage – one 'survives' earthquakes and shipwrecks, but also bomb attacks and attempted murder.

Turning to the protest action, again there are a number of compounds: *women's anger, angry women, feminist anger* and *direct action*. The comments above about *male violence* apply also to *women's anger* and variants of that expression: this is a wording of a politically significant, and mobilizing, category in feminist politics, not simply a way of referring to the fact that some women happen to be angry. Feminists have probably taken *direct action* from the peace movement.

The wording of responses to the women's action draws upon the most obvious feminist political vocabulary – *misogyny, misogynist, patriarchal, anti-woman*. A final point to notice is the extent to which key expressions, such as *male violence* and *women's anger*, are repeated through the text. They include the word *women* itself. There are a number of points in the text where one might expect *women* to be 'pronominalized' (or replaced with a pronoun), or omitted, yet it isn't. The last sentence of paragraph 2 is an example – *their 'violence', they are dividing* could substitute for *the 'violence' of women, the women are dividing*.

CONCLUSION

In a society as complex as ours, tendencies in the societal order of discourse will not be a simple matter of progression in one direction, but contradictory and difficult to sum up. This chapter has offered only broad and preliminary answers to the neglected question of what characterizes the contemporary order of discourse and the direction of its movement, but I hope that readers will at least take from it a sense of the importance of this question within the more general social exploration of the present.

REFERENCES

For tendencies in contemporary capitalism, new social movements, *strategic* versus *communicative* discourse, I have drawn upon Habermas J 1984. Mey J 1985 is focused around the question, 'what kind of language do we use in a modern, industrialized economy?'. I have found both Leiss W *et al.* 1986 and Williamson J 1978 useful on consumerism and advertising. My comments on the state and the welfare state draw upon Hall S 1984, as well as Habermas. The notion of 'discourse technologies' is based upon Michel Foucault's analyses of the technologies of power; see Dreyfus H L, Rabinow P 1982. Steedman C *et al.* 1985 includes some interesting discussion of the strategy of discipline through self-discipline. On the sociology of 'taste', see Bourdieu P 1984. For 'social skills training', I have drawn upon Argyle M 1978. The first of the counselling texts is taken from 'Some of the directions evident in therapy' in Rogers C 1967. The unattributed quotations about counselling are from Vaughan T D 1976. On postmodern culture and 'postmodernism', see Jameson 1984.

NINE

Critical language study and social emancipation: language education in the schools

In this final chapter, I look at how critical language study (CLS) might contribute to the emancipation of those who are dominated and oppressed in our society. After a brief general discussion of the potential contribution of CLS to social emancipation, the chapter focuses in on one domain in which this potential could be developed: language education in the schools. I argue that *critical language awareness*, based upon CLS, should be a significant objective of language education, and there are some suggestions about methods for developing it. The main reason for this choice of focus is its current relevance, given the major changes in educational policy and practice which are being implemented or planned, and given more specifically the report of the Kingman Committee and the deliberations of the Cox Committee on the teaching of English in schools. The last section of the chapter contains some ideas and suggested readings for those who would like to extend their acquaintance with CLS.

In the opening chapter of this book, I said that one of my purposes in writing it was to help increase consciousness of how language contributes to the domination of some people by others, because consciousness is the first step towards emancipation. That consciousness of language in particular is a significant element of this 'first step' follows from the way domination works in modern society: it works, as I have been arguing increasingly through 'consent' rather than 'coercion', through ideology, and through language. Increasingly, but by no means entirely: it will not do to reduce domination to the generation of consent and to the vehicles of ideology and language, any more than it will do to reduce emancipation to 'seeing through', and changing, the practices of discourse. Even while we focus upon language and discourse, let us remind ourselves that social emancipation is primarily about tangible matters such as unemployment, housing, equality of access to education, the distribution of wealth, and removing the economic system from the ravages and whims of private interest and profit.

If CLS or any other mode of critical social analysis is to make any contribution to social emancipation through the raising of consciousness, certain conditions must obtain. We can distinguish 'objective' and 'subjective' conditions. The main objective condition is perhaps obvious, but nevertheless worth reiterating: the wider social situation must be such as to make progress towards social emancipation feasible. The emancipatory potential of CLS in a fascist dictatorship, or even in a democracy where the position of the dominant bloc is unassailable, is strictly limited! Subjective conditions involve, first, dominated groupings of people: they must be open to critique and raising of consciousness, and this depends on their experience of social struggle. Oppressed people will not recognize their oppression just because someone takes the trouble to point it out to them; they will only come to recognize it through their own experience of it, and their own activity in struggling against it. Thus struggle and the raising of consciousness are dialectically related: struggle opens people to the raising of consciousness, which empowers them to engage in struggle. Then there are subjective conditions relating to those who act as catalysts in the raising of consciousness: there must be people who have the theoretical background to enable them to act in this way, as well as sharing the experience of the oppressed to a sufficient extent for them to be accepted as catalysts. Very often they will be educators in some formal or informal sense, but this is not necessarily so. Part, but only part, of their equipment might be a familiarity with CLS, and the capacity to mediate books like this one to people without the background to read them.

There are many social contexts in our society where CLS might play a part in struggles for social emancipation. Some of these are educational (schools, colleges, contexts of 'on-the-job' or 'in-service' training, etc.); others might be the activities of trade union branches, political organizations, women's groups, environmentalist groups, tenants' associations; and a host of informal types of encounter in workplaces, homes, pubs, cafes, or streets. Let me comment very briefly upon three such contexts, before I focus on language education in schools.

One context involving professional teachers is the teaching of

English as a Second Language (ESL). Teachers of ESL are dealing with some of the most disadvantaged sections of the society, whose experiences of domination and racism are particularly sharp. Some of these teachers already see their role in terms of empowering their students, in the words of one practitioner, to 'deal with communicative situations outside the classroom in which institutional power is weighted against them, preparing them to challenge, contradict, assert, in settings where the power dynamic would expect them to agree, acquiesce, be silent'. This educational process 'must be grounded in a dialogue about the meaning of power and its encoding in language', which indicates a role for CLS. Thus ESL is one instance where the idea of developing a critical consciousness of discourse as a basis for a mode of discoursal ideological struggle is already established to some extent.

Another example where there is, as far as I am aware, no such established tradition, but where the potential would nevertheless appear to be great, is the training of workers in public services who come directly into contact with dominated social groupings – nurses, for instance. Many such workers are currently being subjected to enormous pressure to adapt their practices in order to meet the purely instrumental criteria of bureaucratic rationality, such as 'efficiency' and 'cost-effectiveness'. And for many of them this means that fewer workers are expected to 'handle' more people. Consequently, in so far as discourse or 'communication' figure in training, they tend to figure in the form of 'communication' or 'social skills' whose primary motivation is efficient people-handling. Recall the discussion of 'skills' in Chapter 8. CLS could be a significant resource for those who are concerned about such developments.

A further case, which is outside official schooling or training, is the potential which exists for building upon the critique of the media which is to be found in the trade union movement in Britain. Many trade unionists hold the view that media practices are damaging to the interests of trade unions in particular, and working-class people in general. This negative attitude is in part based upon bitter collective experience of the way in which the media have represented trade union activities and practices, such as ballots, elections, and industrial action. But there is little general access to modes of analysis which would allow trade unionists to undertake detailed monitoring of media output, though such monitoring could strengthen their campaigns for democratic control of the media, for the 'right of reply' to be given to those represented in the media, and so forth. CLS is I think one resource which could help, whose relevance would be clear to many trade unionists.

LANGUAGE EDUCATION IN SCHOOLS: CRITICAL LANGUAGE AWARENESS

I mentioned above the Kingman Committee as one reason for focusing upon language education in the schools. Various factors appear to have contributed to the decision to set up the committee, including the controversy which followed an attempt by the English education inspectors to set out objectives for English teaching, and moves towards a national curriculum in a range of 'core' school subjects. A major factor was complaints about 'standards', and particularly standards of literacy, very often from employers or from politicians echoing employers. Here, for instance, is how the Minister of Education, Mr Kenneth Baker, speaking in November 1986, justified his decision to set up the committee: 'Frequently I hear employers complain that many school-leavers applying for jobs after 11 years of compulsory education cannot write simply, clearly and without obvious error.'

We must all share concern about the poor language capabilities of many children when they leave education, but it is striking that complaints about standards are so often cast in narrowly instrumental terms, as if language capabilities were no more than skills or tools (both commonly used words) for performing tasks ('simply', 'clearly', 'without error', and so forth), and as if language education were no more than the transmission of such skills. Similar instrumental language is to be found in Mr Baker's speech of January 1987, when he announced the membership and terms of reference of the Committee:

> . . . I have been struck by a particular gap. Pupils need to know about the workings of the English language if they are to use it effectively. Most schools no longer teach old-fashioned grammar.

But little has been put in its place. There is no common ground on teaching about the structure and workings of the language, about the way it is used to convey meaning and achieve other effects. We need to equip teachers with a proper model of the language to help improve their teaching.

The picture of language used here is exclusively task-oriented: using language *effectively*, for *effects* such as *conveying* meaning. Even the language training of teachers is put in terms of tools for the job (*equip*). Yet as we have seen in this book, language use – discourse – is not just a matter of performing tasks, it is also a matter of expressing and constituting and reproducing social identities and social relations, including crucially relations of power.

From the perspective of CLS, there is nothing to object to in the idea that the development of children's language capabilities requires that they and their teachers have some 'model' of language, but the view of language and discourse is radically different from the instrumental conception above. And since CLS ascribes richer and weightier social significance to language, it has a correspondingly wider view of language education. I have structured my discussion of language education around the terms of reference of the Kingman Committee, so that this section can be read as a contribution to the debate from a point of view which is very different from some of the thinking behind the Committee. The Kingman Report was published too late for detailed attention here, but it seems to manifest much the same sort of thinking.

The terms of reference are to recommend:

- A model of the English language, whether spoken or written, which would
  (i) serve as the basis of how teachers are trained to understand how the English language works;
  (ii) inform professional discussion of all aspects of English teaching.

- The principles which should guide teachers on how far and in what ways the model should be made explicit to pupils, to make them conscious of how language is used in a range of contexts.

- What, in general terms, pupils need to know about how the English language works and in consequence what they should have been taught and be expected to understand on this score at age 7, 11 and 16.

I shall begin with a discussion of the 'model' referred to in the first of the terms of reference, and then discuss the second and third together under the heading 'Guiding principles', though I shall not suggest specific targets for 7-, 11- and 16-year-old children.

Model

The characterization of discourse in Chapter 2 (pp. 20–27), summed up in Fig. 2.1, provides an appropriate model of language for language education, its main elements being *text*, *interaction*, and *context*. I emphasized two points in that discussion which are relevant here. Firstly, discourse is not just a matter of text, or of language form. It seems that the sort of model envisaged in the terms of reference is just a model of English as a formal system, which would be quite unsatisfactory as an educational model, because it would have nothing to say about interaction or context. Secondly, apropos of context, discourse is determined by social relations, through its dependence upon participants' MR, and it contributes to shaping those social relations. In my view, a model suitable for language education would need to give prominence to this socially constituted and socially constituting nature of discourse and language.

The selection of a model will evidently depend on one's view of language education, and education more generally. There is I think a distinction to be drawn between education and training, and this applies to language as to other elements of the school curriculum. The instrumental views of language education referred to earlier strike me as training-oriented, focusing on the transmission of knowledge and skills, whose content is assumed to be unproblematic and whose social origins are ignored. One finds an analogous conception of literary education, often advocated by the same people, as the transmission of dominant cultural values, teaching children what conventional wisdom regards as 'great literature'. I would say that education, by contrast, is not just passing things on (though it is partly that);

it is developing the child's critical consciousness of her environment and her critical self-consciousness, and her capacity to
contribute to the shaping and reshaping of her social world.

It is therefore no part of education to present to children any
element of their humanly produced and humanly changeable
social environment as if it were a part of the natural environment
over which they have no control. Yet it is precisely such an alienating view of language that has been traditionally transmitted in
the schools. It is the perspective of language as socially constituted and constituting that is all too often missing, leading to
legitimized and naturalized orders of discourse being presented
as legitimate and natural, the social devaluation of the vernaculars
of most children being presented as irrational prejudice rather
than an effect of power relations, and the ideological shaping of
discourse being trivialized and misrepresented as abuse of
'loaded' language by unscrupulous individuals. Such ways of
representing language inhibit children from coming to conceptualize it as an object of critical consciousness – that is, they
prevent a genuinely educational orientation to language.

I would argue that such an orientation must be based upon a
critical model of language such as CLS. The conception of
language education that I am proposing stresses the development
of a critical consciousness among children of the orders of
discourse of their society, or what I shall call *critical language
awareness*. This echoes the now widespread acceptance that
'language awareness' should be an element in the school
curriculum – though the content of existing language awareness
programmes is generally by no means critical!

Guiding principles

Consciousness or awareness are dialectically related to practice
and (as I said earlier) struggle. The point of language education
is not awareness for its own sake, but awareness as a necessary
accompaniment to the development of the capabilities of children
as producers and interpreters of discourse. I am referring here not
just to developing the capabilities of each individual child, but
also to developing the *collective* capabilities of children from
oppressed social groupings. I would regard this as the primary
emancipatory task of language education: critical language awareness is a facilitator for 'emancipatory discourse' (see below) which

challenges, breaks through, and may ultimately transform the dominant orders of discourse, as a part of the struggle of oppressed social groupings against the dominant bloc.

The 'principles which should guide teachers on how far and in what ways the model should be made explicit to pupils' and so 'what pupils should be taught', are rooted in this conception of the relationship between the development of language capabilities and critical language awareness. Figure 9.1 schematically represents a model of language learning which corresponds to this conception, and which can be interpreted as applying either to the learning of individual children, or to the collective learning of social groupings of children.

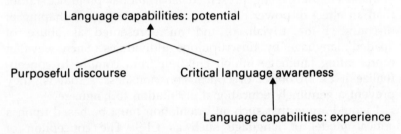

Fig. 9.1 Language learning

This model provides two main guiding principles:

1. *Marrying awareness and practice*: developing children's potential language capabilities depends on a marriage of purposeful discourse practice and critical language awareness.

2. *Building on experience*: critical language awareness should be built upon the existing language capabilities and experience of children.

I shall discuss these in turn.

It will be helpful in discussing the first of these principles to distinguish two levels in the development of critical language awareness:

level 1: awareness of MR in production and interpretation;
level 2: awareness of the social determinants of MR.

Level 1 corresponds to the *interpretation* stage of the procedure I presented in Chapters 5 and 6. It is a matter of helping people become aware of the rich array of resources they have for discourse, and how these are drawn upon in producing and interpreting text. Part of what is involved here is some explicit understanding of language as a formal system. The focus here is upon making unconscious capabilities a focus of attention. The principle of marrying awareness and practice suggests that, on the one hand, this awareness can best be achieved through the development of children's self-consciousness about their own purposeful discourse (i.e. discourse they themselves engage in as producers or interpreters for real purposes, rather than what they might do as an exercise, or what others do); and that, on the other hand, the range of purposeful discourse available to children will be enhanced as their awareness grows.

Level 2 corresponds to the *explanation* stage of the procedure. Once children become more aware of the way their MR function in discourse, questions can be raised about its social origins, the ideological effects upon it of relations of power, and how both MR and the social relations underlying them are reproduced and transformed in discourse. This second level of awareness is essential if the schools are to develop children's language capabilities to the point where the common-sense practices and constraints of currently dominant orders of discourse are probed, challenged, and transformed – rather than simply training children to be good at being conventional. The principle of marrying awareness and practice suggests that consciousness about the social determination and effects of one's own purposeful discourse is an effective route to critical awareness at this level, and that such critical social awareness will facilitate the development in children of emancipatory discourse which stretches and breaks conventions, as part of individual and, especially, collective struggle.

The principle of marrying awareness and practice suggests what children should be taught about language, while the principle of building on experience (as we shall see) suggests how it should be taught. Children ought to have access to an explicit 'model' of language because the development of language capabilities depends on critical language awareness, as I have argued above. Indeed, one might regard the ability to talk or write critically about language as itself an important part of the child's potential language capabilities, as well as facilitating others. This requires a *metalanguage*, a language for talking about language, though one carefully designed not to appear to children as an alien gobbledegook. Given the 'model' I have suggested, it would need to be a metalanguage which enabled children to talk about texts, and interactions, and social context – or all three stages of the procedure I presented in Chapters 5 and 6: description, interpretation, and explanation.

The second principle is that critical language awareness should be built upon the existing language capabilities and experience of the child. Children (and people generally) have a common-sense understanding not only of how to do what they *can* do linguistically, but also of such matters as which discourse types or subject positions are available to them and which are not, how their language is socially (de)valued in comparison with that of others, and so forth. The principle of building on experience claims that language awareness, like social consciousness more generally, can be most effectively developed if children are helped to put such understanding and experience into words, and if these wordings become the basis for building awareness.

This brings us to how children should be taught about language. What I would suggest is a three-part cycle:

(i) *Reflection on experience*: children are asked to reflect upon their own discourse and their experience of social constraints upon it, and to share their reflections with the class.

(ii) *Systematizing experience*: the teacher shows the children how to express these reflections in a systematic form, giving them the status of 'knowledge'.

(iii) *Explanation*: this knowledge becomes an object of further collective reflection and analysis by the class, and social explanations are sought (cf. level 2 of language awareness above).

There is then a fourth element in the cycle identified in the first principle:

(iv) *Developing practice*: the awareness resulting from (i)–(iii) is used to develop the child's capacity for purposeful discourse.

The cycle can be repeated indefinitely: as awareness grows, past experience and developing practice can be subject to increasingly systematic and probing reflection, the teacher's contribution can become more substantial, and so on.

Now an example, necessarily schematic, to illustrate this cycle. One focus might be children's experience of writing, with the aim of extending their capacity to use written language into domains which the majority of people are conventionally excluded from, such as the writing of history. There is nothing novel about this exercise – it is the sort of thing that many English teachers do. But what they do not generally do is systematically tie it to the development of critical awareness in the way I am suggesting. In terms of the cycle, the teacher might proceed with the exercise as follows:

(i) Reflection on experience: ask the children to think about and describe the purposes for which they use writing as opposed to speech, what they think writing 'is for', purposes for which writing is used by others but not by them, and their perceptions of which uses of writing have most social prestige.

(ii) Systematizing experience: present a systematic account of differences of function between speech and writing, the social prestige of various uses of writing, and the distribution of access to prestigious uses.

(iii) Explanation: use (i) and (ii) as the basis for class reflection on the social reasons for access to prestigious uses of writing being restricted; focusing upon history, and social constraints on who writes history, as well as its subject matter, the language in which it is written, and so forth.

(iv) Developing practice: set up a history-writing project for the children, in which they are encouraged to stretch or break conventions for history writing by: (a) writing a history of a grouping, such as women or children in their local community, whose history is not normally written; (b) writing in a language, such as one of the minority languages or a non-standard variety of English, which is not normally used for such purposes; (c) being *serious* historians themselves, by writing for a real purpose rather than just as an exercise -- they might be encouraged, for example, to place copies of their histories in a local library.

Such an exercise is designed to lead, in stage (iv), to children producing what I referred to earlier as 'emancipatory discourse' – discourse which goes outside currently dominant conventions in some way. We can distinguish between emancipatory discourse as a matter of *empowerment*, and emancipatory discourse which contributes to the transformation of existing orders of discourse. In the case of empowerment, people who are conventionally excluded from particular types of discourse or particular subject positions within types of discourse, are helped to infringe conventions, without radically changing them, by 'entering' these discourse types or positions. Empowerment has a substantial 'shock' potential, and it can help people overcome their sense of impotence by showing them that existing orders of discourse are not immutable. The transformation of orders of discourse is a matter of the systematic de-structuring of existing orders and restructuring of new orders, in the terms of Chapter 7.

To sum up, then, what I have suggested on the basis of the two guiding principles set out earlier is that the development of children's language capabilities should proceed through bringing together their existing abilities and experiences, their growing critical awareness of language, and their growing capacity to engage in purposeful discourse.

TAKING IT FURTHER

A discussion of language education in the schools is perhaps an appropriate way of concluding a book on language and power, because what happens in schools can be decisive in determining whether existing orders of discourse, as well as more generally existing relations of power, are to be reproduced or transformed. This final section of the book is addressed particularly to readers who wish to take further their interest in CLS. It contains brief practical notes on *where*, *how* and with *what focus* this might be done, and suggestions for further reading.

The most effective way to develop an interest in CLS is to apply it, to engage in the critical analysis of some specific type or types of discourse. This can be done as a purely personal exercise, but it is more in accordance with the objectives of CLS to do it collectively in some sort of group. Here are just a few of the many possibilities:

Where? school, college, university
         trade union branch
         women's group
         CND branch
         youth centre
         political party
         law centre

How?   class
          informal or extra-curricular seminar
          TV, radio, or newspaper monitoring group
          video or film showings
          visual display, use of notice boards
          role playing (empowerment)

Focus?   racism or sexism (e.g. in casual conversation)
            media (e.g. coverage of trade unions or CND)
            advertising (of children's toys, for instance)
            dealing with officials, tribunals, etc. (for claimants)
            ideological role of images (printed or televised)
            can counselling be non-directive?

In deciding how to launch a CLS initiative, it is worth bearing certain points in mind. Firstly, that CLS is best applied to types of discourse which are perceived by those involved as having real significance in their own lives and experience. Secondly, that people are most open to critical approaches such as CLS where they are most involved in social struggle. And thirdly, that, for most people, focusing on language will initially make little sense; the significance of language will generally need to be painstakingly demonstrated, which is why I have not worded the focuses suggested above explicitly in terms of language.

FURTHER READING

I have given in Chapters 5 and 6 references which readers may find helpful in terms of the procedure for discourse analysis, including the various levels of textual analysis. I have also referred, in Chapter 1 and throughout the book, to major work in social theory which those wishing to take further their interest in CLS will find it helpful to read. I would suggest particularly: Thompson J B 1984; Dreyfus H L, Rabinow P 1982; Foucault M 1972; McCarthy T 1978; Habermas J 1984; Bourdieu P 1977; Bourdieu P 1982.

What follows is a very selective annotated list of books which are about or closely relevant to CLS. I have listed the books approximately in order of difficulty, with the most accessible ones first.

Kress G 1985. A concise account of Kress's view of CLS, bringing difficult theoretical issues down to earth with good illustrative materials. Explores how creativity is compatible with social determination. Valuable as an introduction to CLS.

Fowler R *et al.* 1979. Representative of important work in 'critical linguistics' developed at the University of East Anglia. Ideological analysis of grammatical and vocabulary features of mainly written texts. Designed to give non-linguists a usable analytical framework. Highly recommended.

Kress G, Hodge B 1979. Closely complements Fowler R *et al.* 1979.

Barthes R 1972. Published in French in 1957. Semiological analysis of culturally prominent artefacts and images, instructive for any sort of ideological analysis.

Mey J 1985. A substantial (400 pages) study of language in late capitalism. A wealth of material and ideas, if rather rambling at times. Central concepts are linguistic 'manipulation', 'repression', and 'emancipation'. Main data: news discourse, the discourse of immigrant language education. Linguistic analysis closely integrated into social analysis.

Van Dijk T forthcoming. A comprehensive framework for analysing media discourse, combining text analysis, analysis of processes of production and comprehension, and social analysis. Richly illustrated with an analysis of coverage in the world press of the assassination of President Gemayel of Lebanon.

Chilton P (ed) 1985. A collection of papers on the language of the nuclear arms race, or 'Nukespeak'.

Williamson J 1978. A semiotic approach to advertising, richly illustrated. Highly recommended.

Pateman T 1980. Reissue of 1975 text with added appendices. Topics include linguistic 'exclusion', 'mystification' and 'repression'. Uneven, but valuable insights into 'language worked by power'. Refreshingly self-critical.

Thompson J B 1984. Study by a sociologist of social theorists on the connection between language and ideology. A valuable overview of the work of Bourdieu, Pecheux, Habermas and others.

Shapiro M (ed) 1984. A collection of Anglo-American and Continental papers from various academic disciplines on the language of politics and the politics of language.

Volosinov V I 1973. First published in Russian in 1929. Important and influential account of ideology and language, with a critique of mainstream linguistics which is still remarkably apt.

Jameson F 1981. Collection of papers by Marxist literary critic, with valuable insights on the nature of interpretation.

Pecheux M 1982. Argues against mainstream linguistics and for the analysis of language as social practice. Heavily influenced by Althusser's work on ideology. Difficult theoretical text.

REFERENCES

I have drawn extensively in this chapter on papers dealing with critical language awareness which I have co-authored with colleagues at Lancaster: Department of Linguistics and Modern English Language, University of Lancaster 1987, and Clark R *et al*. 1987. On language awareness, see Hawkins E 1984 and NCLE 1985. I have found Freire P 1972 and Freire P 1985 invaluable for their insights on language education, including the notion of *conscientization*, which I have relied upon above. The quotations on ESL are from Baynham 1986. Objectives for English teaching are set out by the English education inspectors (HMIs) in Department of Education and Science 1984.

Bibliography

Akinasso, F N, Ajirotutu C S 1982 Performance and ethnic style in job interviews. In Gumperz J 1982b

Althusser L 1971 Ideology and ideological state apparatuses. In *Lenin and philosophy*. New Left Books

Argyle M 1978 *The psychology of interpersonal behaviour* (3rd edn). Penguin

Atkinson J M, Heritage J 1984 *Structures of social action: studies in conversation analysis*. Cambridge University Press

Barthes R 1972 *Mythologies* (trans A. Lavers). Paladin

Barthes R 1977 *Image, music, text* (trans S. Heath). Fontana/Collins

Baynham M 1986 Action and reflection: the Freirean argument in ESL. Paper given at the Linguistics and Politics conference, University of Lancaster, April 1986

Bolinger D 1980 *Language – the loaded weapon: the use and abuse of language today*. Longman

Bourdieu P 1977 *Outline of a theory of practice* (trans R Nice). Cambridge University Press

Bourdieu P 1982 *Ce que parler veut dire: l'économie des échanges linguistiques*. Fayard, Paris

Bourdieu P 1984 *Distinction: a social critique of the judgement of taste* (trans R. Nice). Routledge & Kegan Paul

Brown G, Yule G 1983 *Discourse analysis*. Cambridge University Press

Brown P, Levinson S 1978 Universals in language usage: politeness phenomena. In Goody E (ed) *Questions and politeness: strategies in social interaction*. Cambridge University Press

Brown R, Gilman A 1972 The pronouns of power and solidarity. In Giglioli P (ed) *Language and social context*. Penguin

Candlin C N 1986 Beyond description to explanation in cross-cultural discourse. In Smith L (ed) *Discourse across cultures*. Pergamon

Candlin C N, Lucas J L 1986 Interpretations and explanations in discourse: modes of 'advising' in family planning. In Ensink T *et al. Discourse analysis and public life*. Foris, Dordrecht

Chilton P (ed) 1985 *Language and the nuclear arms debate: nukespeak today*. Frances Pinter

Cicourel A 1973 *Cognitive sociology*. Penguin
Clark R, Fairclough N L, Ivanic R, Martin-Jones M 1987 Critical language awareness. *CLSL Working Papers 1*. Centre for Language in Social Life, University of Lancaster
Communist Party of Great Britain 1978 *The British road to socialism*. CPGB
Coulthard M 1977 *An introduction to discourse analysis*. Longman
Culler J 1976 *Saussure*. Fontana/Collins

Davis H, Walton P 1983 *Language, image, media*. Basil Blackwell
Department of Education and Science 1984 *English from 5 to 16*. HMSO
Department of Linguistics and Modern English Language, University of Lancaster 1987 *Submission to the Kingman committee of inquiry into the teaching of English*
de Saussure F 1966 *Course in general linguistics* (trans W Baskin). McGraw-Hill, New York
Downes W 1984 *Language and society*. Fontana Paperbacks
Dreyfus H L, Rabinow P 1982 *Michel Foucault: beyond structuralism and hermeneutics*. The Harvester Press

Edelman M 1974 The political language of the helping professions. *Politics and Society* 4: 295–310
Emerson J 1970 Behaviour in private places: sustaining definitions of reality in gynaecological examinations. In Dreizel H P (ed) *Recent Sociology no 2*. Collier-Macmillan, New York

Fairclough N L 1985 Critical and descriptive goals in discourse analysis. *Journal of Pragmatics* 9: 739–763
Fairclough N L 1988 Register, power, and sociosemantic change. In Birch D, O'Toole M (eds) *Functions of style*. Frances Pinter
Faye J P 1972 *Langages totalitaires: critique de la raison/l'économie narrative*. Hermann, Paris
Foucault M 1971 *L'ordre du discours*. Gallimard, Paris
Foucault M 1972 *The archaeology of knowledge* (trans A. Sheridan Smith). Tavistock Publications
Foucault M 1982 The subject and power. Afterword to Dreyfus H L, Rabinow P 1982
Fowler R, Hodge B, Kress G, Trew T 1979 *Language and control*. Routledge & Kegan Paul
Freire P 1972 *Pedagogy of the oppressed*. Penguin Books
Freire P 1985 *The politics of education*. Macmillan
Fromkin V, Rodman R 1983 *An introduction to language* (3rd edn). Holt, Rinehart & Winston, New York

Garfinkel H 1967 *Studies in ethnomethodology*. Prentice Hall, Englewood Cliffs, New Jersey

Garrod S 1986 Language comprehension in context: a psychological perspective. *Applied Linguistics* **7**: 226–238

Giddens A 1976 *New rules of the sociological method: a positive critique of interpretative sociologies*. Hutchinson

Gramsci A 1971 *Selections from the prison notebooks* (ed and trans by Q. Hoare, G. Nowell-Smith). Lawrence & Wishart

Gumperz J 1982a *Discourse strategies*. Cambridge University Press.

Gumperz J (ed) 1982b *Language and social identity*. Cambridge University Press

Gurevitch M, Bennett T, Curran J, Woollacott J (eds) 1982 *Culture, society and the media*. Methuen

Habermas J 1984 *Theory of communicative action vol 1: Reason and the rationalization of society* (trans T. McCarthy). Heinemann

Hall S 1982 The rediscovery of 'ideology': return of the repressed in media studies. In Gurevitch M *et al*. 1982

Hall S 1984 The state – socialism's old caretaker. *Marxism Today* 28. 11: 24–29

Hall S, Jacques M (eds) 1983 *The politics of Thatcherism*, Lawrence & Wishart

Halliday M A K 1978 *Language as social semiotic*. Edward Arnold

Halliday M A K 1985 *An introduction to functional grammar*. Edward Arnold

Halliday M A K, Hasan R 1976 *Cohesion in English*. Longman

Halliday M A K, Hasan R 1985 *Language, context, and text: aspects of language in a social-semiotic perspective*. Deakin University Press, Victoria, Australia

Harding S 1983 *'Orderly freedom': the 'common sense' of Margaret Thatcher*. Communication Studies Department, Sheffield City Polytechnic

Hawkins E 1984 *Awareness of Language: an introduction*. Cambridge University Press

Henriques J, Hollway W, Urwin C, Venn C, Walkerdine V 1984 *Changing the subject*. Methuen

Heritage J C, Watson D R 1979 Formulations as conversational objects. In Psathas G (ed) *Everyday language: studies in ethnomethodology*. Irvington, New York

Hymes D 1962 The ethnography of speaking. In Gladwin T, Sturtevant W C (eds) *Anthropology and human behaviour*. Anthropological Society of Washington, Washington. Also in Fishman J (ed) *Readings in the sociology of language*. Mouton, The Hague

Irvine J 1979 Formality and informality in communicative events. *American Anthropologist* **81**: 773–790

Jameson F 1981 *The political unconscious*. Methuen

Jameson F 1984 Postmodernism, or the cultural logic of late capitalism. *New Left Review* **146**

Kramarae C, Schulz M, O'Barr W 1984 *Language and power*. Sage
Kress G 1985 *Linguistic processes in sociocultural practice*. Deakin University Press, Victoria, Australia
Kress G, Hodge B 1979 *Language as ideology*. Routledge & Kegan Paul

Laclau E, Mouffe C 1985 *Hegemony and socialist strategy*. Verso
Lakoff G, Johnson M 1980 *Metaphors we live by*. University of Chicago Press
Leech G N 1974 *Semantics*. Penguin Books
Leech G N 1983 *Principles of pragmatics*. Longman
Leiss W, Kline S, Jhally S 1986 *Social communication in advertising*. Methuen
Leith D 1983 *A social history of English*. Routledge & Kegan Paul
Levinson S 1983 *Pragmatics*. Cambridge University Press
Lyons J 1977 *Semantics*. Cambridge University Press

McCarthy T 1978 *The critical theory of Jürgen Habermas*. Hutchinson
McLellan D 1986 *Ideology*. Open University Press
Marx K, Engels F 1968 *Selected writings*. Lawrence & Wishart
Mey J 1985 *Whose language? a study in linguistic pragmatics*. John Benjamins Publishing Company, Amsterdam/Philadelphia

National Congress on Languages in Education (NCLE) 1985 *Language awareness*. Centre for Information on Language Teaching and Research

Pateman T 1980 *Language, truth and politics* (2nd edn). Jean Stroud
Pecheux M 1982 *Language, semantics and ideology: stating the obvious* (trans H. Nagpal). Macmillan

Quirk R, Greenbaum S, Leech G N, Svartvik J 1972 *A grammar of contemporary English*. Longman
Quirk R, Greenbaum S, Leech G N, Svartvik J 1985 *A comprehensive grammar of the English language*. Longman

Rogers C 1967 Some of the directions evident in therapy. In *On becoming a person*. Constable

Sacks H, Schegloff E A, Jefferson G 1974 A simplest systematics for the organization of turn-taking for conversation. *Language* 50: 696–735
Schank R, Abelson R 1977 *Scripts, plans, goals and understanding*. Lawrence Erlbaum, Hillsdale, New Jersey

Schenkein J 1978 *Studies in the organization of conversational interaction.* Academic Press, New York

Searle J R 1969 *Speech acts: an essay in the philosophy of language.* Cambridge University Press

Shapiro M (ed) 1984 *Language and politics.* Basil Blackwell

Sinclair J, Coulthard M 1975 *Towards an analysis of discourse: the English used by teachers and pupils.* Oxford University Press

Steedman C, Urwin C, Walkerdine V 1985 *Language, gender and childhood.* Routledge & Kegan Paul

Stubbs M 1983 *Discourse analysis: the sociolinguistic analysis of natural language.* Basil Blackwell

Tannen D 1979 What's in a frame? Surface evidence for underlying expectations. In Freedle R O (ed) *New directions in discourse processing.* Ablex, Norwood, New Jersey

The New York Times (eds) 1973 *The Watergate hearings.* Bantam Books, New York

Therborn G 1980 *The ideology of power and the power of ideology.* Verso

Thomas J forthcoming *Speaker meaning: an introduction to pragmatics.* Longman

Thompson J B 1984 *Studies in the theory of ideology.* Polity Press

van Dijk T (ed) 1985 *Handbook of discourse analysis*, 4 vols. Academic Press

van Dijk T forthcoming *News as discourse*

van Dijk T, Kintsch W 1983 *Stategies of discourse comprehension.* Academic Press

Vaughan T D 1976 *Concepts of counselling.* Bedford Square Press

Volosinov V I 1973 *Marxism and the philosophy of language.* Seminar Press, New York

Widdowson H G 1979 *Explorations in applied linguistics.* Oxford University Press

Williams R 1976 *Keywords.* Fontana/Croom Helm

Williamson J 1978 *Decoding advertisements.* Marion Boyars

Zimmerman D, West C 1975 Sex roles, interruptions and silences in conversation. In Thorne B, Henley N (eds) *Language and sex: difference and dominance.* Newbury House, Rowley, Massachusetts

Index